Web Design Blueprints

Build websites and applications using the latest
techniques in modern web development

Benjamin LaGrone

PUBLISHING

BIRMINGHAM - MUMBAI

Web Design Blueprints

First published: April 2016

Production reference: 1270416

Published by Packt Publishing Ltd.

Livery Place
35 Livery Street
Birmingham B3 2PB, UK.

ISBN 978-1-78355-211-5

www.packtpub.com

Credits

Author
Benjamin LaGrone

Reviewer
Kryštof Doležal

Commissioning Editor
Edward Gordon

Acquisition Editor
Reshma Raman

Content Development Editor
Sumeet Sawant

Technical Editor
Mohit Hassija

Copy Editor
Madhusudan Uchil

Project Coordinator
Shweta H Birwatkar

Proofreader
Safis Editing

Indexer
Priya Sane

Production Coordinator
Shantanu N. Zagade

Cover Work
Shantanu N. Zagade

About the Author

Benjamin LaGrone is a web developer who lives and works in Texas. He got his start in programming at the age of 6 when he took his first computer class at the Houston Museum of Natural Science. His first program was "choose your own adventure book", written in BASIC; he has fond memories of the days when software needed you to write line numbers. Fast forward to about thirty years later: after deciding that computers are here to stay, Ben has made a career combining two of his favorite things, art and coding — creating art from code. One of his favorite projects was using the GMaps API to map pathologies to chromosomes for cancer research. Fascinated with mobile devices for a long time, Ben thinks that the responsive Web is one of the most exciting, yet long time coming, new aspects of web development. He now works in a SaaS development shop and is the mobile and responsive Web evangelist of the team. When he's not working on some Internet project, Ben spends his time building robots, tinkering with machines, drinking coffee, surfing, and teaching Kuk Sool martial arts.

About the Reviewer

Kryštof Doležal is a web developer from Prague, the capital of the Czech Republic. He has been interested in creating websites since he got his first computer.

Kryštof has been a qualified specialist in computer science applications since 2006. He has worked in a TV studio for the ministry of education and AVG Technologies. Now, he works in web development and IT consulting as a freelancer.

www.PacktPub.com

eBooks, discount offers, and more

Did you know that Packt offers eBook versions of every book published, with PDF and ePub files available? You can upgrade to the eBook version at www.PacktPub. com and as a print book customer, you are entitled to a discount on the eBook copy. Get in touch with us at customercare@packtpub.com for more details.

At www.PacktPub.com, you can also read a collection of free technical articles, sign up for a range of free newsletters and receive exclusive discounts and offers on Packt books and eBooks.

https://www2.packtpub.com/books/subscription/packtlib

Do you need instant solutions to your IT questions? PacktLib is Packt's online digital book library. Here, you can search, access, and read Packt's entire library of books.

Why subscribe?

- Fully searchable across every book published by Packt
- Copy and paste, print, and bookmark content
- On demand and accessible via a web browser

Table of Contents

Preface

Web design is becoming a fragmented and dispersed topic. There are many trends within the industry that allow professional developers to build websites for clients with a growing set of demands. There is currently no documentation that draws all of this information into one place, provides web designers with a panoramic view of their industry, and gives them the necessary skills to go out and make a given website.

What this book covers

Chapter 1, *Responsive Web Design*, discusses responsive elements, layouts, media, typography, and navigation. It provides the elements to create a good starter template for a responsive website. It discusses RWD basics, the user agent, the media query, responsive images with CSS, responsive images with SRCSET, responsive video, responsive typography, responsive layouts, and responsive menus with CSS and JavaScript.

Chapter 2, *Flat UI*, teaches you flat user interfaces: what they are, the changes in them, and using color schemes. This chapter takes you through creating a responsive Flat UI layout you can use.

Chapter 3, *Parallax Scrolling*, begins with taking elements from the two previous chapters and creating a Parallax Scrolling website using modern web elements and graphics.

Chapter 4, *Single Page Applications*, takes the flat UI layout and turns it into a real dynamic single-page application using nothing but plain vanilla JavaScript.

Chapter 5, *The Death Star Chapter*, is a challenging boss-level chapter that takes a cumulative approach to all the subjects in the book by building a flat UI, multi-level parallax scrolling, interactive video game.

What you need for this book

You will need an integrated development environment (IDE), a local host webserver, a browser, and your thinking cap.

Who this book is for

This book is a must-have for web developers who want to stay on top of the latest trends in web app and site development. This book is for web developers already familiar with HTML CSS, and functional JavaScript and wanting to learn the latest trends in web development.

Conventions

In this book, you will find a number of text styles that distinguish between different kinds of information. Here are some examples of these styles and an explanation of their meaning.

Code words in text, database table names, folder names, filenames, file extensions, pathnames, dummy URLs, user input, and Twitter handles are shown as follows: " Add a selector for the navButton class to the media query for viewports larger than 480px."

A block of code is set as follows:

```
<!doctype html>
<html lang='en'>
    <head>
        <title>Responsive Web Design</title>
        <meta name="viewport" content="width=device-width,
            initial-scale=1.0, user-scalable=no">
    </head>
</html>
```

New terms and **important words** are shown in bold. Words that you see on the screen, for example, in menus or dialog boxes, appear in the text like this: " Next, launch the file in your browser. Open the **Inspector** (right-click, and select **Inspect Element**) and go to the **Network** Tab."

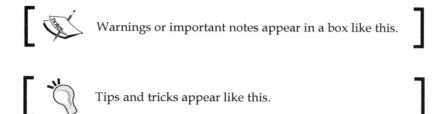

Warnings or important notes appear in a box like this.

Tips and tricks appear like this.

Reader feedback

Feedback from our readers is always welcome. Let us know what you think about this book—what you liked or disliked. Reader feedback is important for us as it helps us develop titles that you will really get the most out of.

To send us general feedback, simply e-mail feedback@packtpub.com, and mention the book's title in the subject of your message.

If there is a topic that you have expertise in and you are interested in either writing or contributing to a book, see our author guide at www.packtpub.com/authors.

Customer support

Now that you are the proud owner of a Packt book, we have a number of things to help you to get the most from your purchase.

Downloading the example code

You can download the example code files for this book from your account at http://www.packtpub.com. If you purchased this book elsewhere, you can visit http://www.packtpub.com/support and register to have the files e-mailed directly to you.

You can download the code files by following these steps:

1. Log in or register to our website using your e-mail address and password.
2. Hover the mouse pointer on the **SUPPORT** tab at the top.
3. Click on **Code Downloads & Errata**.
4. Enter the name of the book in the **Search** box.
5. Select the book for which you're looking to download the code files.
6. Choose from the drop-down menu where you purchased this book from.
7. Click on **Code Download**.

Once the file is downloaded, please make sure that you unzip or extract the folder using the latest version of:

- WinRAR / 7-Zip for Windows
- Zipeg / iZip / UnRarX for Mac
- 7-Zip / PeaZip for Linux

Downloading the color images of this book

We also provide you with a PDF file that has color images of the screenshots/diagrams used in this book. The color images will help you better understand the changes in the output. You can download this file from `https://www.packtpub.com/sites/default/files/downloads/WebDesignBlueprints_ColorImages.pdf`.

Errata

Although we have taken every care to ensure the accuracy of our content, mistakes do happen. If you find a mistake in one of our books — maybe a mistake in the text or the code — we would be grateful if you could report this to us. By doing so, you can save other readers from frustration and help us improve subsequent versions of this book. If you find any errata, please report them by visiting `http://www.packtpub.com/submit-errata`, selecting your book, clicking on the **Errata Submission Form** link, and entering the details of your errata. Once your errata are verified, your submission will be accepted and the errata will be uploaded to our website or added to any list of existing errata under the Errata section of that title.

To view the previously submitted errata, go to `https://www.packtpub.com/books/content/support` and enter the name of the book in the search field. The required information will appear under the **Errata** section.

Piracy

Piracy of copyrighted material on the Internet is an ongoing problem across all media. At Packt, we take the protection of our copyright and licenses very seriously. If you come across any illegal copies of our works in any form on the Internet, please provide us with the location address or website name immediately so that we can pursue a remedy.

Please contact us at copyright@packtpub.com with a link to the suspected pirated material.

We appreciate your help in protecting our authors and our ability to bring you valuable content.

Questions

If you have a problem with any aspect of this book, you can contact us at questions@packtpub.com, and we will do our best to address the problem.

Responsive Web Design 1

Welcome to *Web Design Blueprints*. This book is meant to introduce you to some really cool new web design patterns that have arisen in web development. In this book, you will learn how to create responsive websites, how to create websites using the principles of flat design, make deep-dive sites using parallax scrolling, and use Ajax in single-page apps. Finally, we'll combine all these together into an awesome *choose-your-own-adventure-style* game.

Introduction to responsive web design

Let's be honest, you already know what responsive web design means. But for the sake of the age-old tradition of pedagogy, I'll explain. **Responsive web design** is designing a website to optimize for multiple different viewports. What this means is that in this part of the book, I'll be discussing various techniques for creating a webpage that will look good on mobile devices, tablets, desktops, and laptops, and so on.

I'm not a fortune-teller, but I suspect that mobile devices are not disappearing any time soon. In fact, in my work, I've seen the traffic move from desktop to mobile. In many areas, we see that mobile is the primary tool for people's search for information. If it's not the primary one, it's at least a growing audience. Or else, they are the audience that leaves a site that doesn't have a mobile Web presence. Therefore, the demand for web developers who understand responsive design is paramount to the industry. This skill is a must-have if you want to stay current in the developer workforce.

In this chapter, I will discuss responsive elements, layouts, media, typography, and navigation. You can jump ahead to a section you are particularly interested in or read the whole thing from beginning to end. If you follow along through the entire chapter, you should have a good starter template for a responsive website. We'll learn the following:

- Responsive web design basics
- The user agent
- The media query
- Responsive images with CSS
- Responsive images with `srcset`
- Responsive video
- Responsive typography
- Responsive layouts
- Responsive menus with CSS and JavaScript

Getting familiar with the basics

Before we start, let's go over some basic stuff. There are some trivial and not-so-trivial things that you will need to do to get your responsive site working.

Using the inspector

The first foundational thing you should learn is using your browser's inspector to emulate different devices. There are a number of tools available in this toolset. Let's look at Chrome; first: click on the Chrome menu in the top-right corner of the browser window:

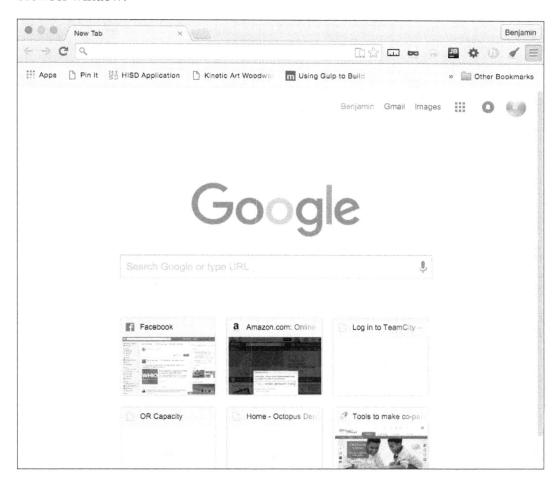

Next, select **More Tools | Developer Tools**. Then you can right-click on any element and select **Inspect Element**:

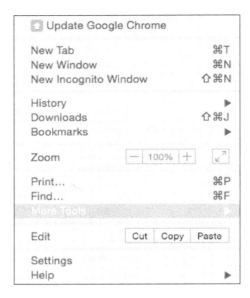

With this tool, you can inspect elements; use the JavaScript console; look at source code, network requests and responses, the timeline, and resources such as session and local storage; and even connect to a device and debug its Chrome browser.

Likewise, in Firefox, select **Tools** from the menu bar, and then select **Developer Tools**. You should see this:

Understanding the viewport meta tag

Now, on to our next task: creating the **viewport meta tag**. Every function of any responsive site you create will depend on this tag. Without it, your site won't be responsive at all!

The viewport meta tag was initially implemented only in Safari but was quickly adopted by other browsers. This clever little tag instructs your browser to render the webpage scale and size in specific ways.

Learning about the viewport meta tag by example

It may be easier to learn about the meta tag by demonstrating what the viewport will look like without it. Without the tag, your webpage will be rendered at full width in mobile viewports. The result will be the text being so small that you will have to pinch out to expand the text to a readable size.

For the sake of proving the point, let's start with a paragraph of text (you can go generate some ipsum text from `http://www.lipsum.com/`) styled to have a font size of 12px, using the following code:

```
<!DOCTYPE html>
<html>
<head>
<title>Viewport META Tag Test</title>
<style>
    p{
        font-size:12px;
    }
</style>
</head>
<body>
    <p>
    Lorem ipsum dolor sit amet, consectetur adipiscing elit.
    Phasellus feugiat tempor dui, ac volutpat lacus tempus id.
    Suspendisse feugiat est felis, vitae ultrices neque accumsan
    non. Curabitur lacus erat, suscipit eget sagittis eu,
    tincidunt eget urna.
    </p>
</body>
</html>
```

Viewing your work on the tag

Now, save the file and launch it in a browser with a good mobile emulator, such as Google Chrome, or use iOS Simulator. You will find that it is not very readable. All of the text is very tiny. This is what the world would look like without the viewport meta tag. See it illustrated in this screenshot:

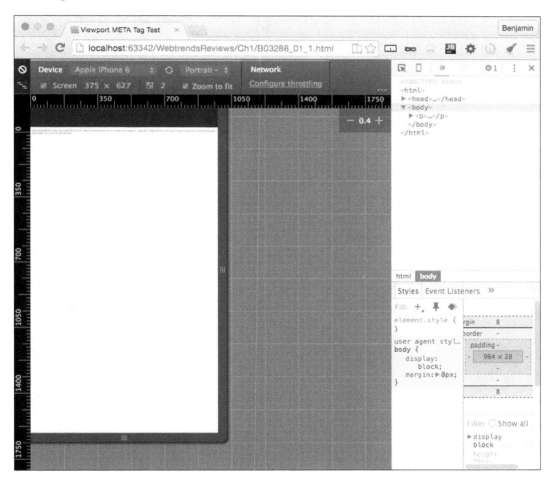

Compare it to normal desktop browser rendering. There's a very big difference in the readability. The pixel density of mobile devices changes the way this is rendered, so you will need to account for this by defining the viewport's properties in the meta tag. Here's the desktop browser rendering:

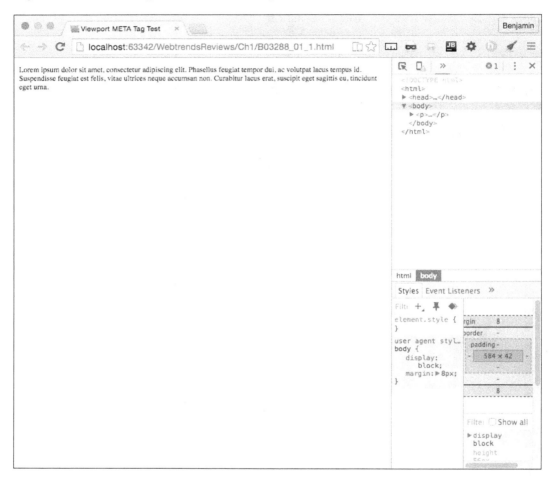

Fixing the problem by adding the proper meta tag

Now let's see what a wonderful world it would be with the addition of the viewport meta tag. Add a very simple version of the tag to the same code in the header, as I have in the following code sample:

```
<head>
    <title>Viewport META Tag Test</title>
    <meta name="viewport">
</head>
<body>
    ...
```

There are a few options for the viewport meta tag; however, only use them if you know what you are doing. These can end up causing more damage than you might anticipate. If you are not sure what you are doing, just keep it simple, Slick.

Further explanation of the viewport meta tag

Let's look at the viewport options in detail, starting with setting the width. You can set the width to a specific number, but that's not recommended. So set the `content` attribute equal to the device width, as illustrated in the following sample code:

```
<meta name="viewport" content="width=device-width">
```

Next, we look at the scaling. This is when you squeeze your two fingers together and apart on the screen to zoom out and in. You can prevent this behavior in the viewport or limit it by setting the `maximum-scale` attribute equal to 1. You can also predetermine the scale of the webpage when it's rendered initially, by setting the `initial-scale` attribute. In most cases, I set both as 1; see it in this sample code:

```
<meta name="viewport" initial-scale=1 maximum-scale=1>
```

This meta tag will not affect the rendering in the viewport unless it is viewed on a mobile device or proper emulator or simulator. Now, relaunch the file, and you will see that the page behaves much better. See it in this screenshot:

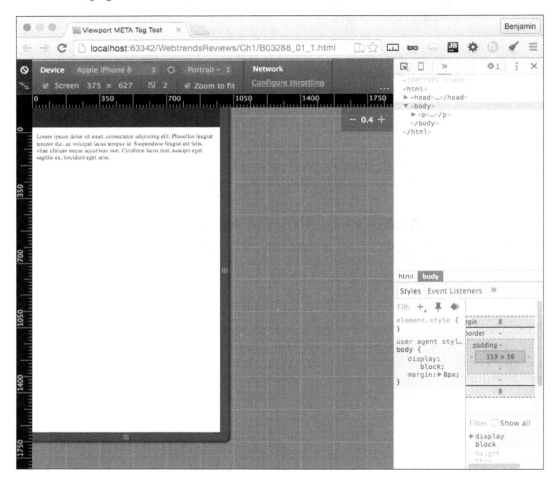

Understanding and changing the user agent string

Every time your audience's browser makes an HTTP request to your server to obtain a webpage, it identifies itself and reveals some things about itself to the server. This information can be used by your code to help create an optimized rendering of the site. The most important information revealed in the **user agent string** is the browser product name and version (such as Chrome/32.1), the layout engine and version (Gecko/1.1), and usually, the device system product name and version.

Using the user agent string for testing

When creating your responsive website, you will most likely be working directly on your computer, not on a mobile device, and either hosting locally or deploying to a server for production. No matter whether it's local or hosted, even if you're the Nikola Tesla (`https://en.wikipedia.org/wiki/Nikola_Tesla`) of CSS, you can't guess everything, so you will eventually want to do some visual testing on your site.

Manipulating the user agent string is a good way of simulating what your responsive website will look like in production. There are plenty of tools available to switch the user agent. The Chrome debugger includes a device mode you can toggle in order to simulate the mobile device. In addition to changing the viewport size to match the selected device, this wonderful little tool will switch the user agent string for you, re-rendering your website on the fly (usually, however, you may need to refresh).

How to change the user agent string in Chrome

You can access the toggle device mode from Chrome's developer tools. There are a few ways to get here. First, from the system menu, select **View**, then **Developer**, and then **Developer Tools**. Or you can right-click on an element in the viewport to launch the contextual menu and can then select **Inspect Element**. Finally, you can use keyboard shortcuts: on a Mac, use *Cmd + Opt + I*, and on Windows, use *F12* or *Ctrl + Shift + I*.

Once you have the developer tools open, you'll see in the top-left corner of the developer tools section of the viewport an icon of a magnifying glass and, next to it, an icon of a mobile phone. When you click on it, it will toggle the device mode or change the user agent. See this in the following screenshot:

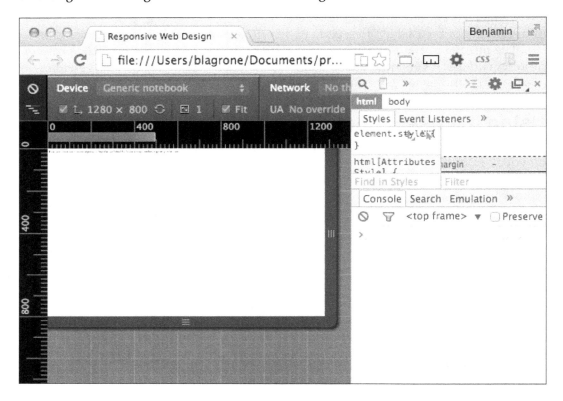

Once you activate this new interface, you will see some new options. First, you may be prompted to refresh the page. Otherwise, on the top, you will see a **Device** select option, where you can toggle through a list of common devices. Next to it is a **Network** select option element. With this tool, you can throttle the download speed in order to emulate different network types and speeds to see how slower downloads will affect the rendering of your responsive webpage.

What next?

Other cool features of the inspector are the rulers on the sides that let you get precise reads on the rendering and the touch emulation so that you can see how the user will truly interact with the user interface. Once it is launched, you can keep it running and toggle between different user agents and see how your page is rendered. There are even some views that emulate notebooks. This tool will prove to be one of the most useful tools in your toolbox. You will likely use it for many of the projects following this section.

Using media queries for responsive design

The media query is the philosopher's stone of responsive design. With its logical expression, you can create a webpage that responds and transforms to fit different viewports. A media query contains a media type and one or more expressions that, if true, can invoke new CSS attributes for that expression.

Some background information

There are possibly hundreds of permutations of these expressions; for a moment, take a look at the W3C website for the possible attributes. All of these are available for you to browse through over at http://www.w3.org/TR/css3-mediaqueries/. Here's that list for easy reference:

- `width`: This describes the width of the targeted viewport of the device. It can accept `min`/`max` prefixes.

- `height`: This describes the height of the targeted viewport of the device. This can accept `min`/`max` prefixes.

- `device-width`: This describes the width of the rendering surface of the device. It can accept `min`/`max` prefixes.

- `device-height`: This describes the height of the rendering surface of the device. It can accept `min`/`max` prefixes.

- `orientation`: This describes the height being larger or smaller than the width. When larger, the value is `portrait`; when smaller, the value is `landscape`.

- `aspect-ratio`: This is defined as the ratio of the value of `width` to the value of `height`. It can accept `min`/`max` prefixes.

- `device-aspect-ratio`: This is defined as the ratio of the value of `device-width` to the value of `device-height`. It can accept `min`/`max` prefixes.

- `color`: This describes the number of bits per color component on the output device. It can accept `min`/`max` prefixes.

- `color-index`: This describes the number of entries in the color lookup table. It can accept `min`/`max` prefixes.

- `monochrome`: This describes the number of bits per pixel in a monochrome frame buffer. It can accept `min`/`max` prefixes.

- `resolution`: This describes the resolution of the output device. It can accept `min`/`max` prefixes.

- `scan`: This describes the scanning process of TV output devices.

- `grid`: This can be used to query whether the output device is a grid or bitmap.

A small example

A media query can be executed as a condition in a link reference to a stylesheet or within a stylesheet itself. First, let's look at an example of the stylesheet link:

```
<!-- CSS media query on a link element -->
<link rel="stylesheet" media="screen and (max-width:720px)"
  href="example.css" />
```

In the example, the stylesheet will be applied to viewports on devices with widths of 400px or lower. The CSS stylesheet `link` element lives in the `<head>` tag, before the `<body>` tag.

The `media` attribute is the actual query. Here, you can set the conditions that, if `true`, will load the linked stylesheet. You can add more logic to this media query conditional expression in the `media` attribute by including `and`, `not`, or `only` to the query expression. You can also specify the media type; however, there are not too many universally useful options here beyond `screen` and `print`.

Media queries are most useful when included in the CSS. Here is the place you can make them really work for you and make a fully responsive website.

A better example

Enough explaining; let's jump into some learning by doing. Open up your favorite IDE and create a new HTML file. It should look something like the following code sample. Remember to include your viewport meta tag!

```html
<!doctype html>
<html lang='en'>
    <head>
        <title>Responsive Web Design</title>
        <meta name="viewport" content="width=device-width,
            initial-scale=1.0, user-scalable=no">
    </head>
    <body>
        ...
    </body>
</html>
```

That was easy, I hope. We need to add some content and markup to that skeletal HTML. Next, within the body, insert a `paragraph` element with some ipsum text to fill it up, as I have in the following code sample:

```html
<body>
    <p>
    Lorem ipsum dolor sit amet, consectetur adipiscing elit.
    Suspendisse eget finibus dolor. Cum sociis natoque penatibus
    et magnis dis parturient montes
    </p>
</body>
```

Adding style

You've created a simple webpage; next, let's create a stylesheet and try some media queries. Back in the header of the HTML page, add a CSS stylesheet link. This time, include `screen` and `max-width` as a feature of the inline media query. See this in the following code sample:

```html
<head>
    <link rel="stylesheet" media="screen and (max-width: 720px)"
        href="style.css" />
</head>
```

In the same directory, create a new file, `style.css`. Open it in your text editor or IDE and add some style for the `<p>` element. Give it a `font-size` value of `12px`. This is illustrated in the following code:

```
p {
    font-size: 12px;
}
```

Next, we will add a media query to the CSS. The media query will begin with `@media` and then the operator in parentheses. A bracket { . . . } will follow, containing the style attributes you want applied for that media query. Let's go through the media queries listed previously. I'll show this in the following code sample:

```
@media (width:360px) {
    p {
        font-size:20px;
    }
}
```

This media query will apply only when the viewport `width` is `360px`. The result is that the font of the paragraph will render at `20px`. That's great, but honestly, it is not very useful, because it will apply only when this condition is `true`. If the viewport is `361px` or `359px`, then it is `false`. This is too laborious to test. Instead, recall that this feature can accept `min`/`max` prefixes. So, you can probably guess that I'm going to tell you to prefix the `width` feature with `min` or `max` and show it in a code sample, like this:

```
@media (max-width:360px) {
    p {
        font-size:20px;
    }
}
```

Viewing your example

Demonstrating this feature will be a snap. Launch the HTML file in your browser and compare the desktop version to what you see when you toggle the display mode in the inspector to a viewport size that is less than `360px`. You should be seeing a larger font size when the page is viewed on a mobile device. Try out some of the other media queries mentioned in the previous list to see how they apply; at least try the ones you can test.

Adding complexity to your stylesheet

Next, let's work on some combinations of features to demonstrate how they work together. We will combine two media query features using the conjunction and. Our purpose will be to have a specific style attribute apply only to viewports between two size values. To make a combined media query that applies style attributes only to tablets, we might want the style to apply to all viewports between 360px and 600px. So, let's create a media query for viewport sizes greater than 360px and less than 600px, as I have in the following code:

```
@media (min-width:360px) and (max-width:600px) {
    p {
        font-size:16px;
    }
}
```

Refresh your browser and you will see that there are now three distinct font sizes rendered in the viewport. Look at this set of screenshots for an example:

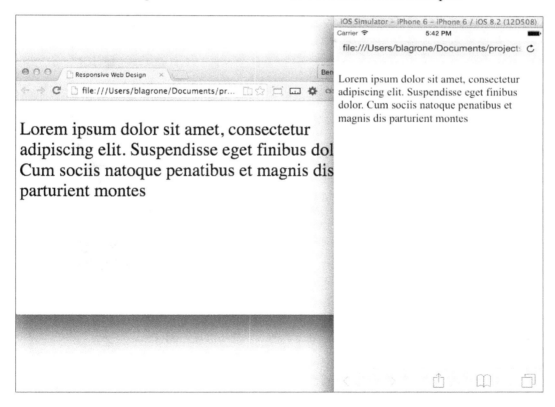

Adding more media queries

Let's add just one more media query to get a more complete picture. This next media query should apply to tablets only, so create a new media query for viewports greater than 600px. Take a look at the following code example:

```
@media (min-width:600px) {
    p {
        font-size:14px;
    }
}
```

See how the sample media queries work:

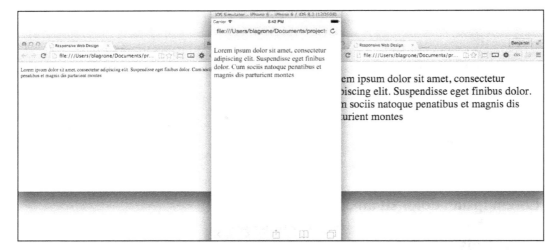

It is typical to combine many media queries in a stylesheet in order to create a fully responsive web application. I often even create media queries to apply style attributes for larger screens. This is W3C often an overlooked aspect of responsive design, as most discussion is centered on mobile. But just as screens have gotten smaller, they have also gotten larger. Your specific project may need to consider the audience using a viewport larger than 1400px.

> In this sample project, if you need to create a media query for anything over 720px, you will need to remove the inline media query.

More complicated examples

The following sample code is an example of a series of media queries to cover a broad spectrum of viewport sizes:

```
@media (max-width:600px) {
    p {
        font-size:12px;
    }
}
@media (min-width:600px) and (max-width:900px) {
    p {
        font-size:14px;
    }
}
@media (min-width:900px) and (max-width:1280px) {
    p {
        font-size:16px;
    }
}
@media (min-width:1280px) and (max-width:1440px) {
    p {
        font-size:18px;
    }
}
@media (min-width:1440px) {
    p {
        font-size:15px;
    }
}
```

This series of media queries would combine to make a starter template for a responsive design that covers a broad spectrum of most device viewports. There are some other media queries that could be useful, such as orientation; here, you can make media queries that apply styles depending on whether the orientation is portrait or landscape. See this code for an example:

```
@media (orientation: landscape) {
    p {
        font-size:16px;
    }
}
@media (orientation: portrait) {
    p {
        font-size:20px;
    }
}
```

Armed with these media queries, you should be able to create a framework that works pretty well for most responsive design scenarios. Now, let's move on to working with some media. You will be using media queries in the upcoming sections to apply responsive styles to your webpage.

Working with responsive media

Media is a big deal in web design and development and is therefore a big deal in responsive web design and development. Our concern with preparing for media in our web development concerns optimization. We want to consider many factors, such as bandwidth use, but also, and perhaps more importantly, the size and pixel density of the device the media will be viewed on. This next section on responsive media will prepare you to handle these concerns.

Creating responsive images with srcset

Not too long ago, when developers wanted to make a truly responsive image, we had to construct server-side and client-side code to deliver a responsive image to the viewport. The client would detect and store the viewport size and send the data to the server when making requests for images. Much of the developers' discussion was centered on delivering the "right-sized" image to the device, and consideration of the user's bandwidth was a factor. This solution was burdensome enough that many developers opted to just send the large file anyway, instead of choosing among three (or more) versions of each picture, and let the CSS scale the image to fit in the viewport.

How things have changed

In recent history, the advent of high-density displays changed the focus of the discussion, and "right-sized" took on a new meaning. Now, high-density displays mean that you need to deliver a much larger file to the viewport—a game changer for sure. Now the larger file is more appropriate for mobile devices' high-density displays. This is a polar change from the original story, where the developer was considerate of the viewers' bandwidths.

The emerging technology of high-density displays is the driving force in this change in how we develop mobile apps. Now, responsive web design is liberated from the chains of developing for bandwidth limits, and we can now develop for more beautiful displays.

A brand-new solution

With that said, let's leave behind our cares about bandwidth for a moment and take a look at a new solution, srcset — a new attribute of the img element. It has only recently been implemented in select browsers. Not every browser has implemented this attribute, only the browsers that need it have it: the primary mobile browsers. If you want to know exactly which ones have it, take a look at **Can I Use _____?** (http://caniuse.com/#feat=srcset) for the most recent versions that have implemented this feature.

The srcset attribute allows the developer to define a list of sources for the image attribute, selected by the user agent based on the device's viewport pixel density ratio for each CSS pixel. Sounds convoluted, yes; it's sort of a pink unicorn hocus pocus, whatever that means.

Instead of me struggling to explain the hocus pocus, let's go through an example that demonstrates the property.

Enough theory, let's do something

Before we start with any code, let's get the content created. Get a hold of a large high-resolution image. If you don't have any, perform an advanced imaged search on Google; search for the subject, select **Images**, then **Search Tools**, and then set **Size** to **Large**. Then select an image you like, and save it to your hard drive.

Next, open it in your favorite image-editing software. If you don't have an image-editing software, or a favorite for that matter, you can download a free, open source image editing software from http://www.gimp.org/. GIMP has versions for Windows, Mac, and Linux. It's good enough for the purposes of resizing an image. In your new favorite photo-manipulating software, create the largest-sized image. I chose 1024 pixels and named it robot-large.png (because I think robots are really cool). Next, scale down the image to make two smaller images, one of 600 pixels, named robot-medium.png and the other of 300 pixels, named robot-low.png. Now that you have your images ready, place them into the img subdirectory of your project for later. From here, we can get on with the code.

Layout basics

You should already be familiar with the basics of layout, such as picking out your IDE and basic HTML tags. So launch your IDE and create an HTML page, as I have in the following code example. Remember your viewport; it's important:

```
<!DOCTYPE>
<html>
    <head>
    <title>Trying out SRCSET</title>
    <meta name="viewport" content="width=device-width" initial-
        scale=1 maximum-scale=1>
    </head>
    <body>
        //TODO add the content
    <body>
</html>
```

That was easy, wasn't it? I hope so. If not, go back to the beginning of the section and start over. Otherwise, your training has begun.

We are going to add the image soon, but first, let's get our CSS out of the way, as the bulk of the operation is a content issue, not a style issue. In your header, right before the closing `header` tag, add a `style` tag with CSS for the `img` element. Display it as block and with a `width` of `50%`. You can add media queries later if you want to do some more involved work for the responsive design. These instructions are implemented in the following code:

```
<style>
img{
    display:block;
    width:50%;
}
</style>
```

That simple block of CSS is all we are going to do with CSS. Everything else will be handled within the `img` tag. The next sensible thing to do is add the `img` tag to our HTML. We will add an `img` tag with the `src` attribute set to `robot-large.png`. Don't forget your `alt` attribute for Section 508 compliance. See this demonstrated in the following code:

```
<img
    src='./img/robot-large.png'
    alt='a picture of a robot'
/>
```

The `src` attribute is the fallback called when the code is viewed on a browser that has not implemented `srcset`. This is an acceptable depreciation, as you will find this occurs only on some of the not-so-cool desktop browsers.

Making the img element responsive

Finally, let's get into the meat and potatoes of this subsection: the new attribute, `srcset`. We are going to list all three of the images we created, matched to the pixel density ratio we previously described. The attribute will take a comma-separated list of image name and pixel-density ratio pairs. For the very large pixel density screens, say those with three times as many pixels as a regular CSS pixel, we will use `robot-large.png`. Then, add the comma. For `robot-medium.png`, set it to be used with screens with twice the pixel density. Comma again. For the smallest version of your image, `robot-low.png`, attach it to the screens with comparable pixel density, such as normal monitors.

We use the x descriptor after the image name in `srcset` to determine the appropriate pixel density to match the image against. Look at this code sample:

```
<img
    srcset='./img/robot-high.png 3x,
    ./img/robot-medium.png 2x,
    ./img/robot-low.png 1x'
    src='./img/robot.png'
    alt='a picture of a robot'
/>
```

Viewing your responsive image

Next, launch the file in your browser. Open the **Inspector** (right-click, and select **Inspect Element**) and go to the **Network** tab. Refresh, and you will see that the browser has loaded `robot-low.png`, if you are working on a laptop with a normal pixel density.

Click on the mobile phone icon in the inspector window to start the mobile user agent emulator. Now, as you toggle between different types of device emulators, you will see that the appropriate image is loaded for devices with larger pixel densities. For example, the Samsung S4 loads the high-resolution file, while the iPhone 3 loads the medium-resolution image. If you do not see the change automatically, you may need to refresh the screen after you select a different device emulator. The following screenshots demonstrate the different renderings:

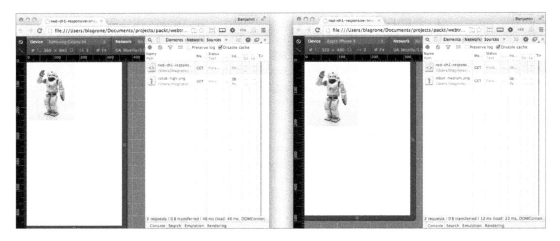

Beyond this cursory lesson, there are other features for images that are not yet implemented, so it's impractical to go beyond the x descriptor too much. There is another descriptor, the w descriptor, but it is not implemented in many browsers. In the future, this may be implemented, and then you can integrate with the `sizes` attribute.

The `srcset` attribute is a really big leap forward for interface development. It is difficult to conceptualize at first, but once you do, and match it to some clever media queries, such as ones we'll discuss soon, you can create some outstanding responsive UI work.

Creating responsive images with CSS

Images are a big deal in responsive design. Once we have the right image delivered to the viewport, we can use CSS to manage how the viewport renders the image. This is simple in theory. In practice, however, responsive design for images can be a little more complicated. It is important to have a good plan for how you want your design to handle images responsively.

In this section, we will go through some of the more complicated strategies; first, let's get started with the simple aspects of responsive design for images.

Getting started coding

The first part of this exercise is to create a simple webpage with an image in it. You can use the `srcset` example from the previous chapter if you already have it. If not, use the following example code. You should also place an image in a folder named `img` in your root directory:

```
<img
    srcset='./img/robot-high.png 3x,
            ./img/robot-medium.png 2x,
            ./img/robot-low.png 1x'
    src='./img/robot.png' alt='a picture of a robot'
/>
```

In your header, create a section for the CSS. You don't need a separate text file for your stylesheet; it won't be so complicated as to justify the extra complexity. Inside it, add a CSS style for the `img` element.

Responsive style

The `img` element is easy to make responsive. Simply give it a width of `100%`, and set the height to `auto` so that the aspect ratio stays proportional. The `100%` width will stretch the image to fill its wrapping element. Keep this in mind, as we will discuss it later. Look at the code in the following code sample:

```
<style>
    img{
        width: 100%;
        height: auto;
    }
</style>
```

Open your HTML document in your browser, and you will see the image stretched fully across your screen. Technically, this is responsive, but it does not respond in a good way. If the viewport area is wider than the image, then the image may become pixelated and blurry. This is certainly not optimal. So let's work on this some more.

Above and beyond

To prevent the image from exploding all over your viewport, you can add some more complexity to the CSS. Try limiting the width of the img element to the width of the actual image. To do so, you will need to change the width attribute to a max-width value of 100%. This small change allows the image to be responsive with the viewport changes limited to the maximum size of the image. This means that if the image is really only 300px, then that's as big as it will get. This starts to make sense if you can work out some good patterns along with the srcset attribute of the img element. You can see the additional CSS in the following code sample:

```
<style>
    img{
        max-width: 100%;
        height: auto;
    }
</style>
```

Often, you will not want your image to take up 100% of the viewport. Of course, there are a number of layouts where an image takes 100% of the viewport width. That aside, in your content area, your image may not be the most important piece of content in the viewport.

Responsive images can be difficult to manage, and you may want to have a more universal control over how the images look in a template. Additionally, you would probably never simply leave the image by itself on a page; you would likely have some wrapper around it for thoughtful layout control.

With that in mind, add a wrapping div element around your image and give it a class identifier. In this example, we can use foo:

```
<div class="foo">
<img
    srcset='./img/robot-high.png 3x,
            ./img/robot-medium.png 2x,
            ./img/robot-low.png 1x'
    src='./img/robot.png' alt='a picture of a robot' />
</div>
```

Now that the image is naturally resting inside of the layout element, you will change the CSS so that the image is maximized inside the wrapping `div` element, and the wrapping `div` element is used therefore for control of the layout. For this simple example, make the wrapping element to have a width of 30% of the viewport. Restyle the `img` to be a width of 100%.

```
<style>
    div.foo {
        width: 30%;
    }
    img{
        width: 100%;
        height: auto;
    }
</style>
```

Now we have better layout control of the image and how it is placed in the layout. Look at the example illustrated in the following screenshots:

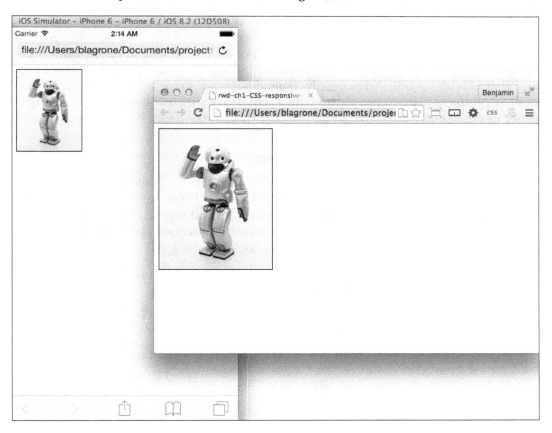

Calculating the responsive image size

Speaking of layout, before we move on, let's briefly take a look at an example of how to determine the percentage width of an image for responsive design. Take a look at, or create a static layout (low-fidelity) version of, the page that is 1024px wide. Take an image and place it in the layout at 300px. To calculate the percentage of the image width, or the wrapping `div`, for our image, we simply need to divide the image width, 300 (px), by the layout width, 1024 (px). This gives us 0.2929, or roughly 29%. This is expressed as *300/1024 = 0.2929*. And do not forget that if you are adding margins as padding, each must be doubled for both sides and added to the space it takes. Therefore, a 300px image with 2px horizontal padding and 2px horizontal margins will take up 308px of the horizontal width of the 1024px screen, which comes to 0.3001 or 30.01%. Keeping the vertical padding and margins as static pixels is recommended.

Adding responsive video to your site

This book would be incomplete without a section on how to create a responsive template for video. Video, as a medium, has become one of the most prolific forms of communication using the Internet. Hordes of people are seeking to become Internet-famous with their own YouTube channels, and these videos are posted all over blogs and shared with friends. Additionally, businesses want to include live-action shots of their products to demonstrate how they will help their customers. In fact, nearly every new site will likely have some video component.

Working with two use cases

This section will demonstrate how to create the template for embedding a video and controlling how it will display in your responsive site. There are different use cases to consider: first, you are hosting the video yourself, and second, you are embedding it hosted on another site using an `iframe` element. The second is more common as people often use a video-hosting service such as YouTube.

Use case #1 – self-hosted video

If you are hosting the video yourself, this is easy—just like a responsive image. Set up your video, and an example of the layout code is as follows:

```
<video width = "320" height = "240" controls = "controls">
    <source src = "movie.mp4" type = "video/mp4">
    <source src = "movie.ogg" type = "video/ogg">
    Your browser does not support the video tag.
</video>
```

Then, use CSS to give the video a percent width and an automatic height, as I have demonstrated here:

```
video {
    max-width: 100%;
    height: auto;
}
```

That was simple, but perhaps it is not the most pertinent of the use cases.

Use case #2 – embedded through the iframe element

Let's examine the use case of embedding the video through an `iframe` element. The typical method for embedding the video is as follows:

```
<iframe src = "http://player.vimeo.com/video/123456789" width =
    "800" height= "450" frameborder = "0">
</iframe>
```

The `iframe` element itself is not a responsive element, so we need to wrap it with an element that we can exert control over. Create a wrapping `div` with a `video-wrap` class, as I have in the following code:

```
<div class="video-wrap">
    <iframe src = "http://player.vimeo.com/video/52948373?badge=0"
        frameborder = "0">
    </iframe>
</div>
```

Responsive video CSS

This will allow us to use CSS to force the `iframe` element to behave responsively. For `iframe` itself, the CSS is simple: assign it an absolute position to the top at 0px and a 100% height and width. The wrapping `div` is where the magic happens. First, give it a relative position to the top at `0` also so that the `iframe` element is an absolute within a relative position. Then, assign it a `55%` padding to the bottom and `30px` to the top. Finally, hide the overflow. The code is shown here:

```
<style>
    .video-wrap {
    position:relative;
    padding-bottom: 55%;
    padding-top:30px
    height: 0;
    overflow:hidden;
    }
```

```
    .video-wrap iframe,
    .video-wrap object,
    .video-wrap embed {
    position:absolute;
    top:0;
    width:100%;
    height:100%;
    }
</style>
```

Modifying the layout

We have laid a good foundation for controlling the video `iframe` element. Next, we can make it responsive. Like a responsive image, we control the width of the video by making it consume 100% of its parent element width, and then we make the parent width responsive.

The next step will be to add another wrapping `div` element to the video. Give it a `video-outer-wrap` class, as I have in this sample code:

```
<div class="video-outer-wrap">
    <div class="video-wrap">
        <iframe src =
          "http://player.vimeo.com/video/52948373?badge=0"
          frameborder = "0">
        </iframe>
    </div>
</div>
```

Then add to the CSS attributes for `video-outer-wrap`, like the following code demonstrates:

```
.video-outer-wrap {
    width: 50%;
}
```

Viewing the example

Now, launch the file in your browser. This is a big improvement: we can control the size of the video in the viewport now. Look at the example in the following screenshots:

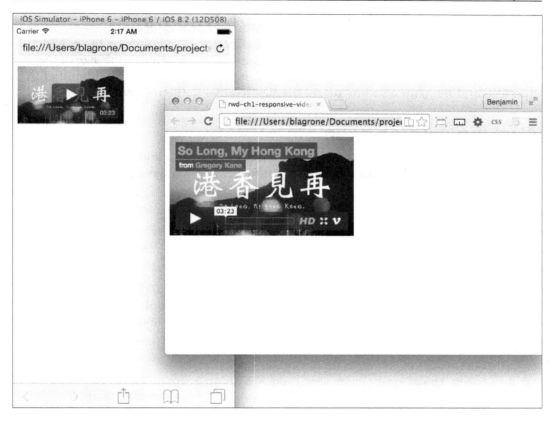

The next step to do on your own is to add some media queries so that, for different devices, you can have a different-sized video.

Communicating with responsive typography

In your responsive project, you must consider your typography. Typography is probably the most important part of responsive design, as the Internet's primary purpose is to convey information. Sure, there are plenty of pictures and video, but type is what makes the Internet useful. Therefore, a certain level of attention to type should be expected.

A question would arise: is there more to it than just setting the font just a few pixels bigger or smaller for the mobile viewport? Yes, of course. Think about the fact that the devices for which you will be designing can be quite diverse and will have different factors that affect your content's usability.

A good solution for responsive typography

A shiny happy new font size was introduced in CSS3, rem. It is similar to em, which means relative to the font size of the element. rem means relative to the size of the root element. This means that you set the font size at the root or HTML identifier in your CSS and then, for an element, set the size relative to the root with rem.

Working with an example

To try a bold experiment, create a new HTML document and add three paragraphs of text. Give them each a different class identifier. See how I have done it in the following code:

```
<p class="foo">
    Lorem ipsum dolor sit amet, consectetur adipiscing elit.
    Suspendisse eget finibus dolor. Cum sociis natoque penatibus
    et magnis dis parturient montes
</p>
<p class="bar">
    Lorem ipsum dolor sit amet, consectetur adipiscing elit.
    Suspendisse eget finibus dolor. Cum sociis natoque penatibus
    et magnis dis parturient montes
</p>
<p class="gup">
    Lorem ipsum dolor sit amet, consectetur adipiscing elit.
    Suspendisse eget finibus dolor. Cum sociis natoque penatibus
    et magnis dis parturient montes
</p>
```

Create the typography's CSS

Next, create the CSS for the root HTML element and the three p elements. The root needs to have the font size defined. Give it a font-size value of 60% of its default size. Then, for each paragraph, assign a font-size attribute of 1rem, 2rem, and 3rem. This is demonstrated in the following code:

```
<style>
    html{font-size:60%;}
    p.foo{font-size:1rem;}
    p.bar{font-size:2rem;}
    p.gup{font-size:3rem;}
</style>
```

Different `rem` font sizes will appear differently in the viewport. Now that we've illustrated a point, let's change the demonstration to be a responsive demonstration of `rem` font sizes. Next, we will add media queries to our CSS to demonstrate responsive typography. Add new media queries for breakpoints at `320px`, `768px`, and `1024px`. Look at the following code sample:

```
<style>
    @media screen and (max-width:320px)
    {
    }
    @media screen and (min-width:320px) and (max-width:768px)
    {
    }
    @media screen (min-width:768px) and (max-width:1024px)
    {
    }
    @media screen (min-width:1024px)
    {
    }
</style>
```

Next, add the font size by `rem` CSS to each of the series of media queries, like this:

```
<style>
    @media screen and (max-width:320px)
    {
        html{font-size:60%;}
        p.foo{font-size:3rem;}
        p.bar{font-size:3rem;}
        p.gup{font-size:3rem;}
    }
    @media screen and (min-width:320px) and (max-width:768px)
    {
        html{font-size:60%;}
        p.foo{font-size:2rem;}
        p.bar{font-size:2rem;}
        p.gup{font-size:2rem;}
    }
    @media screen and (min-width:768px) and (max-width:1024px)
    {
        html{font-size:100%;}
        p.foo{font-size:1rem;}
        p.bar{font-size:1rem;}
        p.gup{font-size:1rem;}
    }
```

```
    @media screen and (min-width:1024px)
    {
        html{font-size:60%;}
        p.foo{font-size:1rem;}
        p.bar{font-size:1rem;}
        p.gup{font-size:1rem;}
    }
</style>
```

Finished!

Now, save you progress and refresh your screen. Launch your mobile device emulator and you will be able to run a battery of tests to see how this typography is effected on different devices. Look at these sample screenshots:

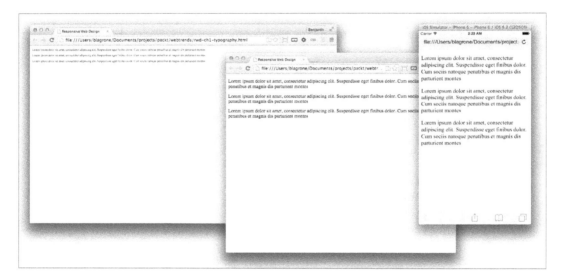

Building responsive layouts

This penultimate section in responsive design will be about creating layouts for your responsive design. Creating the layout is the exciting and challenging part of creating a responsive web design. There are a number of ways to go about this. We'll go through them, starting with some very simple methods of creating a responsive layout for your project.

Creating responsive padding with the box model property

The first aspect of responsive layout we will cover is the use of padding and margins to control your responsive layout. This is indeed a low-level form of responsive design. First, let's review some of the mathematic principles you should keep in mind when using padding in your responsive layout. These are referred to as the **box model properties**. The total offset width of your object should include the actual width plus its left and right padding, its left and right border, and its left and right margin, or *2 x (margin + border + padding) + Element = total width.* Next, divide one side of the padding by the total width of the box model property.

To make the padding responsive, a static width will not be a useful attribute. A 10px width may look first right for your desktop design, but on a mobile device, it is preferable to make the padding a percentage of the viewport. We can use the box model property to calculate the padding percentage. The percentage is easily calculated by one side of the padding divided by the total with of the page viewed in standard desktop format, or 1024px. Let's look at a real-world example.

A real-world example

Start by creating a new HTML document, and include an image followed by a paragraph of text. Next, we'll work on creating the responsive padding in CSS. I have shown the setup below:

```
<html>
    <head>
        <meta name="viewport" content="width=device-width initial-
        scale=1 maximum-scale=1">
        <style>
        </style>
    </head>
    <body>
        <img src="img/robot-med.png"/>
        <p>
            Lorem ipsum dolor sit amet, consectetur adipiscing
            elit, sed do eiusmod tempor incididunt ut labore et
            dolore magna aliqua. Ut enim ad minim veniam, quis
            nostrud exercitation ullamco laboris nisi ut aliquip
            ex ea commodo consequat. Duis aute irure dolor in
            reprehenderit in voluptate velit esse cillum dolore eu
            fugiat nulla pariatur. Excepteur sint occaecat
            cupidatat non proident, sunt in culpa qui officia
            deserunt mollit anim id est laborum
```

```
        </p>
    </body>
</html>
```

Within the style tag, add a style for the `img` and `p` tags. And add a 4px padding, 4px margin, and 1px border around the `img` tag. This is a standard non-responsive design for layout padding. Look at the following code example:

```
<style>
    img{
        padding:4px 4px;
        border:1px solid #ccc;
        margin:4px;
    }
    p{}
</style>
```

Let's take this simple example of a static design and turn it into a responsive design. In this example, we want to convert the static padding width in pixels into a width measured by a percentage of the viewport.

Applying the box model property

To calculate a percentage that will be proportional to the desktop design, apply the box model properties formula to this example, as follows:

4px / [2 x (4px + 1px + 4px) + 300px] = 0.0126

Take the fraction and convert it to a percentage, and then apply it to your padding of the `img` element. You can also apply it to the margin. To apply it to the margin, I would recommend you only apply it to the left and right margins, not the top and bottom. Otherwise, your vertical alignment could become distorted and produce some unintended consequences. See it done in the following code sample:

```
<style>
    img{
        padding:1.26%;
        border:1px solid #ccc;
        margin:1.26%;
    }
</style>
```

Finished!

Upon launching the HTML in your browser and in the mobile device emulator, you will see that this makes a good layout control for the image that looks good on both desktop and mobile viewports.

Going further

A useful variation of this will be to add a media query to keep the padding static for desktop viewports. This will prevent the padding and margins from blowing up on larger desktops. I have done this in the following sample code:

```
<style>
    @media screen and (max-width: 620px){
        img{
            padding:1.26%;
            border:1px solid #ccc;
            margin:1.26%;
        }
    }
    @media screen and (min-width:620px){
        img{
            padding:4px;
            border:1px solid #ccc;
            margin:4px;
        }
        p{
        }
    }
</style>
```

This is a good start; however, it does not really utilize the space very well. There are some problems to fix in order to make this a good responsive design. The first problem I see is that the paragraph of text clears the image on mobile and desktop. We need to better utilize the space if this is going to be a good responsive design. Start by cleaning up the CSS. There are some redundant attributes, such as the `border` attribute. To clean this up, we should have only the attributes that change inside the media queries. See it illustrated in the following sample code:

```
<style>
    @media screen and (max-width:620px){
        img{
            padding:1.26%;
            margin:1.26% 4px;
        }
```

```
        }
        @media screen and (min-width:620px){
            img{
                padding:4px;
                margin:4px;
            }
        }
        img{
            border:1px solid #ccc;
        }
    </style>
```

Now, in your `min-width` media query, add a left and right float to the `img` and `p` selectors, adding a paragraph selector. In the same media query, add a percentage width to each element. You will need to account for the box model properties you calculated previously. In our example, our margin and padding were 1.26%, and the 1px border would altogether make it about 2.53%. To be safe, you can round the percentage width of the `img` down to 47%, as I have in this sample code:

```
    <style>
        @media screen and (max-width:620px){
            img{
                padding:1.26%;
                margin:1.26%;
                width:95%;
            }
        }
        @media screen and (min-width: 620px){
            img{
                padding:4px;
                margin:4px;
                width:47%;
                float:left;
            }
            p{
                float:right;
                width:50%;
            }
        }
            img{
                border:1px solid #ccc;
            }
    </style>
```

Viewing your example

Launch the new version of your HTML document and you will see how, on viewports larger than 620px, both elements are floating left and right. When viewed on a mobile viewport, you will see they are aligned horizontally. This is a basic responsive layout.

Adding more complexity

You can add more complexity through additional media queries. Let's add another media query for additional practice. We want to add a media query for all viewports over 1024px. This also means that we need to prevent conflicts with the `min-width:620px` media query. Add to it another query parameter that limits the style to a `max-width` value of 1024px, like in the following sample code:

```
@media screen and (min-width:620px) and (max-width:1024px)
```

You will also need to add the new media query for viewports over 1024px, like in the following sample code snippet:

```
@media screen and (min-width:1024px)
```

In this media query, add the same selectors as for the 620px to 1024px viewports; only change the width to make the image take up a smaller proportion of the screen than before. In my example here, I make them `17%` and `80%`:

```
@media screen and (min-width:1024px){
    img{
        padding:4px;
        margin:4px;
        width:17%;
        float:left;
    }
    p{
        float:right;
        width:80%;
    }
}
```

Finished! Now view your work

Launch this in your viewport, and you will see your responsive layout optimizing itself for these three differently sized viewports. Look at the example illustrated here:

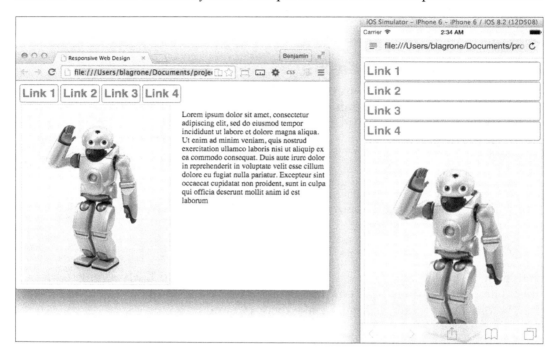

Next, it will be up to you to use the same principles to make more creative and exciting layouts.

Creating responsive navigation with CSS and JavaScript

A usable navigation element is vital to your audience being able to find what they want on your site. A top-horizontal navigation layout may work on a desktop-only site, but it will be difficult to see on a mobile device. Due to the differences in the viewports of desktops and mobile devices, the navigation design should be different and optimized for each.

Jump into an example

This subsection builds on top of the previous one on responsive layouts. If you have not been following along by section, you can just as easily start with a new file.

In this example, we will add a navigation element to the work we did in the previous chapter on responsive layouts. Inside the body tag at the top, insert a nav element. Next, inside the nav element, add a list of links. This is demonstrated in the following code snippet:

```
<nav>
    <ul>
        <li><a href="#">Link 1</a></li>
        <li><a href="#">Link 2</a></li>
        <li><a href="#">Link 3</a></li>
        <li><a href="#">Link 4</a></li>
    </ul>
</nav>
```

Your navigation HTML is complete, so let's double our efforts and add the CSS to make it responsive.

Creating the responsive CSS with media queries

In a media query for viewports under 480px, add a selector for the nav with the display:block style and a selector for nav LI with the display:inline-block style. Also, let's add some style to this menu so that it does not look so plain Jane. Add a section in the CSS outside of any media queries, and in it, add the html, li, and li a selectors.

In the non-responsive area of the CSS, give the HTML a font-size value of 100%, the li a 1px solid green border with a 4px border-radius value, and the li a a block display, Helvetica font, bold font-weight value, font-size value of 1.5 rem, green color, and none for text-decoration. You can also invert it on hover by adding a hover pseudo-element to the li element with a green background color, and to the li a with a white font color. Look at the non-responsive CSS in the following sample code:

```
html{
    font-size:100%;
}
li{
```

```
    border-radius:4px;
    border:1px solid green;
}
li a{
    font-family:Helvetica;
    font-weight:bold;
    font-size:1.5REM;
    color:green;
    text-decoration:none;
    display:block;
}
li:hover{
    background-color:green;
}
li a:hover{
    color:white;
}
```

Next, inside the smaller media query, one with the max-width value of 480px, add an LI and an `li a` selector. Inside the `li` selector, add a block `display` attribute and a top and bottom margin of 2px. Give the `li a` selector a padding of `1.26%`. This is done in the following code:

```
@media screen and (max-width: 480px){
    li{
        display:block;
        margin:2px 0px;
    }
    li a {
        padding:1.26%;
    }
    img{
        padding:1.26%;
        margin:3px 0;
        width:98%;
    }
}
```

Conversely, inside the larger of the media queries, the one with a min-width value of 480px, add the `li` and `li a` selectors. Then, give the `li` selector an inline-block display. And add a 4px padding to the `li a` selector. Cue a corresponding code snippet:

```
@media screen and (min-width:480px){
    li{
        display:inline-block;
    }
    li a {
        padding:4px;
    }
}
```

Your first version is complete

Congratulations, you have created a simple responsive menu! Open it on your desktop and mobile browsers and see whether it looks like these examples:

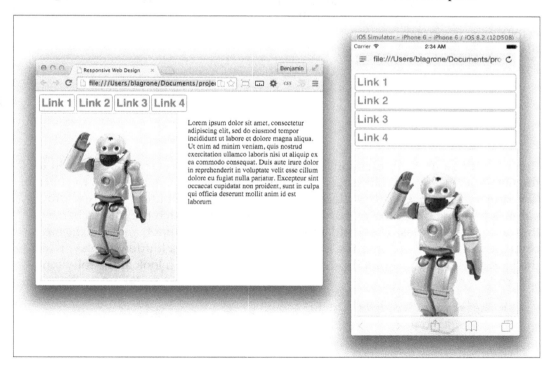

It is optimized for each of our defined viewport sizes. Even though it works, it can still be better, so let's keep working on this responsive menu.

Going further

The problem with our current responsive menu is that on the mobile display, the menu takes up too much vertical space on the viewport. Imagine the frustration of a viewer having to scroll down on every page just to be able to view your content. So, this menu is incomplete. To make it more complete, let's convert it into a hidden menu that is revealed by the user clicking on a button.

Adding interaction

To begin, add a `button` element with a parent `div` element with a `navbutton` class to the top of the page directly beneath the `body` opening tag. Also, add an ID called menu to the `nav` element. We will be using an ID because we will be writing some simple JavaScript to the UI. This JavaScript is so simple we won't be using any libraries such as jQuery. Inside the `button` body, add an inline `onclick` JavaScript code block that activates a function called `menuButton()`. Take a look at the new HTML code example:

```
<body>
    <div class="navButton">
        <button onclick="menuButton()">=</button>
    </div>
    <nav id="menu">
    ...
```

Before writing out the interaction function, let's finish our style in the CSS. Add to the max-width: 480px media query selectors for the `navButton` class and the button. Give the `navButton` selector a block display. Next, give the button a 30px width value, a padding of 4px, a 4px border-radius value, and match the color scheme to the navigation buttons. Then, add a selector for the `nav` element, and add the `nav` element with a class of `show`. The `nav` selector should have a hidden display, while the `nav.show` selector should be displayed as a block. Take a look at the following CSS code example:

```
@media screen and (max-width: 480px){
    .navButton{
        display:block;
    }
    button{
        background-color:green;
        color:white;
```

```
        width:30px;
      padding:4px;
        border-radius:4px;
    }
    nav{
        display:none;
    }
    nav.show{
        display:block;
    }
    ...
```

We do not want this element to be displayed on the larger viewports at all. Add a selector for the navButton class to the media query for viewports larger than 480px. Look at this example code:

```
@media screen and (min-width:480px){
    .navButton{
        display:none;
    }
    ...
```

Finally, the interaction function

Finally, let's build that interaction JavaScript function. Immediately following the closing style tag, add an opening and closing script element. Inside it, define your menuButton() function. Its function starts by defining the theMenu variable as the element with the menu ID. Next, add the conditional test to check whether theMenu does not have the class with the property className of show. If this is true, add the string show to the className property. Otherwise, if the condition is false, and the element does in fact have the show class, set the className property to be a blank string. This will make the button click activate the function to add the show class, show the element if it is not already showing, and if it is visible, to remove the show class, hiding it again. Take a look at this example script:

```
<script>
    function menuButton(){
        var theMenu = document.getElementById("menu");
        if(theMenu.className!="show"){
            theMenu.className = theMenu.className + "show";
        } else {
            theMenu.className = "";
        }
    }
</script>
```

Viewing your interactive responsive navigation

Now, launch your completed page and test it on a mobile device or emulator, and compare it to a desktop view. You will see the menu completely changed, or optimized, for the different views. See the example screenshots here:

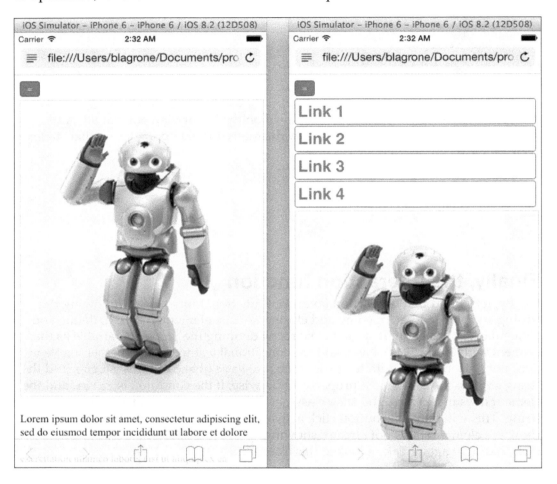

There are still a number of further customizations you can add to this to make it look even better, such as adding transition animations, changing the position of the menu, and, of course, adding more style to the menu. I will leave these improvements to your creative mind.

Summary

We covered a lot of material in this chapter. While there's a lot to swallow, this is possibly one of the most important and useful aspects of modern web development. Combined together, the techniques discussed can deliver an amazing user experience optimized for all types of viewports. With your creativity and this new knowledge, you should be able to deliver clever designs that use responsive media, typography, layout, and navigation. So go forth and create!

2
Flat UI

Flat design is an increasingly popular trend in web design and is currently the dominant design style in mobile interfaces. Based on simplicity, minimalism, and efficiency, flat UI design eliminates much of the third dimension from the design. According to its advocates, it no longer is necessary to mimic the familiar third dimension in UI design, as people have accepted and adopted the mobile device or are practically born with it in their hands and don't need the third dimension anymore. The mobile device is now ubiquitous and can stand on its own.

No discussion of flat design is complete without a reference to what flat design is not. However, let's start our discussion not by defining it by what is not, but by what it is. Flat design is minimal and basic communication of the interactive and content elements of a design, be it native or web. What it does not exhibit is that ugly word, **skeuomorphism** — using 3D objects to represent elements in a way that mimics interacting with the 3D world. Flat design sheds drop shadows, 3D objects, textures, gradients, and (mostly in theory) z-indexing.

I'm not so bold as to predict what people will do. History has a way of unfolding plenty of unexpected weirdness that simple and logical folks like me could never expect. However, there are always plenty of fools willing to make bets on trends. The wristwatch was panned a "passing fancy." Some say that Flat UI is only a passing trend and eagerly wait for their familiar world of skeuomorphic mimicry to return. Others say that people's interests are as fickle as a pendulum and predictably swing back and forth. Some cowards take a more hedged approach and say that it will lose its hotness and become just another design option, and some other new trend will be the new excitement. The hipsters were flat before it became cool.

A brief history of flat design

Flat UI has its roots in the minimalist art movement beginning in the 1920s in Northern Europe and reached its heyday in the mid-twentieth century in Swiss design. It featured sans-serif typography, grids, and asymmetrical layouts. This new design trend used simplicity as a method of conveying clear messages. In this era, people began to look at the text content and type as the most important aspect of the design. This was about the time of the invention of new typefaces such as Helvetica.

Flat UI color

Flat UI brings about a dramatic change in the way color is used in web design. Since the designs are no longer skeuomorphic, designers are more reliant on color and color contrast to relay information on the screen.

Flat UI tends to use more saturated, bright colors instead of grey, white, or black. You can use many different shades, as long as the tone and depth of the colors match. Often, the more simple color palettes are used, but the primary objective is to use colors that help convey the content as opposed to using color to mimic a 3D everyday object. The key is to go for simplicity.

There are a number of online tools to help you create a flat UI color palette. You can take a look at `http://flatuicolors.com` for a good sample of color codes. You can also visit `http://www.colorhexa.com/` for a good color-matching tool.

Sample color swatches for flat UI

This section has a few sample color swatches for you to view. Each swatch has descriptions and reasons you might want to use it. Over at DesignModo, a design company and blog that focuses on flat UI design, there are more swatches like these you can look at:

`http://designmodo.com/flat-design-colors/`

Let's take a look at the color swatches now.

The vivid color swatch

Many style guides on flat UI design recommend using vivid colors to convey simplicity and let the actual content tell the story. This is a good swatch to start with:

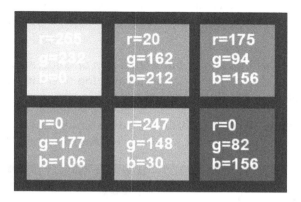

The retro color swatch

Another popular color trend that mixes well with Flat UI is using retro colors. Retro colors have less saturated hues—bright with white added to make them muted and faded. Be careful; these are not pastel, but old school. Use lots of orange, yellow, some red, and blue. It is common to see primary and secondary colors because of the toning down of color.

Retro colors are best when they are the dominant color element and are paired with images or muted colors. The most popular are orange, peach, plum, and dark blue.

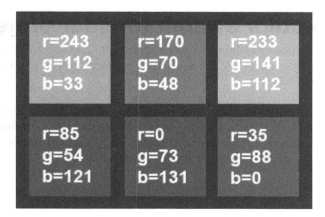

The monotone color swatch

A design trend I like and is very popular, especially for app design, is monotone colors. This color scheme relies on only a single color with black and white to create a bright, distinct palette. Use a base color and two or three tints for effect. As it is regarded a soothing color, the most popular color is blue, followed by green and grey.

Sometimes, a designer will pick grey but with a pop of color, such as red, for buttons and calls to action. Another option is to use a variation of color, for instance, a primary such as blue, but add tints of green.

Monotone color schemes need to include contrast, so mix tints so that each different color is distinct from the parent color. Go from 100% to 50% to 20%.

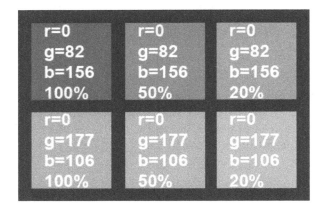

Creating a color swatch for your project

You can also look at other online color guides for flat UI color schemes; `https://flatuicolors.com/` is an excellent source for colors to use in your flat UI design project.

Finally, when you have decided on your style and created a color palette, you will next want to create a CSS style for them. Let's make it easy so you don't have to jump back and forth between your markup and style just to add colors. So, launch your IDE and create a new project for your flat UI design.

Inside the header of the HTML page you created, add a style tag. Inside it, we'll start adding some colors. Get your list of colors you have picked and list them inside the style sheet as selectors. For illustration, I'll use the colors in a code snippet. The Peter River color from `https://flatuicolors.com` really stands out. Let's use that to create a monochrome color palette for our flat UI project. We can also use the Wet Asphalt color for some of the darker colors. Here's the code snippet:

```
<style>
    .peter-river{
    background-color:#3498DB; /* r=52, g=152, b=219, 76% */
    }
    .wet-asphalt{
    background-color:#34495E; /* r=52, g=73, b=94, 45% */
    }
</style>
```

From here, let's create some tints for our Peter River color by modifying the tint by 10% increments.

The additional colors are as follows:

```
.color-1 {
    background-color: #85C4ED; /* r=133, g=196, b=237, 44% */
}
.color-2 {
    background-color: #58ADE3; /* r=88, g=173, b=227, 61% */
}
.color-3 {
    background-color: #0F85D1; /* r=15, g=133, b=209, 93% */
}
.color-4 {
    background-color: #0665A2; /* r=6, g=101, b=162, 96% */
}
```

The color swatch for this is as follows:

Instead of assigning a color to `div` through CSS, we are going to assign the colors by creating a color for the class and assigning the class to the element. You will see how this works in the next section.

Creating a flat UI layout

Before we jump headfirst right into the icy cold waters of layout design, let's talk briefly about what we are making, as it wouldn't be useful to just start laying out a grid without a purpose. In our work, we want to make content or data useful. Often in application development, someone asks for a high-level view of some data set—the ubiquitous dashboard or executive view. So let's make this our practice today: to make a layout for a useful application that gives a decision-maker an at-a-glance view of a daily capacity-utilization metric. See what I did there? I said a lot of things that an executive would like to hear, without saying too much.

Without further ado, let's make this dashboard!

Get your code editor spun up, and let's create this dashboard. Since this is a data visualization tool, we want the audience to focus on the data being presented; therefore, we will use the monochromatic blue color scheme we selected in the previous section.

But first, be sure to create your viewport meta, or this will all be for naught! We can do this using the following code:

```
<meta name="viewport" content="width=device-width, initial-
   scale=1">
```

In the project we created in the previous section, we should have a style section in our header for our monochromatic color scheme:

```
<style>
    .peter-river{
    background-color:#3498DB; /* r=52, g=152, b=219, 76% */
    }
    .wet-asphalt{
    background-color:#34495E; /* r=52, g=73, b=94, 45% */
    }
    .color-1 {
    background-color: #85C4ED; /* r=133, g=196, b=237, 44% */
    }
    .color-2 {
    background-color: #58ADE3; /* r=88, g=173, b=227, 61% */
    }
    .color-3 {
    background-color: #0F85D1; /* r=15, g=133, b=209, 93% */
    }
    .color-4 {
    background-color: #0665A2; /* r=6, g=101, b=162, 96% */
    }
</style>
```

To add to the color setup we already have, we will need to define our layout areas. This is a web application, but it will be a mobile-first responsive web application. Therefore, we want to define different layout displays for portrait versus landscape. Next, in your CSS, add the media queries for portrait versus landscape:

```
@media (orientation:portrait){

}
@media (orientation:landscape){

}
```

That's a good start; next, let's create some of the actual layout elements, and then we will come back to style them. We will want out app to have two responsive sections, each with two `div` elements for dynamic at-a-glance content, a `footer`, and finally, inside each of the next two `div` elements, we want to split them in half by adding two subordinate `div` elements:

```
<body>
    <section>
        <div>FOO</div>
        <div>
            <div>FOO</div>
            <div>FOO</div>
        </div>
    </section>
    <section>
        <div>FOO</div>
        <div>
            <div>FOO</div>
            <div>FOO</div>
        </div>
    </section>
    <footer>FOOTER</footer>
</body>
```

That's the simple form of the layout. It's lovable in its simplicity. Take a good look at it because it will only grow in complexity from here. First give the body some color; give it the class `color-4`. We next want to add some class attributes to the `div` elements for color and to identify the sections later. The first `div` element is for a clock, and we want it to be the `color-0` color as identified in the flat UI color section. The next `div` is a parent element for two `div` elements, so leave it blank, but give its first child `div` element the class name `news` and `color-1` and the last child `div` element the class `tasks` and `color-2`. Jump inside the next section, and assign to the first `DIV` element the class `weather` and `color-3`. The following class is a parent, and like before, we will assign attributes to its children. The first child will have the class `travel` and `color-1`, and the last child will have the class `stock` and `color-4`. In the text, I am referring to the second child as the last child because this is how we will select them later in `CSS`. Finally, for `footer`, let's give it the class for the `wet-asphalt` color. Your layout with the classes will now look like this:

```
<body class="color-4">
    <section>
        <div class="time color-0">FOO</div>
        <div>
            <div class="news color-1" >FOO</div>
            <div class="tasks color-2" >FOO</div>
```

```
        </div>
    </section>
    <section>
        <div class="weather color-3">FOO</div>
        <div>
            <div class="travel color-1">FOO</div>
            <div class="stock color-4">FOO</div>
        </div>
    </section>
    <footer class="wet-asphalt">FOOTER</footer>
</body>
```

Briefly, let's calculate our element dimensions using the golden ratio. Start with our first number 1, add 1 to it to get 2, and then add the previous to it to get 3. Then add to it the previous number to get 5. Follow this pattern until we have a series that looks like this:

```
1, 1, 2, 3, 5, 8, 13, 21, 34, 55, 89, 144, 233, …
```

These numbers, and combinations of them, will be used to define the heights of our areas.

Now back to our CSS: we will make our markup look beautiful. Let's append to our style a body selector and a footer selector. In your body selector, set the padding to 0 and the font color to white. In the footer selector, set the height to 34px. Also, set the footer selector to clear both left and right. The code should look like this:

```css
body{
    margin:0;
    color:white;
}
footer{
    height:34px;
    clear:both;
}
```

Working with our elements, we will use the pseudoselectors first-of-type and last-of-type to select these, as shown in the following code. These will go inside our media queries, so don't put them in just yet:

```css
div:first-of-type{
}
div:last-of-type{
}
section:first-of-type{
}
section:last-of-type{
}
```

And we will also select the `div` elements using the parent selector `>`. This will prevent confusion as we add complexity later in the chapter. Again, do not add these yet:

```
section > div {
}
div > div {
}
```

Next, let's get to work inside our media queries and define the responsive layout for the sections. First, let's work on the simpler portrait mode. The sections should be 100% of the width of the viewport. When viewed in landscape, the sections should each be only 50% of the width. Additionally, set the first of the selectors to float to the left and the second to float to the right. Now, we can add the following code:

```
@media (orientation:portrait){
    section{
        width:100%;
    }
}
@media (orientation:landscape){
    section{
        width:50%;
    }
    section:first-of-type{
        float:left;
    }
    section:last-of-type{
        float:right;
    }
}
```

Now for the `div` elements. In portrait mode, the `div` elements that are children of the section parents need their heights defined. Give the first a height of 110px (89 + 21) and give the same height to the `div` elements that have parent `div` elements, like this:

```
@media (orientation:portrait){
    section{
        width:100%;
    }
    section > div:first-of-type{
        height:110px;
    }
    div > div{
        height:110px;
    }
}
```

The landscape mode is more complicated, as its layout has divided subsections. Assign a height of 144px to the first `div` with a section parent. To the `div` elements with `div` element parents, give a 50% width and a height of 199px (144 + 55 from our Fibonacci sequence above). Finally, float the first and last `div` elements that are children of `div` elements left and right. You should have this:

```
@media (orientation:landscape){
    section{
        width:50%;
    }
    section:first-of-type{
        float:left;
    }
    section:last-of-type{
        float:right;
    }
    section > div:first-of-type{
        height:144px;
    }
    div > div{
        width:50%;
        height:199px;
    }
    div > div:first-of-type{
        float:left;
    }
    div > div:last-of-type{
        float:right;
    }
}
```

Now, aside from applying our selected color palette, our layout is complete. Before we look, let's apply some color to our page. Since we have already created the CSS color palette, we can simply add the CSS classes to our elements in the HTML document. Add the `color-0` class to the first div element, `color-1` to the second, and so on for the other `div` elements, as per your liking. Then assign the `wet-asphalt` class to the footer.

Now, refresh the project in your browser and, now that the simple layout has been laid, you will see our flat UI starting to take shape. This is what it should look like at this point:

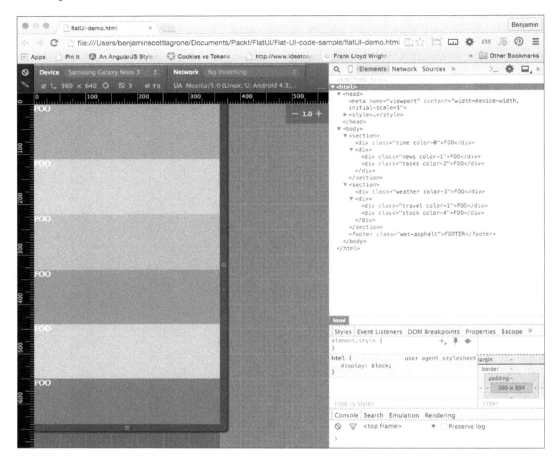

And here it is in landscape mode:

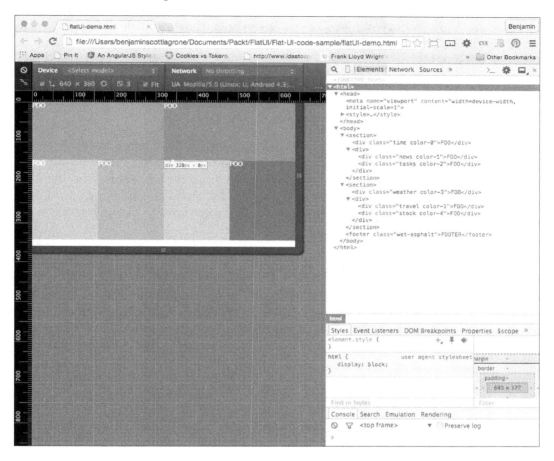

Adding content

In our flat UI design, our focus should be on the content and how it is used. The application we are designing needs to be able to present the most useful information on this at-a-glance screen. Our world is such that we need filters to filter out the rattle and hum of useless data from our newsfeeds. We need an app that gives us the most useful information without any extra clutter.

The content of our executive view is the central aspect of our design. This is why we are studying the Flat UI, so we can focus on being able to display the most import data, without letting design clutter get in the way.

Let's create an app that will display the most useful things you need to see while waking up and getting ready for work, sort of a good morning app. It will display the time and date, important news, upcoming events from your calendar, the weather, stocks, and tasks. This is similar to, but not as sophisticated as, the **Cards** function of Google.

Like the Swiss style I mentioned earlier, our design should be information-oriented, logical, and concerned with the presentation of information. So, let's create some extremely useful fake content for our heads-up display.

Open up your flat UI project; let's add some fake content. First, let's take an inventory of the spaces we have. There is a first main content area, with two sub areas, and a second main content area, also with two sub content areas. And then there is a `footer` area. For this project, we will use the areas to display our most useful information, which we described earlier. Let's go through them one by one and adjust our markup as needed.

Creating a working JavaScript clock

The first large section will display the time and date. We want this to be the largest item and the most visible. For fun, let's make it a working clock. If you don't care to go through this JavaScript code, you can just make your clock a static text like the following, by inserting this inside the `div` element. But you will miss out on the fun.

```
<span>7:45</span> 
<span>Tuesday</span> 
<span>August</span> 
<span>5</span> 
<span>2015</span>
```

If you want to join in the fun, back in your IDE, add a `<script>` tag in your header and add some code. Start with a new function called `getTime()`. We will be working with the JavaScript `Date` object. Because the `Date` object does not return the word values for the day of the week, or the month, we will need to create an array for both to match up against the numerical value. Next, create a new variable, `today`, which will equal `new Date()`:

```
var dayArray =
  ["Sunday","Monday","Tuesday","Wednesday","Thursday","Friday",
  "Saturday"];
var monthArray =
  ["January","February","March","April","May","June",
  "July","August","September","October","November","December"];
```

```
function getTime() {
    var today=new Date();
};
```

Next, we will build our custom nice date text. We'll need to get each part of the date from the `today` date object. Create new variables `h`, `m`, `s`, `d`, `mo`, and `y`. Each of them will access a part of the date object, as listed. The `new Date()` method has a number of methods; we will use `getHours()`, `getMinutes()`, `getSeconds()`, `getDay()`, `getMonth()`, and `getFullYear()`. We will use the numerical values returned by the `getDay()` and `getMonth()` methods to access their respective values from the arrays. These following lines of code show how to put it together:

```
var h=today.getHours();
var m=today.getMinutes();
var s=today.getSeconds();
var d=dayArray[today.getDay()];
var mo=monthArray[today.getMonth()];
var y=today.getFullYear();
```

Next, you will need to build and insert the times into your markup. The following lines of code will get an element by its ID and insert inside the `innerHTML` code. You will create the HTML by combining the times and some wrapping `span` elements into a string. We will add style to these later.

```
document.getElementById('time').innerHTML =
    "<br><h1>"+h+":"+m+":"+s+"</h1> <span>"+d+",</span> 
<span>"+mo+"</span> <span>"+y+"</span>";
```

You will need to add the `id` attribute to the `div` element to make this work. In your HTML, find the first section, and it into it, the first `div`, and add to it the `id` `time` value. This will be found by the JavaScript, and the string containing the time and HTML markup will be added to the `innerHTML` code. Additionally, you will need to cause the function to execute, so inside the `body` tag, add a little inline script, `onload="getTime()"`. These changes can be seen here:

```
<body onload="getTime()" class="color-4">
<section>
    <div class='time color-0' id="time">
```

This is great so far, but there are a couple of things left to do to make this functionality excellent. The clock executes using the `onload` function of JavaScript, which means it works once when the DOM loads. If we leave it like this, it can only be correct two times every day. We need the clock to continue to function and create new time values at set periods of time. To create this rhythmic clock, add another variable `t` for time, which will employ the JavaScript `setTimeout()` method to call `getTime()` at an interval of 500 seconds:

```
var t = setTimeout(function(){getTime()},500);
```

The other problem, and the final step in creating the clock, is that the single-digit numbers are returned in the minimal number of digits necessary, that is, 7 is 7, when 07 is what should be displayed. To correct this, a separate function, correctDigit(), must be created to check whether the number is single-digit, and if so, add the preceding 0 as a string. Also note that the type of the value i returned will be a string.

```
function correctDigit(i) {
    if (i<10)  i = "0"+i;
    return i;
}
```

To use this function to change the second and minute values, add two lines that set the m and s variables to equal the function call with the values before the existing line that places the innerHTML portion in the DOM:

```
m = correctDigit(m);
s = correctDigit(s);
document.getElementById('time').innerHTML =
"<br><h1>"+h+":"+m+":"+s+"</h1> <h2><span>"+d+"</span> 
<span>"+mo+"</span> <span>"+y+"</span></h2>";
```

Our clock is now fully operational and should be a nice-looking feature for the site, but it's only one of the six sections. It is the most complex, I promise, but let's continue and make some more sample content for our other sections.

Adding textual content

The next section will display important news for the viewer. This will be static text. Start with an unordered list of three-line items and in each add an h3 header element around the Title 1 text, and follow it with a short one-line paragraph of Ipsum text (go to http://www.lipsum.com/ to get some Ipsum). Repeat this three times, and the news div element will look like this:

```
<div class="news color-1">
    <ul>
        <li>
            <h3>Title 1</h3>
            <p>Lorem ipsum dolor sit amet, consectetur
            adipiscing elit, </p>
        </li>
        <li>
            <h3>Title 2</h3>
            <p>sed do eiusmod tempor incididunt ut labore
            et dolore magna aliqua.</p>
```

```
            </li>
            <li>
                <h3>Title 3</h3>
                <p>Ut enim ad minim veniam, quis nostrud
                exercitation ullamco laboris nisi ut aliquip
                ex ea commodo consequat.</p>
            </li>
            <li>
                <h3>Title 3</h3>
                <p>Ut enim ad minim veniam, quis nostrud
                exercitation ullamco laboris nisi ut aliquip
                ex ea commodo consequat.</p>
            </li>
            <li>
                <h3>Title 4</h3>
                <p>Ut enim ad minim veniam, quis nostrud
                exercitation ullamco laboris nisi ut aliquip
                ex ea commodo consequat.</p>
            </li>
        <ul>
    </div>
```

The next `div` element will contain upcoming reminders and calendar events for the day. Create another list like the previous one. This one will be a little different. Instead of the title in the `h3` element, put a time value in an `h4` element, and follow it with a paragraph describing the event or task. This `div` element should look something like this:

```
<div class="tasks color-2">
    <ul>
        <li>
            <h4>8:00am</h4>
            <p>Wake up, fall out of bed</p>
        </li>
        <li>
            <h4>9:00am</h4>
            <p>Run the comb across your head</p>
        </li>
        <li>
            <h4>10:00am</h4>
            <p>Find your way downstairs and Drink a
              cup</p>
        </li>
        <li>
            <h4>11:00am</h4>
```

```
            <p>Looking up, notice you are late</p>
        </li>
        <li>
            <h4>12:00am</h4>
            <p>Find your coat and grab your hat</p>
        </li>
    </ul>
</div>
```

Let's talk about the weather, travel, and the stock market

In the next section, the first div element will display weather information. This element will have an unordered list with two columns of data in unordered lists, but both will be the same single solid color. The left-hand column's list will have an h2 title, WEATHER, and following it will be an unordered list with two list items, each with an h3 element for the current temperature, and then a p element with High and Low.

The right-hand column list will have two unordered lists. The first will have the weather points Pollen, Humidity, Precipitation (or Precip), and Wind, each in an h4 element, followed by a number value in a p element. The second list will have four list items, each one with a number for the hour of the day, an icon placeholder, and the temperature for that day. This code for the entire weather div will look like this:

```
<div class="weather color-3">
    <ul>
        <li>
            <ul>
                <li>
                    <h2>WEATHER</h2>
                </li>
                <li>
                    <ul>
                        <li>
                            <span>104</span>
                            <br>
                            <span>High</span>
                        </li>
                        <li>
                            <span>94</span>
                            <br>
```

```
                        <span>Low</span>
                    </li>
                </ul>
            </li>
        </ul>
    </li>
    <li>
        <ul>
            <li>
                <ul>
                    <li>
                        <span>Pollen</span>
                        <span>3.5</span>
                    </li>
                    <li>
                        <span>Humidity</span>
                        <span>90%</span>
                    </li>
                    <li>
                        <span>Precip</span>
                        <span>90%</span>
                    </li>
                    <li>
                        <span>Wind</span>
                        <span>0</span>
                    </li>
                </ul>
            </li>
            <li>
                <ul>
                    <li>
                        <span>9</span>
                        ICON
                        <span>95</span>
                    </li>
                    <li>
                        <span>12</span>
                        ICON
                        <span>100</span>
                    </li>
                    <li>
                        <span>3</span>
                        ICON
                        <span>105</span>
```

```
                          </li>
                          <li>
                              <span>6</span>
                              ICON
                              <span>105</span>
                          </li>
                      </ul>
                  </li>
              </ul>
          </li>
      </ul>
  </div>
```

The last two `div` elements will be much simpler, as they each will only have one data point. In the first one, add the text TRAVEL in an `h3` element as an icon placeholder, and then an `h4` element with a time value in minutes, followed by a paragraph containing the text Minutes to work, indicating the time to drive to work. The second `div` element will have an `h3` element with your favorite stock price, followed by an unordered list with two list items: one for the current price and the second for how much it has gone up that day. If it keeps going up, you won't need to make that long drive to work today. Keep your fingers crossed! Finally, add a list item with the text MORE inside. This block of code will look like this:

```
<div>
    <div class="travel color-1">
        <h2>TRAVEL</h2>
        <h3>45</h3>
        <h4>Minutes to work</h4>
    </div>
    <div class="stock color-4">
        <ul>
            <li>
                <h2>FOO</h2>
            </li>
            <li>
                <ul>
                    <li>
                        <span>104</span>
                    </li>
                    <li>
                        <span>+5.5</span>
                    </li>
                </ul>
```

```
        </li>
        <li>MORE</li>
      </ul>
    </div>
  </div>
```

Congratulations, you have created your content. It still looks messy, but in a following section, we will style it. This is what it should look like:

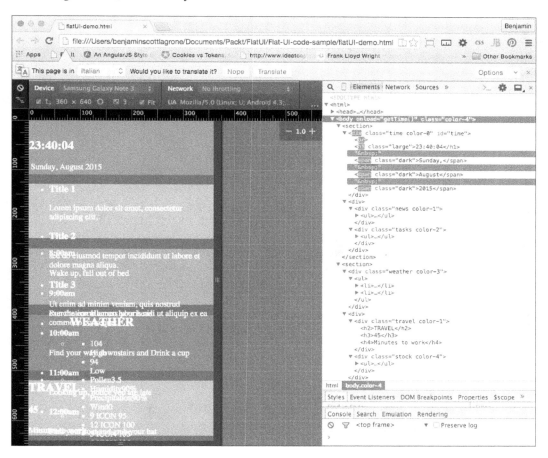

And here it is in landscape mode:

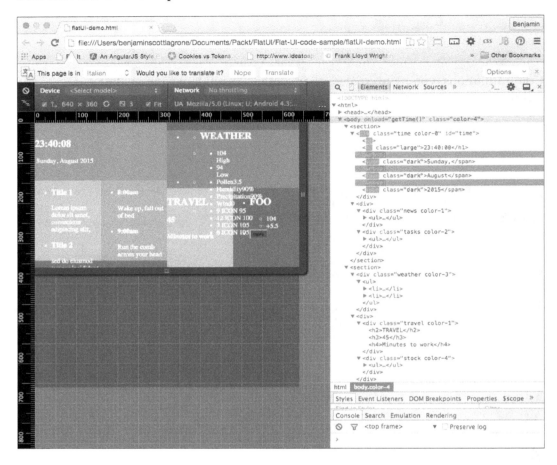

Flat UI typography

Typography is a key component of flat UI design, and choosing the right font can make or break a design. In the distant past, you were limited to your system fonts in your typography choices, and even then, it was advisable to use a font family because there was no guarantee that the font was on any particular system. Or you could have used an image of the text. No, just no.

But lo! Those days are in the past. Now you can use webfonts to make your desires a reality and ensure they are indexed by Google. So choose wisely. For a flat UI project, choose simple and minimalistic.

Adding webfonts

How do you get webfonts? Fortunately, you live in the modern era where you don't have to know how to do anything to actually do anything. You just Google it. But because I'm old school, and this is a book, I'll tell you: Google. Or, more precisely, Google Fonts is an online repository of webfonts you can quickly deploy on your project. There are other providers, such as http://www.cssfontstack.com/, but the link to their actual font is back on Google. So I'd rather go back to the source so that you know it's not going away:

```
<link rel="stylesheet" type="text/css"
  href="//fonts.googleapis.com/css?family=Abel" />
```

Take a look at https://www.google.com/fonts to find a font that suits your taste.

For this project, I have chosen the very popular and good-looking, minimalist webfont from Google, Lato. Lato was created in 2010 by Warsaw designer Łukasz Dziedzic and means "summer" in Polish. I also like it because it's easy to add to your project. The Google page for this font is https://www.google.com/fonts/specimen/Lato.

With that expectation set, let's easily add it to your project. Add the link provided for the webfont to your header before your CSS:

```
<link href=
  'http://fonts.googleapis.com/css?family=Lato&subset=latin,latin-
  ext' rel='stylesheet' type='text/css'>
```

Next, in the body selector in your style code, add the font-family attribute Lato and sans-serif. Your body selector will now look like this:

```
body{
    font-family: 'Lato', sans-serif;
    margin:0;
    color:white;
}
```

I hope I have fulfilled the expectation that this would be easy. Now launch your project in your viewport and take a look at how your typography has transformed. We'll continue to clean this up when we get to the CSS cleanup at the end of the chapter:

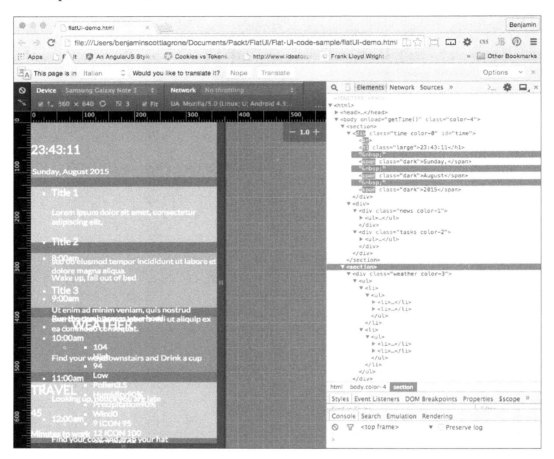

And here it is in landscape mode:

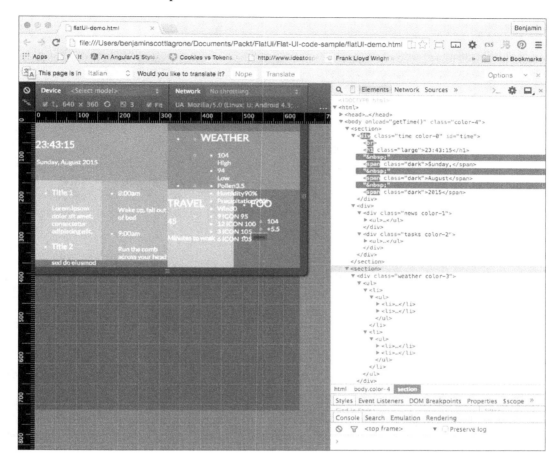

Adding flat UI elements

At this point, the project looks like a big mess. We'll still need to do some cleanup at the end of the project to make this app look amazing.

Let's get to the first and most simple part of the app. Let's add a button to the last `div` element, the `stock div` element. This in theory will be to launch into a browser or pull up a page with more information about the stock you are watching. We want it to be a very dark blue with a white font. So add a `button` with the class `wet-asphalt` to call up the color selector in the CSS:

```
<button onclick="doSomething()" class="wet-
    asphalt">more</button>
```

So far, this is simple enough and a good start. Since we iterate, fail often and early. This means the button looks bad, but we'll take care of that soon enough.

And that's it for the button, for now. Let's continue with our flat UI improvements by adding elements. The next step is much cooler than adding a button. We are going to get into SVG icons. Specifically we are going to use the web-hosted SVG font icon library, **Font Awesome**. These fonts are great because they are completely scalable via CSS and there is no pixelation in doing so. Also, they are easy to deploy and not technically cumbersome.

If you have not heard of Font Awesome yet, then let's fix that. Font Awesome, according to their website, gives you scalable vector icons that can instantly be customized — size, color, drop shadow, and anything that can be done with the power of CSS. Sounds awesome? Well, it *is* awesome. This is a great tool that can help you make great UI, not just flat UI. I don't want to get too much into what it is in theory. Let's jump straight to the how-to section.

We want to add some good-looking graphics to our flat UI. Font Awesome provides a great way to do it. Go to the Font Awesome site and take a few minutes to read the instructions. The project webpage is at `http://fortawesome.github.io/Font-Awesome/`. Play around and look at the example page for some ideas for variations of the fonts. Once you are ready to go into action, go to the icons page and take look at what it has to offer. This is where we will be working from.

The first order of business is to add the reference to the Font Awesome CSS in our header. After the link we added previously for the typography, add a new CSS link to the Font Awesome CDN:

```
<link rel="stylesheet" href="https://maxcdn.bootstrapcdn.com/font-
    awesome/4.4.0/css/font-awesome.min.css">
```

Now, Font Awesome is "installed". We can start inserting cool font icons. Let's skip the clock section and add some icons to each of the other areas. Start with the news section.

On the Font Awesome icons page, search for the word `newspaper` and find the `newspaper-o` icon. Then, right-click on it to open the inspector and look at the code for the icon. The code looks like this:

```
<a href="../icon/newspaper-o"><i class="fa fa-newspaper-o"></i>
    newspaper-o</a>
```

You will need to copy the `i` element and its class information and paste it into your code. You will paste it into the header `h4` tags in your news section and follow it with a space. You could style the `i` element inside the `h4` tag if you wanted its style to be different from the title. It would look like this:

```
<li>
    <h4>
        <i class="fa fa-newspaper-o"></i>
         Title 1
    </h4>
    <p>
        Lorem ipsum dolor sit amet, consectetur adipiscing elit...
    </p>
</li>
```

In each list item of the news section, do the same thing. You could also just copy the class information from the `i` element and paste into the `h4` element. This will save you some space, and it would have the same style as the `h4` text:

```
<li>
    <h4 class="fa fa-newspaper-o">
         Title 1
    </h4>
    <p>
        Lorem ipsum dolor sit amet, consectetur adipiscing elit...
    </p>
</li>
```

Next, jump to the task's `div` element. We want to add a calendar icon to represent tasks. Search the page for a calendar, and you will find a `calendar-check-o` icon. Repeat the same process as before for this icon and add it to the list item headers:

```
<li>
    <h4>
        <i class="fa fa-calendar-check-o"></i>
         8:00 am
    </h4>
    <p>Wake up, fall out of bed</p>
</li>
```

In the section for the weather, we will add a large icon that will indicate the current weather. This icon can be changed on the client on the fly as our data source tells the application the weather has changed. Since it's hot here in Texas, I want some clouds (if only it were this easy to change the weather). Perform a search for cloud, and you will find a cloud icon. Copy it and replace the word WEATHER with the icon and its class. I want this to look bigger, so I will add a Font Awesome class to increase its font size. Add fa-3x to the i element's class. If you want it to be sunny, look for the sun icon and you will find the sun-o icon. This list item will look like this:

```
<li>
    <h2>
        <i class="fa fa-cloud fa-3x"></i>
    </h2>
</li>
```

Skip the list that has the data on pollen humidity and so on, and in the next list, which will show the temperature outlook for the day at different times, add either a cloud or a sun icon to the middle of each list item. You will set it in between the existing spans. This list will look like this:

```
<ul>
    <li>
        <span>9</span>
        <i class="fa fa-sun-o"></i>
        <span>95</span>
    </li>
    <li>
        <span>12</span>
        <i class="fa fa-sun-o"></i>
        <span>100</span>
    </li>
    <li>
        <span>3</span>
        <i class="fa fa-cloud"></i>
        <span>105</span>
    </li>
    <li>
        <span>6</span>
        <i class="fa fa-cloud"></i>
        <span>105</span>
    </li>
</ul>
```

The next section contains the travel and stock div elements. In the first header, travel, we want to add an icon to represent our transportation. I want you to look cool, so instead of a car, search the Font Awesome page for a bicycle and copy the icon code into the first header in the travel div, replacing the TRAVEL text:

```
<h2>
    <i class="fa fa-bicycle fa-4x"></i>
</h2>
```

We will simply do the same for the stock section. Find the `line-chart` icon and copy its code into your stock symbols header:

```
<h2>
    <i class="fa fa-line-chart"></i>
    FOO
</h2>
```

Now, let's take another look. Your flat UI is starting to shape up with our new flat font icons. Next, we need to pull it all together and get the layout sharpened up with some additional CSS. It is fairly normal that at the end of any project, we have to get the last 20 percent of the code together to make it complete. Here is the page in portrait mode:

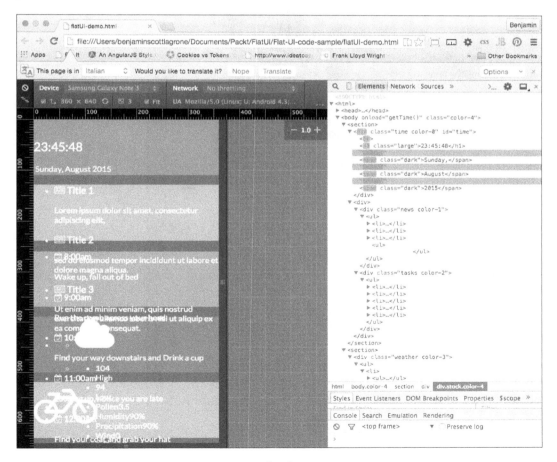

And here it is in landscape mode:

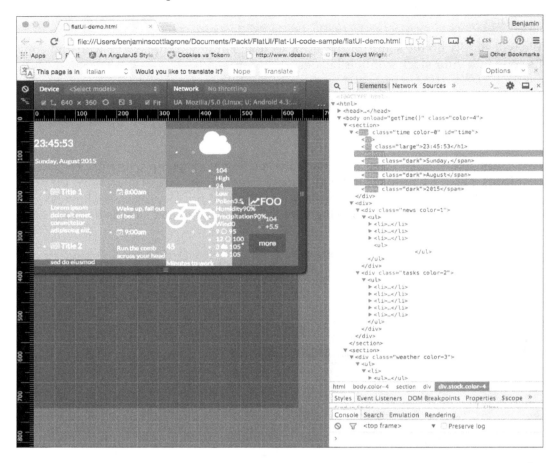

Flat UI CSS cleanup

Now that we have our flat UI mostly built out, you will see that it still looks half-baked. This means we need to build out our CSS to clean up the page. As stated before, flat UI is all about simplicity, so we need to focus our styling on the clear presentation of content, not on making it look like a leather-bound notebook.

Let's start with the button. It's sticking out like a sore thumb. The style will affect all the buttons, except the color, which is assigned throughout the color classes we have defined. The style will look a lot like the **Bootstrap** buttons, because they work well for mobile and flat UI.

It needs padding of 13px on top and bottom and 21px on each side, a margin of 8% vertically, and auto horizontally. Set border-color to match the wet-asphalt color, font-color to white, border to none, width to 75%, font-size to 1.1REM, and finally, make the cursor a pointer. The button CSS will look like this:

```css
button{
    padding: 13px 21px;
    margin:8% auto;
    border-radius: 5px;
    border-color: #357ebd;
    color: #fff;
    background-color: #1abc9c;
    border: none;
    width:75%;
    cursor: pointer;
    font-size:1.1REM;
}
```

The new button style helps, and it makes a big difference. So let's take this lesson and roll forward with it, and keep churning away at style.

Creating universal classes

Let's hit the points that will give us the most value first. These are the universal classes that we can assign to elements, similar to the way we did the colors. One of the big problems with our flat UI project is the unordered lists that are breaking out of their parent DIV elements. So, let's create a class selector that we can assign to these breakout DIV elements. In each media query, portrait and landscape, create a selector called scroll. This will apply differently to portrait and landscape modes. Inside the portrait media query, the selector will have the overflow on the X-axis scroll, and in landscape orientation, the overflow on the Y axis will scroll. Look at the following sample. The new coded is appended to the existing CSS media queries:

```css
@media (orientation:portrait){
    ...
    .scroll{
overflow-x:scroll;
}
}

@media (orientation:landscape){
    ...
    .scroll{
overflow-y:scroll;
}
}
```

Now, of course, for this to have any affect, you have to add these classes to the elements you want to scroll. Add the `scroll` class to the `DIV` elements `news` and `tasks`. This solves one big ugly problem. So let's forge ahead and add more style.

The next set of styles will be even more universal classes. These will not be inside any media queries and will apply just fine to portrait or landscape. In your CSS, at the end and outside of any media queries, add a selector for paragraphs, a class called `ellipsis`, and a selector for pseudo elements after `ellipsis`. Give the paragraphs the style attributes of a 94% width, and hide the overflow. In `ellipsis`, add the attributes ellipsis for text-overflow, no-wrap for white-space, and hide the overflow. For the subsequent pseudo class, add "..." to content, a right float, a relative position, 24px from the bottom. This new CSS will look like the following code sample:

```
p {
    width:94%;
    overflow:hidden;
}
.ellipsis{
    text-overflow:ellipsis;
    white-space: nowrap;
    overflow:hidden;
}
.ellipsis::after{
    content:"...";
    float: right;
    position: relative;
    bottom: 24px;
}
```

Next, add the `ellipsis` class to every list item inside the news and tasks `DIV` elements. This will apply these styles to the list items. The noticeable change is that the news and tasks feed will now truncate and add the "..." to the paragraphs of text after cutting them off at the first line and taking up most of the width of the parent element. We are on the path to getting control of our white space, or blue space if we want to be technically correct.

We want to add some size to certain fonts, so let's make it easy to make it consistent across the page. This is helpful when we want to change it; we won't need to hunt for it across the page. Let's add a class to enlarge our text in some areas. In your CSS, add a selector class called `large`. Assign it the attribute of a `2.1REM` font size:

```
.large{font-size:2.1REM}
```

To use this, let's add the class large to the clock time:

```
document.getElementById('time').innerHTML = "<br><h1
class='large'>"+h+":"+m+":"+s+"</h1> <span
class='dark'>"+d+",</span class='dark'> <span
class='dark'>"+mo+"</span> <span class='dark'>"+y+"</span>";
```

Now, as you refresh your viewport, you will see that these two elements are now larger.

Finally, for the universal CSS, let's get rid of the dots for the list styling. Add list-style-type with a value of none for all unordered lists. This should be added outside of the media queries:

```
ul{
list-style-type:none;
}
```

That's better, but it still doesn't work, and we don't want to stop here because then this flat UI will remain unconvincing as a good UI. So let's start by fixing the clock. Orient your page to portrait mode and let's start fixing the time. *Tempus fugit.*

Fixing time

The clock loads and reloads after the page is rendered, but we can still style it. So, in the portrait media query in your CSS, add the selectors for the H1 element in the time DIV element, and add one for the first of the spans (first-of-type) pseudo-class selector. Give the H1 element a top margin of 5% and side margin of 3%, 0 padding, and float it to the left. Next, give the span a block display. It should look like this:

```
@media (orientation:portrait){
//...other CSS...//
/* TIME */
        .time h1{
            margin:5% 3%;
            padding:0;
            float:left;
            }
        .time span:first-of-type{
display:block;
}
}
```

Next, in landscape mode, append code to the CSS style to simply align the text to the center, like this:

```
@media (orientation:landscape){
//...other CSS ...//
        /* TIME */
        .time{
text-align:center;
}
    }
```

Fixing the news and tasks elements CSS

Let's continue working down the elements of the portrait view. Next are the news and tasks DIV elements. In the portrait mode media query, only the unordered list needs attention: give it a width of 1500px and inline-block for display. The list items should float to the left, have a fixed width of 226px, and a right margin of 35px, and the rest should be 0. Give the paragraphs a 5px margin and the H4 headers a margin of 2px:

```
@media (orientation:portrait){
//...other CSS...//
/* TIME */
/* NEWS & TASKS */
.news ul, .tasks ul{
display:inline-block;
width:1500px;
}
.tasks ul li p, .news ul li p{
margin:5px;
}
.tasks ul li h4, .news ul li h4{
margin:2px;
}
}
```

In the landscape media query, the unordered lists should have a 5% padding and margin of 0. And give them a font-size value of 0.7REM.

```
@media (orientation:landscape){
//...other CSS...//
/* TIME */
/* NEWS & TASKS */
```

```
.news ul, .tasks ul{
padding:5%;
margin:0;
}
.news, .tasks{
font-size:0.7REM;
}
}
```

Adding CSS for the weather section

The next section, the weather section, contains many data points in embedded unordered lists; this will take some fancy footwork to clean up. So let's get working on the portrait-mode code. We'll be using parent selectors in this part as we need to make sure we are precise in our attribute assignments.

We will first create the CSS to affect the weather DIV element in both portrait and landscape modes. In essence, it is outside of the media queries. Let's start at the top of the list and work deeper. Create a selector for the unordered list with the weather parent class, and give it the attributes 5% margin and 0 padding. Then create a selector for its first-child list item with a width of 34% and a right margin of 5%, with the rest 0. Make the last child have 60% width. Next, make the unordered list that is the child of the list item have 5% 0 padding and a margin value of 0. Be sure you use the parent selectors:

```
.weather > ul{
margin:0;
padding:5% 0;
}
.weather > ul > li:first-child{
width:34%;
margin:0 5% 0 0;
}
.weather > ul > li:last-child{
width:60%;
}
.weather > ul > li > ul {
padding:0;
margin:0 0 0 5%;
}
```

Copy the last child list item selector; `.weather > ul > li:last-child`, and add to it an unordered list with a child list item using the `first-child` pseudo selector. Give it a width of 60% and float it to the left. Add another similar selector, but for the last child pseudo selector, assign a 40% width value and float it to the left. Next, make another selector, otherwise identical except for the child pseudo, which you should replace with an unordered list child:

```
.weather > ul > li:last-child > ul > li:first-child{
width:60%;
float:left;
}
.weather > ul > li:last-child > ul > li:last-child{
width:40%;
float:left;
}
.weather > ul > li:last-child > ul > li > ul {
margin:0;
padding:0;
}
```

And finally, for the weather class outside the media queries, add a selector for H2 and give it a padding value of 10% 0 0, vertical margin value of 0 and auto horizontal, and align the text to the center:

```
.weather h2{
padding:10% 0 0 0;
margin:0 auto;
text-align:center
}
```

In the portrait media query, first add a selector for the LI item, and make sure to use the parent selector so it only applies to the LI descendant. Display the list items inline and floated to the left.

```
@media (orientation:portrait){
//...other CSS...//
/* TIME */
/* NEWS & TASKS */
/* WEATHER */
.weather > ul > li{
display:inline;
float:left;
}
}
```

Next, copy that selector and add to it the first-child pseudo selector, and then follow it with parent selectors for the next unordered list and list item and the first child again. Do the same again, but replace the last first-child with `last-child`. In the first selector, the list item should have 25% width, a left float, right-aligned text, and a 13% left margin. The second selector should occupy 60% width, float to the right, and have text center aligned. Take a look at this sample:

```
@media (orientation:portrait){
//...other CSS...//
/* TIME */
/* NEWS & TASKS */
/* WEATHER */
...
.weather > ul > li:first-child > ul > li:first-child{
width:25%;
float:left;
text-align:right;
margin-left:15%;
}
    .weather > ul > li:first-child > ul > li:last-child{
width:60%;
float:right;
text-align:center;
}
}
```

Finally, at least for portrait mode, make a selector for the `weather` DIV element's E2 element and give it a font-size attribute of `0.8REM`:

```
.weather h2{
font-size:.8REM;
}
```

Creating more universal classes

Before we get into the specific CSS selectors, let's go back to the strategy of creating universal classes with attributes in the landscape orientation. This will save us some code. I want to first add a class for dark text, so let's add the class `dark` with the color attribute the same as the `wet-asphalt` color. Next, add classes for left and right floating objects. They should clear left and right also. Then, create a class called `center` to center the text within:

```
.dark{
color:#34495e;
}
```

```
.left{
float:left;
clear:left;
}
.right{
float:right;
clear:right;
}
.center {
    text-align:center;
}
```

To make them work, we need to add these classes to the markup. Add left and right classes to the list items containing two temperatures under the Font Awesome cloud:

```
<ul>
        <li>
<h2>
<i class="fa fa-cloud fa-3x"></i>
</h2>
</li>
        <li>
            <ul>
                <li class="left">
<span>104</span>
<br>
<span>High</span></li>
                <li class="right">
<span>94</span>
<br>
<span>Low</span>
</li>
            </ul>
        </li>
    </ul>
```

Also add the left and right classes to the two list items containing the stock information under the line chart icon from Font Awesome:

```
<ul>
        <li>
<h2 class="large">
<i class="fa fa-line-chart"></i>
FOO
</h2>
```

```
        </li>
            <li>
                <ul>
                    <li class="left">
<span>104</span>
</li>
                    <li class="right">
<span>+5.5</span>
</li>
                </ul>
            </li>
            <li>
<button onclick="doSomething()" class="wet-asphalt">more</button>
</li>
        </ul>
```

This helps with the left and right floats. We could pursue this more with other elements as needed, and it would save us from getting too much bloat in our CSS.

Next, let's add some contrast to our text in landscape mode. Adding dark text to the day of the week and calendar date and some of the headers will make them stand out.

First, in your JavaScript for the clock, add the dark class to the spans wrapping the d, mo, and y variables when they are written to the document:

```
    document.getElementById('time').innerHTML = "<br><h1
class='large'>"+h+":"+m+":"+s+"</h1> <span
class='dark'>"+d+",</span class='dark'> <span
class='dark'>"+mo+"</span> <span class='dark'>"+y+"</span>";
```

Next, within the news and tasks elements, add the dark class to the headers:

```
<div class="news color-1 scroll">
                <ul>
                    <li class="ellipsis">
                        <h4 class="dark">
<i class="fa fa-newspaper-o"></i>
 Title 1
</h4>
                        <p>
Lorem ipsum dolor sit amet, consectetur adipiscing elit,
</p>
                    </li>
                    <li class="ellipsis">
                        <h4 class="dark">
```

```
<i class="fa fa-newspaper-o"></i>
 Title 2
</h4>
                        <p>
sed do eiusmod tempor incididunt ut labore et dolore magna aliqua.
</p>
                    </li>
                    <li class="ellipsis">
                        <h4 class="dark">
<i class="fa fa-newspaper-o"></i>
 Title 3
</h4>
                        <p>
Ut enim ad minim veniam, quis nostrud exercitation ullamco laboris
nisi ut aliquip ex ea commodo consequat.
</p>
                    </li>
                    <li class="ellipsis">
                        <h4 class="dark">
<i class="fa fa-newspaper-o"></i>
 Title 4
</h4>
                        <p>
Ut enim ad minim veniam, quis nostrud exercitation ullamco laboris
nisi ut aliquip ex ea commodo consequat.
</p>
                    </li>
                <ul>
            </div>
            <div class="tasks color-2 scroll">
                <ul>
                    <li class="ellipsis">
                        <h4 class="dark">
<i class="fa fa-calendar-check-o"></i>
 8:00am
</h4>
                        <p>
Wake up, fall out of bed
</p>
                    </li>
                    <li class="ellipsis">
                        <h4 class="dark">
<i class="fa fa-calendar-check-o"></i>
 9:00am
```

```
                </h4>
                        <p>Run the comb across your head</p>
                </li>
                <li class="ellipsis">
                        <h4 class="dark">
<i class="fa fa-calendar-check-o"></i>
 10:00am
</h4>
                        <p>Find your way downstairs and Drink a cup</
p>
                </li>
                <li class="ellipsis">
                        <h4>
<i class="fa fa-calendar-check-o"></i>
 11:00am
</h4>
                        <p>Looking up, notice you are late</p>
                </li>
                <li class="ellipsis">
                        <h4 class="dark">
<i class="fa fa-calendar-check-o"></i>
 12:00am
</h4>
                        <p>Find your coat and grab your hat</p>
                </li>
            </ul>
        </div>
```

In the weather section, do the same for the SPAN elements wrapping the High and Low text under the cloud:

```
<ul>
<li>
<h2>
<i class="fa fa-cloud fa-3x"></i>
</h2>
</li>
<li>
<ul>
<li class="left">
<span>104</span>
<br>
<span class="dark">High</span>
</li>
```

```
                    <li class="right">
<span>94</span>
<br>
<span class="dark">Low</span>
</li>
                </ul>
            </li>
</ul>
```

And add the class within the `weather` DIV to the spans wrapping the text `Pollen`, `Humidity`, `Precip`, and `Wind`:

```
                    <li>
                        <ul>
                            <li>
<span class="dark">Pollen</span>
<span>3.5</span>
</li>
                            <li>
<span class="dark">Humidity</span>
<span>90%</span>
</li>
                            <li>
<span class="dark">Precipitation</span>
<span>90%</span>
</li>
                            <li>
<span class="dark">Wind</span>
<span>0</span>
</li>
                        </ul>
                    </li>
```

Finally, within the `travel` DIV element, add the `dark` class to the `H4` header wrapping the text `Minutes to Work`:

```
            <div class="travel color-1 center">
                <h2>
<i class="fa fa-bicycle fa-4x"></i>
</h2>
                <h3>45</h3>
                <h4 class="dark">Minutes to work</h4>
            </div>
```

Add the `center` class to the `travel` and `stock` DIV elements:

```
<div class="travel color-1 center">
            <h2>
<i class="fa fa-bicycle fa-4x"></i>
</h2>
            <h3>45</h3>
            <h4 class="dark">Minutes to work</h4>
        </div>
        <div class="stock color-4 center">
            <ul>
                <li>
<h2 class="large">
<i class="fa fa-line-chart"></i>
FOO
</h2>
</li>
                <li>
                    <ul>
                        <li class="left">
<span>104</span>
</li>
                        <li class="right">
<span>+5.5</span>
</li>
                    </ul>
                </li>
                <li>
<button onclick="doSomething()" class="wet-asphalt">more</button>
</li>
            </ul>
        </div>
```

Final cleanup of the landscape orientation

That covers some good ground in the layout, so let's carry on, tallyho, to cleaning up the landscape orientation of the landscape mode. We're nearly there, I promise, so go make a cup of coffee to get you through this last stretch of CSS.

In the landscape media query, add a selector for the unordered list and child list item immediately descended from the weather class. Give them the left float and 0 margin attributes. Copy that selector and add the first child pseudo selector, and under it, add the selectors for its descendant unordered list and first child descendant list item, giving it a width of 100%. Make another selector for the last child with attributes of 100% width and text aligned to the center. Create yet another selector and add a descendant unordered list, and assign it the attributes of 100% width and 0 padding. And create a selector for the H2 headers within the weather DIV element with a font-size of 1.5 REM.

```
/* WEATHER */
.weather > ul > li {
float:left;
margin:0;
}
.weather > ul > li:first-child > ul > li:first-child{
width:100%;
}
.weather > ul > li:first-child > ul > li:last-child{
width:100%;
text-align:center;
}
.weather > ul > li:first-child > ul > li:last-child ul{
width:100%;
padding:0;
}
.weather h2{
font-size:1.5REM;
}
```

We are nearing the home stretch, so dry those eyes and do not despair. We are done with the weather div element and its children. We are now going to style the stock and travel sections.

First, back in the portrait media query, you will need some trick to easily affect all the direct descendant children of the travel div element. So create a selector including the travel class and a wildcard * as a direct descendant. The style to apply to them is a left float and a top and left margin of 5%, like this:

```
.travel > *{
    float: left;
    margin:5% 0 0 5%;
}
```

Final cleanup of the portrait orientation

The last bit of CSS in the portrait media query should be for the stock DIV element. First, create a selector for `stock` and give it a bottom margin of -5%. Next, we need one for the list items that are direct descendants of the stock unordered list. They will each float left, be one third of the width, have 0 padding and margin, and be displayed inline. Just like this:

```
.stock > ul > li {
    float: left;
    width: 33%;
    margin: 0;
    padding: 0;
    display: inline;
}
```

And finally, for the landscape view, in your landscape media query, append to the end selectors for unordered list in the `stock` class and the same wildcard direct descendant under the `travel` class. In the stock list, apply a 5% padding and 0 margin. In the travel wildcard selector, make a -10% margin.

Now we're looking good!

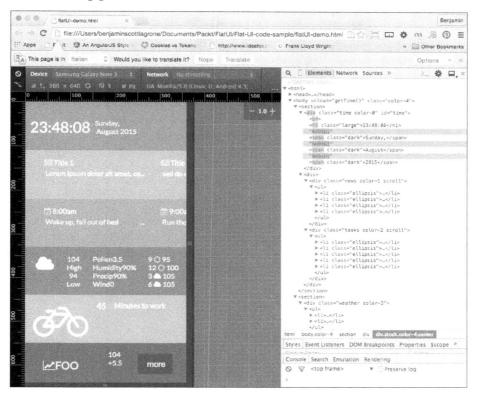

Here it is in landscape mode:

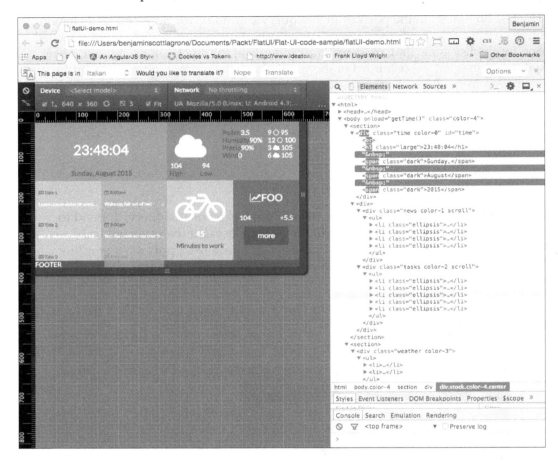

Summary

Congratulations! If you made it this far, you have done excellent work. This chapter was a challenge as there was some tricky CSS involved in making it work. This flat UI project is something you can use as a basis for creating your own personal dashboard. We will keep this project and use it later.

3
Parallax Scrolling

Our next web trend, parallax scrolling, is not really a new concept; it is simply the visual effect where objects that are closer to you appear to move faster when you are moving than objects that are farther. It can be more simply put as the effect you see as you look out your car window and watch the closer objects zip by more quickly than objects off in the distance. In our case, or at least this chapter, we'll replace the car with a rocket blasting off through the clouds and into a sky full of stars as the earth falls beneath us. Does this sound far-fetched for the scope of a single chapter? Not at all! We're going to do it with some clever (if I do say so myself) JavaScript and helpful scalable vector graphics.

The parallax 3D effect in animation was created in the early days of movies to produce more realistic background scenes in the cartoons produced for the early movie theaters. It has also been used widely in video game development, especially in side-scrolling video shooters.

This project is so far the most exciting and challenging in this book for me to create. I wanted it to be as cool and as lightweight as possible while giving you a good framework for continuing the project in you own direction or modifying its functions to suit your own purpose. I hope the code explanation is clear; if you have trouble at any point, take a look at the completed code, available in this book's code bundle or on the GitHub project page at `https://github.com/benlagrone/webtrendsSideScroller`. Feel free to contact me with questions or fork the code, and show me ways to improve it. It would be an amazing bonus if I, the author, could learn something from you, the reader, through this book!

Without any more unnecessary history, let's get into the code.

Starting off

I would like to use some of our previous work in order to shave some pages off the chapter and to build on top of what we already know. This will use the principles of responsive design you learned, but we will update some DIV elements as I take you through the chapter. We will make a simple page layout, and there will be no need for any floating or responsive layout elements. To make it much simpler, we want it to look very modern, so we'll use the flat UI colors and basic layout we used in the previous chapter.

The HTML markup

The work will, however, ramp up pretty early, so we need to pick up speed from very early on in the chapter. The initial layout should have a `<main>` block as the direct child of the body element, containing five sections as shown here:

```
<head></head>
<body>
<main>
<section>
</section>
<section>
</section>
<section>
</section>
<section>
</section>
<section>
</section>
</main>
</body>
```

Since we have our work from the previous chapter, we have some color in our CSS ready to apply to our SECTION and DIV elements. Remember: we want to use the monochrome blue color scheme that we created in the Flat UI color section of the previous chapter.

Next, add some id attributes to the HTML5 SECTION elements. The SECTION elements should have these id attributes, in this order from the top: space, stratosphere, sky, objects, and terra. This should give you a hint as of what we are going to build: something spacey.

Let's forge ahead with building up our layout. Inside the space section, add two DIV elements and give them unique id attributes; anything will work. I will use p0 and p1. In the stratosphere section, add five DIV elements, following from the id attributes and beginning with p2. Next, in the sky DIV element, add seven DIV elements, following the same numbering pattern for its id attributes. In the object section, don't add any child DIV elements, and in the terra section, add a single DIV element with the id attribute ground, and then give it two child DIV elements. All these child DIV elements will serve as section dividers to hold the different frames you will scroll through in your parallax scroller. Take a look at the resulting code:

```
<main>
    <section id="space">
        <div id="p0">
        </div>
        <div id="p1">
        </div>
    </section>
    <section id="stratosphere">
        <div id="p2"></div>
        <div id="p3"></div>
        <div id="p4"></div>
        <div id="p5"></div>
        <div id="p6"></div>
    </section>
    <section id="sky">
        <div id="p7"></div>
        <div id="p8"></div>
        <div id="p9"></div>
        <div id="p10"></div>
        <div id="p11"></div>
        <div id="p12"></div>
        <div id="p13"></div>
    </section>
        <section id="objects"></section>
        <section id="terra">
        <div id="ground">
        <div></div>
        <div></div>
    </div>
    </section>
</main>
```

Color classes

Let's add some color so that you can see this project start to take shape. Therefore, add a style element inside the `header` block, and inside it, add the color classes to assign as attributes to elements inside the HTML body. These classes come from the *Flat UI color* section of the previous chapter. The blue shades will work nicely for this project:

```
<head>
<style>
.black {
background-color: black;
}
.color-0 {
background-color: #85C4ED;
}
.color-1 {
background-color: #58ADE3;
}
.color-2 {
background-color: #3499DB;
}
.color-3 {
background-color: #0F85D1;
}
.color-4 {
background-color: #0665A2;
}
.wet-asphalt {
background-color:#34495e;
}
</style>
</head>
```

Next, we need to assign these general color class attributes to some of our elements. Add the `black` class to the `main` HTML5 element. To the next `section` block, stratosphere, add the `wet-asphalt` class to its first child `DIV` element. In the following four `DIV` elements, add the classes `color-4`, `color-3`, `color-2`, and `color-1`, that order. And in the `sky section`, add the `color-1` class and give all of its direct child `DIV` elements the `color-0` class. In addition, give all of the `DIV` elements in the `space`, `stratosphere`, and `sky` elements the `row` class. This should give you the following:

```
<main class="black">
<section id="space">
    <div id="p0" class="row"></div>
    <div id="p1" class="row"></div>
</section>
```

```
<section id="stratosphere" class="wet-asphalt">
<div id="p2" class="row wet-asphalt"></div>
    <div id="p3" class="row color-4"></div>
    <div id="p4" class='row color-3"></div>
    <div id="p5" class='row color-2"></div>
    <div id="p6" class="row color-1"></div>
</section>
<section id="sky" class="color-1">
<div id="p7" class="row color-0"></div>
    <div id="p8" class="row color-0"></div>
    <div id="p9" class="row color-0"></div>
    <div id='p10" class="row color-0"></div>
    <div id="p11" class="row color-0"></div>
    <div id="p12" class="row color-0"></div>
    <div id="p13" class="row color-0"></div>
</section>
<section id="objects"></section>
<section id="terra">
    <div id="ground">
        <div></div>
        <div></div>
    </div>
</section>
</main>
```

Next, let's perform some cleanup and add a section selector to the STYLE element. Add a -1EM margin attribute to it.

```
section {
margin:-1EM;
}
```

Using SVG font icons

The next part is where the fun begins: you have already created the heavens and earth, now let's fill it up with wonderful things. By wonderful things, I mean lightweight SVG web graphics. And by SVG web graphics, I mean Font Awesome!

Getting the fonts

I know there are other and newer ways to create scalable vector graphics, but this is my favorite: jump on over to Font Awesome (https://fortawesome.github.io/Font-Awesome/) and get yourself some web graphics. I recommend downloading the library instead of calling the CDN, as the loading lag time may cause something else to fail. Download it and put it in a lib folder.

Before you can start creating the sun, moon, stars, and clouds, you need to inject the Font Awesome CSS into your HTML. So, in the `head` element, before the CSS, add the link to the CSS file, as in the following example. I'm currently using version 4.4.0, but use the latest one when you try this:

```
<link rel="stylesheet" href="lib/font-awesome-4.4.0/css/font-
awesome.min.css">
```

In the beginning, there was nothing. If you look at the HTML in your browser, you will see only a black box, and I'm sure you are not impressed:

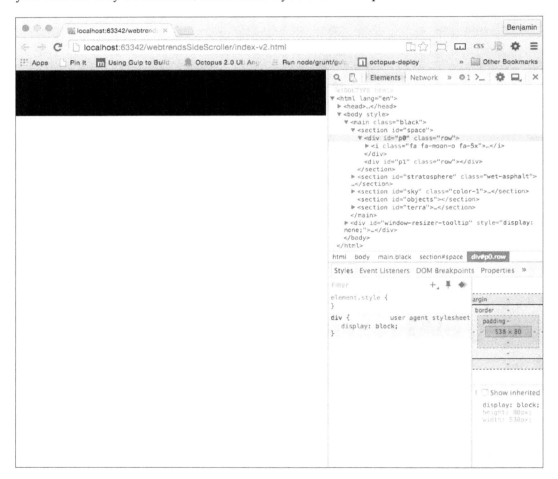

That's no moon!

However, this is good; this is the beginning, and we have more to add. Once you have the library installed on your webhost, we can start filling up space with heavenly objects and the sky with clouds. First, in the p0 div element, add a moon. In Font Awesome, you can go look up the code, or you could just look at my example:

```
<div id="p0" class="row">
    <i class="fa fa-moon-o fa-5x">
    </i>
</div>
```

Let's add some styling so we can make some of these new elements we are adding visible. We are going to work on the CSS now. First, let's get rid of the body margin by adding a body selector with margins of value 0 for style. Next, let's add some selectors for colors: blue, green, white, yellow, grey-1, grey-2, and silver. Add color: #85C4ED for blue and the respective color names for the rest. Then, create left and right selectors, with float left and right for each. Look at this example:

```
.blue {
color: #85C4ED;
}
.green {
color:green;
}
.white {
color:white;
}
.yellow {
color:yellow;
}
.grey-1 {
color:#222222;
}
.grey-2 {
color:#666;
}
.silver {
color:silver;
}
.left {
float:left;
}
.right {
float:right;
}
```

Now add the `yellow` class to the `fa-moon` I element:

```
<i class="fa fa-moon-o fa-5x yellow"></i>
```

Next, refresh your browser, and you will be able to see the moon bright and yellow, like the following example. Excellent!

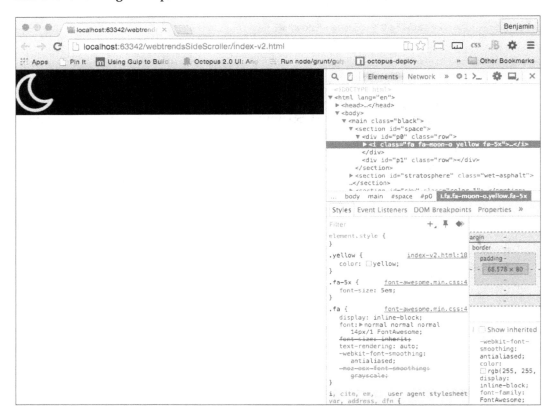

OMG, it's full of stars!

Immediately after the `fa-moon` I element, in the `p1` DIV element, add a DIV element with the id `stars`. Go back to the Font Awesome site and copy the code for the star. Paste it inside the `stars` DIV element and add the `yellow` class to it. Now copy this yellow `fa-star` I element and paste it about 200 more times inside the `stars` DIV element. That will complete the HTML for the `space` section. It will look like my sample here:

```
<section id="space">
    <div id="p0" class="row">
        <i class="fa fa-moon-o yellow fa-5x"></i>
```

```
        </div>
        <div id="p1" class="row">
        <div id="stars">
            <i class="fa fa-star yellow"></i>
            <i class="fa fa-star yellow"></i>
            <i class="fa fa-star yellow"></i>
            <i class="fa fa-star yellow"></i>


    <!--...
    ** repeat 200 times, or a billion if you have the time **
    ...-->
            <i class="fa fa-star yellow"></i>
            <i class="fa fa-star yellow"></i>
            <i class="fa fa-star yellow"></i>
        </div>
        </div>
    </section>
```

You can see in the following screenshot that it's just barely starting to come together. You may be thinking to yourself that it looks lame because all the elements are just lined up. We will take care of that with some JavaScript later in the chapter:

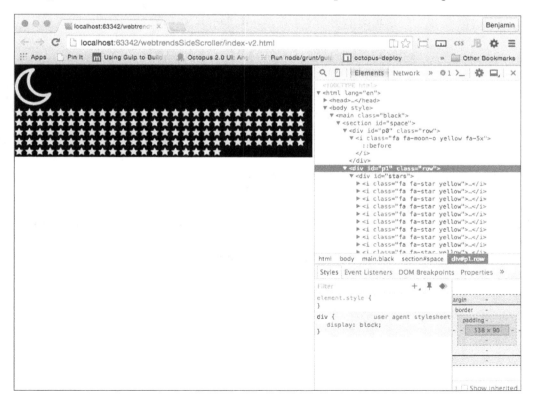

What's next? We have done everything we need for the stratosphere section, so let's put some clouds and birds and an airplane in the sky.

Clouds, birds, and airplanes

In the `sky` section, in the `p9`, `p10`, `p11`, `p12` and `p13` DIV elements (we're skipping `p8`), add a new DIV element with the `clouds` class attribute. In each one, add at least 10 Font Awesome clouds (`fa-cloud`). Font Awesome, being an SVG (Scalable Vector Graphic), can scale up and be modified in several ways; by adding another class, `fa-2x`, you can make the graphic larger. The `fa-3x`, `fa-4x`, and `fa-5x` classes also work the same, with increasing scale. Here is an example of one of the DIV elements with clouds in it:

```
<div id="p10" class="row color-0">
    <div class="clouds">
        <i class="fa fa-cloud fa-3x white"></i>
        <i class="fa fa-cloud fa-2x white"></i>
        <i class="fa fa-cloud fa-5x white"></i>
        <i class="fa fa-cloud fa-2x white"></i>
        <i class="fa fa-cloud fa-4x white"></i>
        <i class="fa fa-cloud fa-5x white"></i>
        <i class="fa fa-cloud fa-3x white"></i>
        <i class="fa fa-cloud fa-2x white"></i>
        <i class="fa fa-cloud fa-5x white"></i>
        <i class="fa fa-cloud fa-2x white"></i>
        <i class="fa fa-cloud fa-4x white"></i>
        <i class="fa fa-cloud fa-5x white"></i>
    </div>
</div>
```

So, by adding the additional classes, you can make the cloudscape more interesting and diverse. We will use this size class to implement the parallax effect later. This being a font, you can also create your own CSS to add to it, treating it like a font. I will also demonstrate this later in the chapter. That being said, add classes with varying sizes like I stated earlier, and add the `white` class to them to make them white. You could also add a `blue` class to them to make them rain clouds.

When we are finished with the clouds, we will want to add some more interesting objects. Add an fa-plane icon to the end of the p12 DIV element, and add four birds using the fa-twitter icon. Add the fa-5x class and the silver color to the plane and add some color classes to the birds. Look at this example:

```
<i class="fa fa-plane fa-5x silver"></i>
<i class="fa fa-twitter"></i>
<i class="fa fa-twitter"></i>
<i class="fa fa-twitter"></i>
<i class="fa fa-twitter"></i>
```

Let's take a look at what this looks like again. I'll show you the code in the inspector as well so that you can get an idea of how it looks.

Continue adding parts. We now arrive at the next section, objects. This SECTION element contains the parts that will do much of the heavy lifting in the animation, or they will at least be visible through most of the parallax effect.

In the objects SECTION element , add a new DIV element with the id attribute sun. Inside it, add three Font Awesome I elements. The first is fa-smile-o; add the green class to it. Then add fa-circle with an additional yellow class, followed by fa-sun-o, and make it yellow as well. That element will look like the following code sample:

```
<section id="objects">
    <div id="sun">
        <i class="fa fa-smile-o green"></i>
        <i class="fa fa-circle yellow"></i>
        <i class="fa fa-sun-o yellow"></i>
    </div>
</section>
```

When you see it in your browser, you can see the three parts of the sun. We will add the style soon enough; don't worry:

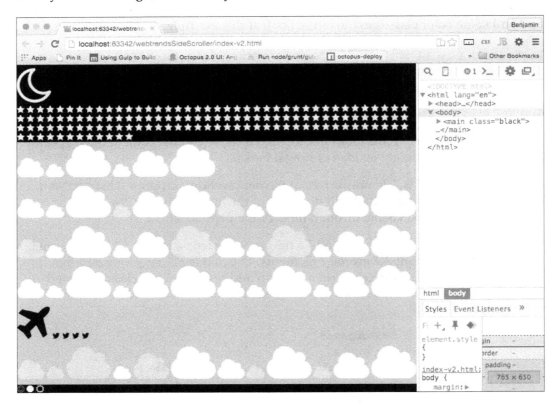

Next, add another DIV element with the id attribute earth. Inside it, add a Font Awesome I globe. Also add additional classes blue, land, and air. I'll explain these additional classes soon. Look at this code sample:

```
<div id="earth">
    <i class="fa fa-globe blue land air"></i>
</div>
```

The rocket

Our final addition to the objects section is the rocket. Add a DIV element with the id attribute rocket. Then put a SPAN element inside it, and inside this, add two separate Font Awesome rockets with the additional class fa-5x for scaling. Next, add a Font Awesome fire I element. Look at the following code sample. Add the color selectors grey-2 and silver to the rockets, and add yellow to the fire.

```
<div id="rocket">
    <span>
        <i class="fa fa-rocket fa-5x grey-2"></i>
        <i class="fa fa-rocket fa-5x silver"></i>
        <i class="fa fa-fire yellow"></i>
    </span>
</div>
```

There is not much to see yet, but refresh your browser and take a look at the new icons on the web page:

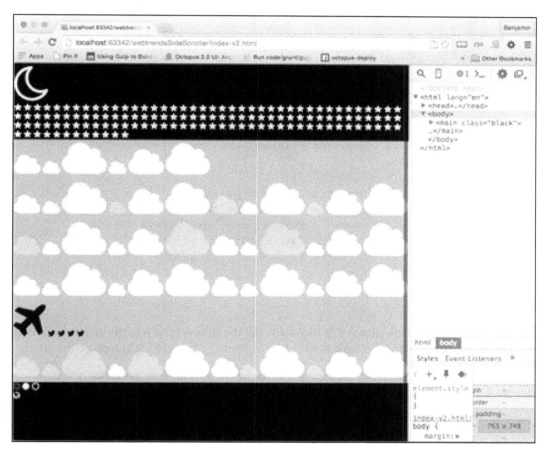

Terra firma

Finally, we will be adding elements to the ground. These will mostly be buildings and trees, and they will be easy to add because they are also Font Awesome SVGs.

In the terra SECTION element, inside the ground DIV element, there are two DIV elements: give the first class left and green, and then give the second DIV element the right class. Then, in the left green DIV element, add a handful of trees from Font Awesome, and in the right DIV element, add a truck and some buildings from Font Awesome. Give the buildings the additional classes small and large. The terra SECTION element code looks like this now:

```
<section id="terra">
    <div id="ground">
        <div class="left green">
            <i class="fa fa-tree"></i>
            <i class="fa fa-tree"></i>
            <i class="fa fa-tree"></i>
            <i class="fa fa-tree"></i>
            <i class="fa fa-tree"></i>
        </div>
        <div class="right">
            <i class="fa fa-truck"></i>
            <i class="fa fa-building small grey-1"></i>
            <i class="fa fa-building small grey-2"></i>
            <i class="fa fa-building large grey-1"></i>
            <i class="fa fa-industry large grey-2"></i>
        </div>
    </div>
</section>
```

So take a break and look at what it looks like in the browser; it's really just a bunch of stacked web icons. Our next task is to bring in some CSS style for the page-the load.

So go get a cup of coffee, and when we get back, we'll jump into some very simple CSS.

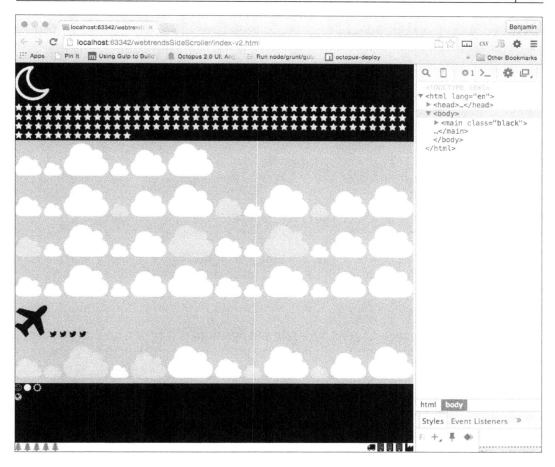

This is great so far, but the birds will not be very interesting if they have no color. So add some color classes to these elements. Look at this example:

```
<i class="fa fa-plane fa-5x silver"></i>
<i class="fa fa-twitter red"></i>
<i class="fa fa-twitter green"></i>
<i class="fa fa-twitter yellow"></i>
<i class="fa fa-twitter silver"></i>
```

Next up, the CSS

Our style sheet will be helpful in some areas, and there is some static styling that we can do here keep the code as lightweight as possible.

Let's start by adding selectors for our sky, ground, sun, rocket, earth, and ground DIV elements. These will have some child selectors to style as well, and we will go through them in this order:

```
#sky{}
#ground{}
#sun{}
#rocket{}
#earth{}
#ground{}
```

In the sky selector, add the overflow:hidden attribute. The sun selector will have the attributes of a fixed position 100px from the top and left and a font-size value of 5px. The sun selector has three I child elements; give the I element a font-size value of 12em.

Give the first child of the sun selector a relative position of 57px left and a font-size value of 13em. Give the second child a relative position of -60px left and 2 px from the top and a font-size of 14em. This will look like the following sample:

```
#sky{
    overflow:hidden;
}
#sun{
    position:fixed;
    top:100px;
    left:100px;
    font-size:5px;
}
#sun > i {
    font-size:12em;
}
#sun > :first-child{
    position:relative;
left: 57px;
    font-size:13em;
}
#sun > :last-child{
    position:relative;
    left: -60px;
    top:2px;
    font-size:14em;
}
```

Styling the objects with CSS

Next, let's work on building our rocket. The Font Awesome rocket is cockeyed, so we need to transform it with a `rotate(315deg)` attribute, fix its position on the screen, and start it 40% from the left. The `rocket` element has two child `fa-rocket I` elements inside it and an `fa-fire I` element.

Style the first child with a fixed position, starting at 3% from the bottom and 40% from the left, and give it a text-shadow value of `1px 1px #666` (for a 3D effect). The rocket's second child will also have a fixed position, 3.2% from the bottom and 39.8% from the left.

Here, we also want to add a 3D effect with a grey background color of #333, a background-clip attribute on the text, and a text shadow of rgb(255,255,255,0.8) at -1px 1px 3px blur. Finally, `fa-fire`, which is the rocket's flame, should also be at a fixed position 12px from the bottom and 12px from the left. Also give it a text shadow to make it look more fiery. I'll put the code in the example and skip describing it. Take a look:

```
#rocket > span{
-ms-transform: rotate(315deg);
-webkit-transform: rotate(315deg);
transform: rotate(315deg);
position: fixed;
left: 40%;
}
#rocket > span > i:first-child{
position: fixed;
bottom: 3%;
left: 40%;
text-shadow: 1px 1px #666;
}
#rocket > span > i:nth-child(2) {
position: fixed;
bottom: 3.2%;
left: 39.8%;
background-color: #333;
-webkit-background-clip: text;
-moz-background-clip: text;
background-clip: text;
color: transparent;
text-shadow: rgba(255,255,255,0.8)
-1px 1px 3px;
}
.fa-fire {
```

```
position: fixed;
bottom: 12px;
left: 12px;
text-shadow: 0 0 20px #fefcc9,
10px -10px 30px #feec85,
-20px -20px 40px #ffae34,
20px -30px 35px #ec760c,
-20px -40px 40px #cd4606,
0 -50px 65px #973716,
10px -70px 70px #451b0e;
}
```

Next, let's style the `fa-plane` icon. Add a selector for `fa-plane` and give it the attributes in the following code sample. It needs to be transformed by rotating it 315 degrees, and let's give it some text shadow and a text background-clip attribute so it blurs in the background.

```
.fa-plane{
-ms-transform: rotate(30deg);
-webkit-transform: rotate(30deg);
transform: rotate(30deg);
background-color: #999;
-webkit-background-clip: text;
-moz-background-clip: text;
background-clip: text;
color: transparent;
text-shadow: rgba(255,255,255,0.8)
-1px 1px 3px;
}
```

Let's pause for a moment and look at what we have so far. So, save the HTML and refresh your browser. It's actually starting to look interesting:

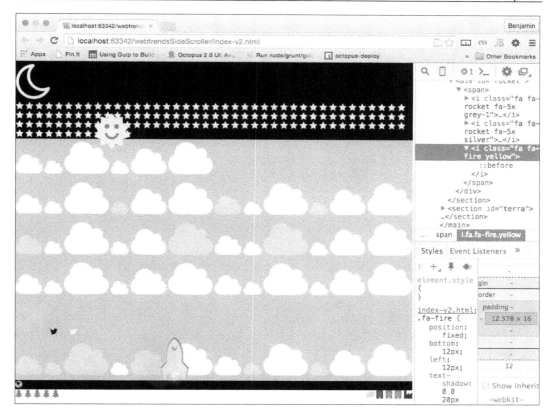

Styling the ground objects

Now that you have added the `fa-*` objects, let's work on the ground and earth elements. These are cool, and you are in for a surprise when you see it come together. First, start with the `earth` element.

This involves a few steps: float it to the left, give it a font size of 1000vw (viewport width), a width of 100%, a height of 100%, and a fixed position 0px from the bottom. Next, we will assign some style attributes to the actual `fa-globe` element itself, make its position relative, floated to the left, 423px from the bottom, and 350% from the right.

Finally, one more step for the earth elements, we will add some style to a pseudo element after `fa-globe` with the land class. Set it to have an absolute position, a blank space string for content, a green background, -1 z-index, 10% from the top, 0% from the left, 100% width, 80% height, and a 50% border radius. Before we continue, I'll pause for the cause and show you what this code looks like:

```css
#earth {
float:left;
font-size: 1000vw;
width: 100%;
height: 100%;
position: fixed;
bottom: 0px;
}
.fa-globe {
position: relative;
float:left;
bottom: 423px;
right: 350%;
}
.fa-globe.land::after {
position: absolute;
content: '';
background: green;
z-index: -1;
top: 10%;
left: 0%;
width: 100%;
height: 80%;
border-radius:50%;
}
```

Finally, let's style the ground `div` element and its children. Make the ground `div` element 100% wide and have a 60px solid brown border at the bottom. Give the direct child `div` elements a width of 50% and height of 0px. Give the ground's left child `i` element a font-size value of 8vw, and float the right `i` elements to the right. Set the first right child -20px to the left and 15px from the bottom. Only two more to go: set the ground `id` element's small right children to a font size of 12vw and the large ones to a font size of 14vw. Look at this code for the ground elements' style:

```css
#ground {
width: 100%;
border-bottom: 60px solid brown;
}
#ground > div {
```

```
width: 50%;
height: 0px;
}
#ground .left I {
font-size:8vw;
}
#ground .right i {
float: left;
}
#ground > .right > :first-child {
left:-20px;
bottom: 15px;
}
#ground .right .small {
font-size: 12vw;
}
#ground .right .large {
font-size: 14vw;
}
```

Before we finish with the CSS, there's one small effect you should add. When the rocket flies through the DIV elements, we want some of them to curve along with the curve of the earth as it falls away. This won't be perfect, but it will add a neat little effect to the stratosphere section elements as we leave them. We will create two new class selectors called curve and curve2. To each, add the attribute for a top-right border with a radius. The curve selector will have 90% and 40% radius values, while curve2 will have 80% and 10%. Look at this code sample:

```
.curve {
border-top-right-radius: 90% 40%;
}
.curve2 {
border-top-right-radius: 80% 10%;
}
```

To use these, add the curve class to the row DIV element with the id p2. Next, add the curve2 class to the SECTION element with the id stratosphere and the row DIV element with the id p7:

```
<section id="stratosphere" class="wet-asphalt curve2">
    <div id="p2" class="row wet-asphalt curve"></div>
    <div id="p3" class="row color-4 curve"></div>
    <div id="p4" class="row color-3"></div>
    <div id="p5" class="row color-2"></div>
    <div id="p6" class="row color-1"></div>
</section>
```

Our CSS is done. It is a small package, and there's a lot of magic inside because it's done in our Font Awesome library and has some JavaScript, which we will go through next. There is now a big blue blob in your viewport—not much to see.

Again, we will put much of the finishing touches together in the JavaScript. You can compare yours to mine here:

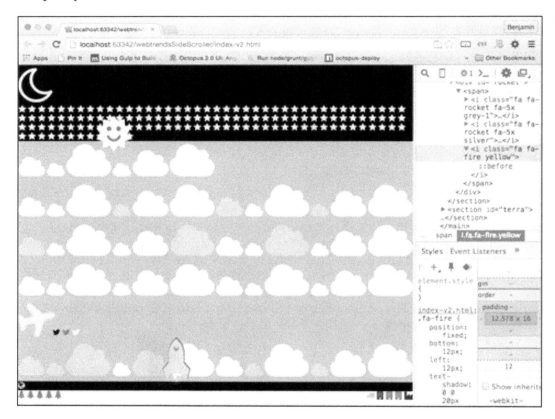

Writing the JavaScript effects

Finally, we arrive at the fun stuff. Let's do some JavaScript. And by the fun stuff, I mean just JavaScript, not jQuery or any heavy libraries—only what we need. The script will go at the bottom of the page, before the close of your body tag. We want everything to load before the script runs.

Setting the row height

Start with the beginning: we need to set the height of the row to equal the height of your viewport. Each row will then take up the height of the screen so that we can scroll through them in a deep-dive fashion. So we want to get the body element and, on load, run a function. The first operation is to get the `row` elements, which we will do by obtaining the elements by the `row` class name, loop through them, add the height style to each one, set to the window's `innerHeight` property, and add the string `px` to it. And then, the only thing that needs to be done is to add an `id` attribute called `body` to the `BODY` element. Look at this example:

```
document.getElementById("body").onload = function() {
        for ( i = 0; i < document.getElementsByClassName("row").
length; i++) {
                document.getElementsByClassName("row")[i].style.height =
window.innerHeight + "px";
        }
}
```

Now, refresh your browser window, and you will see some magic happen. It's still a big blue blob, but it's a very long big blue blob. Look at the following screen grab:

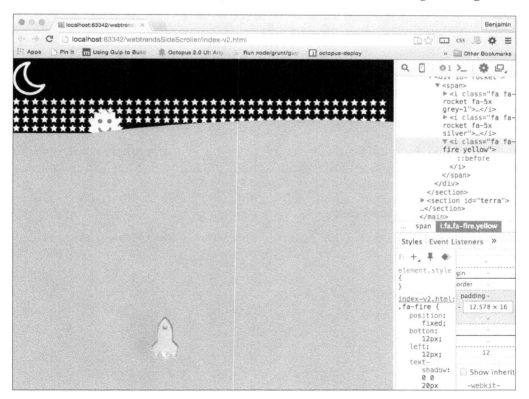

Spreading the objects

Let's continue. Next, we will want to create a function that will spread the objects randomly up and down each row. It will be used on the stars in the space row, the clouds in the sky row, and the buildings and trees at the bottom. The next function will need you to create a new function called spreadObjects() and have it receive the variables x, vm, hm, ha, p, and e.

These variable names represent the data they will receive: x for an array of objects, vm for the vertical multiplier, hm for the horizontal multiplier, va for vertical addition, ha for horizontal addition, p for position type, and e for the extension (px or %).

With x, we will loop through the array of objects and, for each object in the loop, set its style position to the variable p, the style to be a random number multiplied by vm with va added to it, and finally, the e added to the end. We will do the same for the object style left property and vm, vh, and e. Look at this code for the function:

```
function spreadObjects(x, vm, hm, va, ha, p, e){
    for (var I = 0; I < x.length; i++){
        x[i].style.position = p;
        x[i].style.top = Math.floor((Math.random()*vm)+va)+e;
        x[i].style.left = Math.floor((Math.random()*hm)+ha)+e;
    }
}
```

Back to the original onload function; call spreadObjects() with the first variable being the array of the object when you get the element by the stars id attribute, and from that, get the elements by their I tag names. The subsequent variables will be 150, 100, 1, 1, fixed, and %.

Taking a look at the code, I can tell you what will happen: the function will distribute the stars throughout the element they are within 100% from the left and 150% from the top, in a fixed position.

Take a look at the function call:

```
spreadObjects(document.getElementById("stars").getElementsByTagNam
e("i"), 150, 100, 1, 1, "fixed", "%");
```

We are going to call this function a few more times now. All three of the first variables passed start with getting the element by the `ground id` attribute. The first will get the elements inside it that have the `fa-tree` class attribute.

These are only going to be distributed horizontally, not vertically, so the next variable is 0 and then 14, and then, we need some math to determine the inner height of the window, since the elements will be a few pixels from the absolute bottom, divided by 28, then 1 for the horizontal addition, with the position type relative, followed finally by `px` for the extension.

The next two function calls will get the elements that have the class name `right` from within the ground element, select the first of the array, and then get the elements that have the class name `small` and then `large`. The numbers are mostly the same, but the `innerHeight` values are divided by 13 and 15 respectively. I'll show this to you in the following code because I'm trying to keep the explanation brief:

```
spreadObjects(document.getElementById("ground").getElementsByClass
Name("fa-tree"), 0, 14, -(window.innerHeight/28), 1, "relative",
"px");

spreadObjects(document.getElementById("ground").getElementsByClass
Name("right")[0].getElementsByClassName("small"), 0, 14,-
(window.innerHeight/13), 1, "relative", "px");

spreadObjects(document.getElementById("ground").getElementsByClass
Name("right")[0].getElementsByClassName("large"), 0, 14,-
(window.innerHeight/15), 1, "relative", "px");
```

You may be wondering why we are not creating variables and inserting them into the function calls. The answer is we could, but then our code would take up more room, and we would essentially be duplicating something that's already in the DOM, which is unnecessary bloat.

Now, look at your browser, and see how the stars have been scattered throughout space.

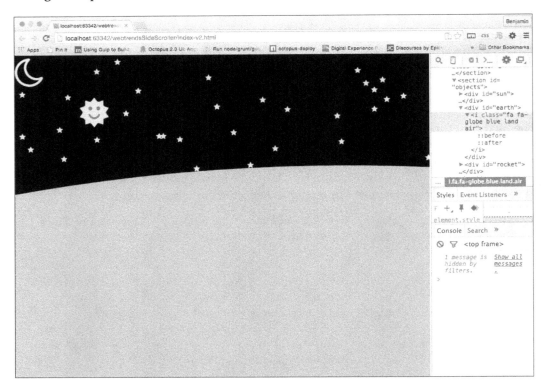

Spreading the clouds

We are not done using that function just yet; we need it once more for the clouds. You will create a loop against an array of the elements with class name `clouds` and, for each one, get the elements by the tag name `I`.

The second variable, the vertical height variable, should be equal to 75% of the `innerHeight` property of the window, and the third variable should be equal to 75% of the `innerWidth` property. The vertical addition variable is `1`, and the horizontal addition variable is half of the window's `innerWidth` property. Set the position variable to relative and the extension to `px`. The code is as follows:

```
for
(var I = 0; I < document.getElementsByClassName("clouds").length;
i++)
{
```

```
spreadObjects(document.getElementsByClassName("clouds")[i].getElem
entsByTagName("i"), window.innerHeight*.75, window.innerWidth*.75,
1, 1-(window.innerWidth/2), "relative", "px");
}
```

Loading the page functions

The first function, the `body.onload` function, will next call another function, called `smoothScrollTo`, as a property of the window, sending the value of the document body's `scrollHeight` property. At the bottom of the script, create that function, and it will make the page scroll smoothly through to the bottom of the full document body.

We will fill it out shortly, but first, we will finish the last line of this function. We will add an `onscroll` attribute to the body with the value calling a function called `updateElement`. The `updateElement` function is the most vital one for our parallax effect, so hang on and we'll write it shortly. Look at this code sample:

```
document.getElementById("body").onload = function(){
    smoothScrollTo(document.body.scrollHeight);
    document.getElementsByTagName("body")[0].setAttribute
    ("onscroll","updateElement()")
};
window.smoothScrollTo = ()
```

Smoothening the scroll

Let's work on the `smoothScrollTo` function. This is the function that detects the scrolling motion to make sure it is smooth. The `smoothScrollTo` function is used to move the scroll to the bottom of the page when the page loads. You could use this function in other scenarios to click a button where its click event uses the function to go to a specific section. In our case, we only want to go straight to the bottom. Let's take a look at the function.

Inside its braces, create a callback function. The first line should list the variables `time`, `start`, and `factor`, left undefined. Next, create a return function, injecting the variables `target` and `duration`. Let's take a quick look at what we have so far:

```
window.smoothScrollTo = (function () {
    var timer, start, factor;
    return function (target, duration) {
    };
}());
```

Inside the return function, create new variables: offset for the window 's
pageYOffset property and delta for the value of pageYOffset subtracted from the
target variable. Next, set duration to be equal to duration || 1000, start equal
to the now() method of Date, and factor equal to 0. Here's the code:

```
var offset = window.pageYOffset,
delta = target - window.pageYOffset; // Y-offset difference
duration = duration || 1000;            // default 1 sec
animation
start = Date.now();                     // get start time
factor = 0;
```

Next, add a logical test that clears an interval on the timer if the timer value is
not false:

```
if( timer ) {
clearInterval(timer); // stop any running animations
}
```

Now, we will create a new function called step to animate the scrolling. Inside it,
first create a new variable called y, then define factor as the value of start subtracted
from the Date's now() method, and divide the result by duration. Next, if factor is
equal or less than 1, use the clearInterval method on timer to stop the animation,
and on the next line, inside the if condition, set factor to equal 1.

After the if conditional statement, set y equal to the result of factor multiplied by
the sum of delta and offset. Finally, in this function, call the scrollBy method of
the window object with the values 0 and y - window.pageYOffset. Check out this
code example:

```
function step() {
var y;
factor = (Date.now() - start) / duration; // get interpolation factor
if( factor >= 1 ) {
clearInterval(timer); // stop animation
factor = 1;            // clip to max 1.0
}
y = factor * delta + offset;
window.scrollBy(0, y - window.pageYOffset);
}
```

After this function, set timer equal to the setInterval method with its variables set
to step and 10. Then, return timer and close the function:

```
***
//previous parts of the function
```

```
timer = setInterval(step,10);
return timer;
}
}());
```

Now, if you reload your browser, you will see some stuff finally happening. But there are a couple of things to see happening here. The first is the obvious big blue blob that does nothing. We will get to that soon.

The other problem is in the developer console. We see that there is an error. The browser is complaining about our function call to `updateElement`, which we have not defined yet. If we take a test-driven development approach, this is a failure that will lead us to success. We need to fix this error. Look at this screenshot:

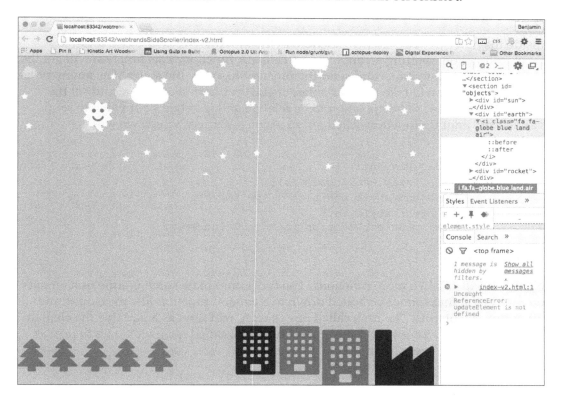

Updating elements on the scroller

To fix the error, start by creating a new function called `updateElement`. You may recall that we added this to the body's `onscroll` method. Now that we have distributed our objects in a random fashion on the screen and created a smooth scroll effect, we need to work on making things change at different rates as we scroll through the rows. This is the meat and potatoes of the parallax effect. In the end, when you scroll through the page, the objects can be programmed to move at different velocities.

This part will involve some fancy footwork and will be explained in a few steps, but it will be lightweight and easy to extend later as you please. The following code contains a function that will be run on every scroll, so we want to keep it as light as possible.

Inside the new `updateElement` function, in the first line, we will create a call to another function, sending an anonymous callback function. This function will get the elements we need to move and send the function to apply the styles. The anonymous callback function will take two variables, `theObject` and `increment`, and set the `theObject` variable's style position to be relative and the style's left value to send variables to another function called `setElementPosition`, which we will define shortly:

```
function updateElement() {
    function (theObject,increment){
        theObject.style.position = "relative";
        theObject.style.left =
        setElementLeftPosition(theObject,increment);
        });
    }
```

Next, we will call two more functions. The functions create some unique movements on each scroll that cannot be boiled down to a general function like the clouds and other moving objects. The first, called `moveEarth`, will send as a variable the element identified by the id earth, and the second function, called `moveRocket`, will take as its variable the element identified by the id rocket:

```
moveEarth(document.getElementById("earth"));

moveRocket(document.getElementById("rocket"));
```

The last part of this function will loop through the Font Awesome I elements inside the DIV element identified by the id stars, and each one will set the style opacity to equal the product of the window's pageYOffest value divided by the window's innerHeight property, multiplied by the total number of elements identified by the class row, and subtracted from 1, and from this final value, 0.3 will be subtracted. This for loop is the last part of the updateElement function. I know it's not easy to read such a description of the math, but you can look here at the code sample to see what I'm building:

```
for (var i = 0; i <
document.getElementById("stars").getElementsByTagName("i").length;
i++)
{
document.getElementById("stars").getElementsByTagName("i")[i].styl
e.opacity = (1-
(window.pageYOffset/(window.innerHeight*
(document.getElementsByClassName("row").length))) -.3);
}
} //closes the function
```

Next, we need to fill in the functions we just referenced; otherwise, the parallax scroller will not be fully operational. The first one, called getMovingElements, takes the variable callback and starts by looping through the elements in the document identified by the row class name. What you will do in this section is determine whether each of the row elements is currently in the viewport. You could add or remove object sets here and control their detection and vertical and horizontal movement.

Inside the for loop, we need to test whether the row it is looping through is actually inside the viewport. Start with this conditional statement: "if the window's pageYOffset property added to the window's innerHeight property is greater than the current row element's offSetTop (distance from top) property and if the window's pageYOffset value is less than the current row element's offSetTop value added to two-thirds of the value of the window's innerHeight property, do the following":

Collecting the moving elements

If the previous condition is true, we need to collect the SVG icons in an array and then get the class of each one. Each class will behave differently. Go through another loop that gathers the current row element's child elements identified by the tag name I. And then loop through each of those children's list of classes collected by the classList method. I will show you how this will look before I tell you what we will do with it. Take a look at the loop in a loop in a loop in this code sample:

```
function getMovingElements(callback){
    for (var i = 0;i<document.getElementsByClassName("row").
length; i++)
{
        if((window.pageYOffset + (window.innerHeight)) >
        document.getElementsByClassName("row")[i].offsetTop &&
        (window.pageYOffset) <
        (document.getElementsByClassName("row")[i].offsetTop +
        (window.innerHeight/2*3)))
{
            for (j = 0; j <
            document.getElementsByClassName("row")
            [i].getElementsByTagName("i"
            ).length; j++)
{
                for (k = 0; k <
                document.getElementsByClassName("row")
                [i].getElementsByTagName("i"
                )[j].classList.length; k++)
{
//Do some thing here
                }
            }
        }
    }
}
```

Inside the nested loop, we will use a conditional set of tests in a switch block to determine what to do. If an element has made it inside the nested conditional statement, we can assume it is in the viewport, so now we need to determine what to do with it.

The types of elements we are dealing with are the moving objects of our project. The clouds (fa-cloud), plane (fa-plane), moon (fa-moon-o), birds (fa-twitter), and whatever else you would want to add. In the switch block, get the current item in the loop of the classList array, and list these cases of results: fa-cloud, fa-plane, fa-moon-o, and fa-twitter. In the case of fa-cloud, we will do something entirely different instead of using the callback we sent earlier.

In the `fa-cloud` case, call a function named `cloudCall`, with the current element identified by the `I` tag name. In the cases of `fa-plane`, `fa-moon-o`, and `fa-twitter`, send the element identified by the `i` tag name and an integer for the velocity to the callback. Send 3 for `fa-plane`, 6 for `fa-moon-o`, and 2 for `fa-twitter`. Look at this code sample:

```
Switch (document.getElementsByClassName("row")
[i].getElementsByTagName("i")[j].classList[k])
{
case 'fa-cloud':
cloudCall(document.getElementsByClassName("row")
[i].getElementsByTagName("i")[j]);
break;
case 'fa-plane':
callback(document.getElementsByClassName("row")
[i].getElementsByTagName("i")[j],3);
break;
case 'fa-moon-o':
callback(document.getElementsByClassName("row")
[i].getElementsByTagName("i")[j],6);
break;
case 'fa-twitter':
callback(document.getElementsByClassName("row")
[i].getElementsByTagName("i")[j],2)
break;
default:
;
}
```

Creating functions for the element types

Let's keep going down this rabbit hole of functions I've created. We have called a function that does not exist yet: `cloudCall`. This function takes the cloud elements, detects the size class we have added, and uses it to determine how fast the cloud should move across the screen. We are going to create an assumption in our parallax 3D effect that the bigger objects are closer and will therefore move faster through the viewport than the slower clouds. The function takes a variable we will identify here as `clouds`. Take the `classList` array, and we will operate on it. Start the function by looping through the clouds' `classList` array.

For each one, use a switch and case test for the Font Awesome class to determine the font's size. Do you remember? It's `fa-2x`, `fa-3x`, `fa-4x`, and `fa-5x`. For each case, call yet another function (have I used the term "rabbit hole" already? What about "labyrinthine"?) as equal to the value of the cloud object's style left property.

The function call is named `setElementLeftPostion` and receives the cloud variable and an integer ranging from 1 to 5. Did you notice there isn't anything for the cloud without an `fa-size` value? There isn't one, but you could send one in the default case. This function can be seen in the following code sample:

```
function cloudCall(clouds){
    for (var k = 0; k < clouds.classList.length; k++)
{
        switch (clouds.classList[k])
{
            case 'fa-2x':
            clouds.style.left =
            setElementLeftPosition(clouds,1);
            break;
            case 'fa-3x':
            clouds.style.left =
            setElementLeftPosition(clouds,2);
            break;
            case 'fa-4x':
            clouds.style.left =
            setElementLeftPosition(clouds,3);
            break;
            case 'fa-5x':
            clouds.style.left =
            setElementLeftPosition(clouds,4);
            break;
            default:
            clouds.style.left =
            setElementLeftPosition(clouds,.5);
            ;
        }
    }
}
```

Hang in there! We really are past the difficult parts now. We only need to create three more functions, and these are going to be small functions. The first is the last one we called, `setElementLeftPosition`.

Setting the left positions

This function will be used to animate the cloud's movement across the viewport by getting the element's left position and adding to it incrementally on each scroll. It receives in the function call the variable's element and increment. In the function, you will first work with the element's style left property using the split method on the string p.

We need to add some failsafe fallback here in case the value is not a number. This could happen if there isn't any value for the style's left property. To verify whether this value is a number, first use the parseInt function on the value you just created and check that it's not NaN (Not a Number). If this logical step passes, return the value of the bounding rectangle's left property of the element, with the string px appended to it.

If the logical test fails, using else, get the integer value of the element's style left property by using the parseInt function and then the absolute value of it, and then add the increment and finally append the string px to it and return it. That was easy enough. Take a look at the code:

```
function setElementLeftPosition(element,increment){
    if
      (isNaN(parseInt(element.style.left.split("p")[0])))
{
        return
((element.getBoundingClientRect().left)+increment) + "px"
      }
else {
        return ((Math.abs(parseInt(element.style.left.split
        ("p")[0]))) + increment) + "px";
      }
    }
```

There are still some errors due to missing functions, but the finish line is in sight. We have two more functions to write, and then the big reveal happens.

Creating the rocket's movement function

Our rocket is the craft we are focusing on in our parallax movement. It should slowly move up or down as we scroll. We want it to slowly move towards the top of the viewport as you move up through the row elements. It will eventually reach to the top of the screen and its final target, the moon. As it moves up, it will also slightly rotate to the right as it arcs up into space. Altogether, this will create a really cool effect.

The function will be named `moveRocket`, and it will take the variable rocket and apply styles to its child elements. It is invoked during the `updateElement` function, so as you scroll through the page, this function will move the rocket.

In the first line, get the `span` elements that are children to the `rocket` element, and apply the style transform equal to the value `rotate` to the first, and here is some more JavaScript math: the window's `innerHeight` property multiplied by the number of rows, minus the rocket's bounding client rectangle's bottom value, divided by the window's `innerHeight` value, all subtracted from the integer 355 and divided by 3. Then, append the string `deg` to the end. This magic algorithm makes the rocket's rotation a factor of if its location in the scrolling.

```
rocket.getElementsByTagName("span")[0].style.transform = "rotate("
+ (355 - (((window.innerHeight *
(document.getElementsByClassName("row").length) -
document.getElementById("rocket").getBoundingClientRect().bottom)/
window.innerHeight))*3) + "deg)";
```

The next line is similar; in fact, I want you to copy and paste it. Then, change the part on the left of the equals sign to get the elements by the tag name `I`, selecting 2 in the array, and to the right of the equals sign, change the integer from 355 to 259. This slightly modifies the rotation of the `fa-flame` I element as it is a different size and orbit.

```
rocket.getElementsByTagName("i")[2].style.transform =
"rotate(" + (259 - (((window.innerHeight *
(document.getElementsByClassName("row").length) -
document.getElementById("rocket").getBoundingClientRect().bottom)/
window.innerHeight))*3) + "deg)";
```

The next line will cause the rockets to move up through the viewport as you scroll up. Instead of selecting the style's transform property, select the style's bottom property. Set it equal to 65 multiplied by the rocket's distance from the bottom divided by the value of the window's `innerHeight` property multiplied by the number of row elements, and then append the string % to the end. Have a look:

```
rocket.getElementsByTagName("span")[0].style.bottom = 65 *
(document.getElementById("rocket").getBoundingClientRect().bottom)
/ (window.innerHeight * (document.getElementsByClassName("row").
length)) + '%';
```

The final function, now that we have moved the heavens, is to move the earth. This function will shrink the earth elements and rotate them as the rocket zooms up into space or as the user scrolls from the bottom to the top. The earth will not be noticeable at first as the rocket will launch from the ground, and the earth is still a very large blue blob obscured in the background.

Finally, moving the earth

Create a new function called `moveEarth` and give it the variable `earth`. First, define the earth variable's style `fontSize` property to be equal to the window's `innerHeight` property multiplied by the number of `row` DIV elements, and subtract from it the element identified by the `id` rocket's bounding client rectangle's bottom property and then divide it by the window's `innerHeight` value; multiply the whole thing by `100`, and then append the string `vw` so that the size is pinned to the viewport width. The function and its first line look like this:

```
function moveEarth(earth){
    earth.style.fontSize=(((window.innerHeight *
     (document.getElementsByClassName("row").length) -
    document.getElementById("rocket").getBoundingClientRect()
    .bottom)/
    window.innerHeight) * 100)+"vw";
}
```

The second line of the `moveEarth` function will set the earth's style left value to be equal to exactly the value of the `fontSize` previously defined, except change `100` at the end to the number of row `DIV` elements multiplied by 2 and instead of `vw`, append the string `px`. Take a look:

```
earth.style.left = (((window.innerHeight *
(document.getElementsByClassName("row").length) -
document.getElementById("rocket").getBoundingClientRect().bottom)
/ window.innerHeight) +
document.getElementsByClassName("row").length * 2) + "px";
```

The next line defines the earth's style height property. Define it as the value of the window's `innerHeight` property multiplied by the number of `row` DIV elements minus the window's `pageYOffset` value, and divide the result by the window's `innerHeight` value plus 1/2, and then append the string `%` to the end. This is illustrated in the following sample:

```
earth.style.height = (window.innerHeight *
(document.getElementsByClassName("row").length)-
window.pageYOffset) / window.innerHeight+.5 + '%';
```

The rest of this function will be used to set style values of the earth's first child element identified by the tag name `I`. The first property to define is transform.

Start with the string `rotate` (and end with the string `deg`), and in between, the value is 15 plus the result of the window's `innerHeight` value multiplied by the result of the number of row elements minus the rocket element's bounding client rectangle's bottom property, which is then divided by the window's `innerHeight` value, and then, that result is multiplied by 4. The code looks like this:

```
earth.getElementsByTagName("i")[0].style.transform = "rotate(" +
(15 + (((window.innerHeight *
(document.getElementsByClassName("row").length) -
document.getElementById("rocket").getBoundingClientRect().bottom)/
window.innerHeight)) * 4) + "deg)";
```

Next, define the right property of the style as the window's `pageYOffset` value divided by its `innerHeight` value and multiplied by the integer 45, then append the string `%`. Whew, that was much easier!

```
earth.getElementsByTagName("i")[0].style.right =
(window.pageYOffset / window.innerHeight * 45) + '%';
```

The next line defines the bottom property of the style. Its definition is the same as the left property, but change the integer 45 to 200:

```
earth.getElementsByTagName("i")[0].style.bottom =
(window.pageYOffset / window.innerHeight * 200) + '%';
```

The final line of code we need to write in this function just happens to be the final line of code we need to write for the application. It sets the style's opacity property of the element, and it's pretty simple compared to most of the previous. It equals 1.3 minus the product of the window's `pageYOffset` value divided by the window's `innerHeight` value, multiplied by the number of `row` DIV elements. And you're done, look at the code here:

```
earth.getElementsByTagName("i")[0].style.opacity = 1.3-
(window.pageYOffset / (window.innerHeight *
(document.getElementsByClassName("row").length)));
} //this closes the function you were working on.
```

Now for the big reveal! Open the file in your browser or refresh it. You will see a number of new things happening. The biggest difference from the previous view is that the earth is no longer a big blue blob, but a big blue-and-green ball that gracefully falls away from the rocket as it exits the stratosphere. And you will see how the rocket arcs in a curve as it shoots away from the earth. In fact, there are a number of moving parts that operate as a function of the updating scrolls.

This project was tonnes of fun for me to create, as I hope it was for you. Again, like I said in the beginning of this chapter, I would like to see what you make of this code, so check out the GitHib code and fork it.

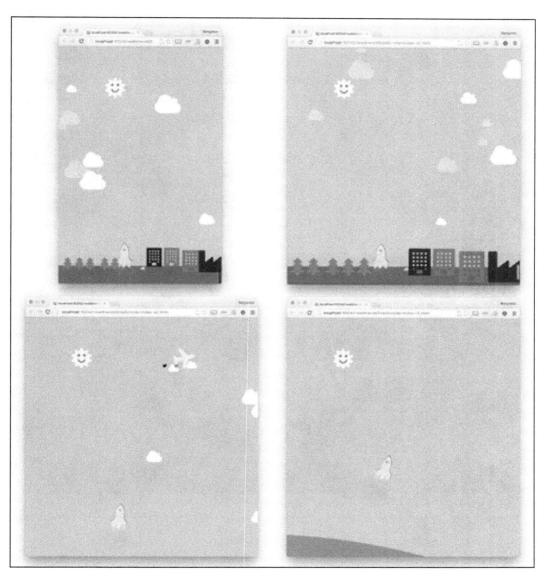

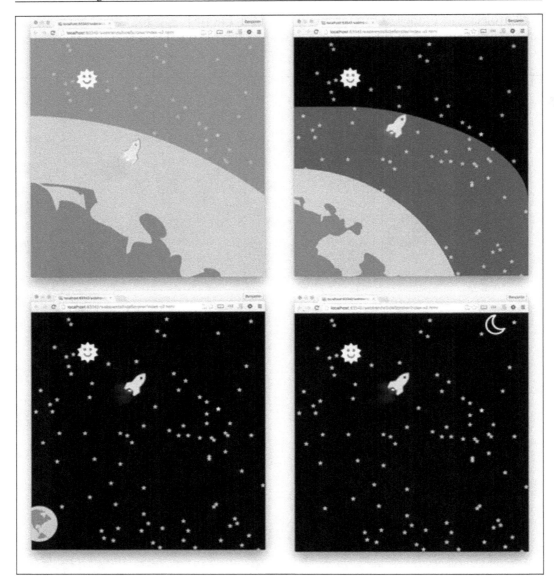

Summary

This chapter was an exciting chapter to create. It's not just useful for a game. It can be used for much more. You could employ the scrollTo functionality to do more, such as linking within and scrolling smoothly down to it. You could also change out the graphics and look to make a different game. Hopefully, you learned some useful information about how to create your own parallax scrolling webpage.

We'll continue to work with this software later. In the final chapter, we will use it to build a larger, more exciting parallax scrolling game. See you there!

4
Single Page Applications

Welcome back! This section is about SPA, Single Page Applications, not a place you go to get your face rubbed. The SPA, if you don't already know, is a web application that loads new pages and content asynchronously. This means that the whole page loads at first, and then uses JavaScript to insert new content inside the page into a defined element.

For this project, let's take an overview of the task at hand. Developing it is not so straightforward; there are a number of steps that we would have to go through before it works. So our development should have some specific milestones of understanding at each step. We will take a UI template we have already built and build it into a Single Page Application framework. First, we will get the template, then break it into the main template and a component loaded through an AJAX function. Then we will break the homepage content into sections that are loaded in a loop from an array containing route information, a routing table. Finally, we will create pages that we can navigate through using the routing table to load the content from links. We will also learn how to use the hash for Single Page Application navigation.

What is an SPA?

Single Page Application is a new and very useful web trend. Using them allows you to build fast and efficient applications and reusable components that are great for mobile and responsive web applications.

Part of the popularity of the Single Page Application is due to its efficiency in front-loading all of the used libraries on the initial load into the DOM and then loading new content as needed. This way, when you want to load a new page, you do not require your user to pull down your CSS or JavaScript file over and over for any new page. You can instead just load the new content, templates, scripts, or data, as you need it. This is a very useful way to build web applications and it makes sense that people want to build them.

The SPA's relevance

The popularity of the Single Page Application has driven the rise of numerous helper libraries for making it. Frameworks are providing routing, loading, and require features that help include scripts, templates, and content, and even provide the framework structure to use to build your app.

You may ask what is the advantage of using a Single Page Application for your project. The advantages are tremendous, and the result is that your SPA web application will load quickly and you do not need to create a whole new file for every link you click, or every post back. The web page and development become streamlined.

Getting to work

In this section, we will get the project started and the filesystem established. For this project, let's take an overview of the task at hand. Developing it is not so straightforward; there are a number of steps that we would have to go through before it works. So our development should have some specific milestones of understanding at each step. We will take a UI template we have already build and build it into a Single Page Application Framework. First we will get the template, and break it into the main template and a component loaded through an AJAX function. Then we will break the home page content into sections that are loaded in a loop from an array containing route information, a routing table. Finally we will create pages that we can navigate through using the routing table to load the content from links. We will also learn how to use the hash for Single Page Application navigation.

Getting the old files

For this application, let's take the Flat UI project we created and turn it into a real working Single Page Application. So go back to the project you built for that project and copy the `index.html` file you created and paste it into the root directory of the Single Page Application project. If you do not have it, you can get it from the GitHub project page, or from the Packt Publishing book page.

Getting the project set up

To get started, create a new project in your IDE, and we will build the app from
there. Let's go over the structure. Inside the base directory, create the folders `app`,
`css`, `images`, and `lib`. The `css` and `images` directories will contain the media
files for CSS and images. The `lib` directory will contain any libraries you choose
to download and use in your project. Finally, the `app` directory will contain the
JavaScript and templates file structures you make when you build the application:

The first thing we can do is create a new CSS file, `style.css`, inside the `css`
directory. In `index.html`, copy the CSS from inside the style element and paste it
into the `style.css` file.

Next, create a link in the `index.html` header to the CSS style sheet, `style.css`:

```
<link type="text/css" rel="stylesheet" href="css/style.css"
media="all">
```

Now, try launching index.html in your browser, and if everything is set up correctly, the application should be working like before.

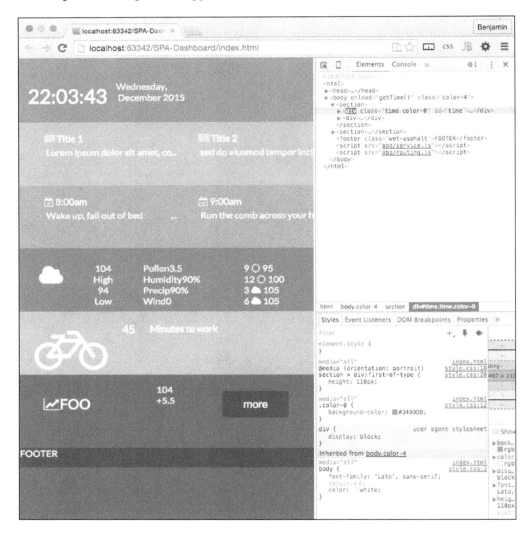

Object and function conventions

In your header file, there is a `script` tag with the clock script in it. Use that for now, and eventually this will grow into a few different scripts as it becomes bigger. Let's get it started in an organized way; there's no sense in creating a debt of disorganization to clean up later.

In the beginning of the script, add a variable object named `home`:

```
var home = {};
```
Then, prepend all variables and functions following this with home instead of leaving them as newly defined. This adds them to that home object. This will prevent confusion and collisions later on. This looks like the following:
```
var home = {};
home.dayArray =
["Sunday","Monday","Tuesday","Wednesday","Thursday","Friday","Satu
rday"];
home.monthArray = ["January","February","March","April","May","June","
July","August"
,"September","October","November","December"];

home.getTime = function(){
var today=new Date();
var h=today.getHours();
var m=today.getMinutes();
var s=today.getSeconds();
var d=home.dayArray[today.getDay()];
var mo=home.monthArray[today.getMonth()];
var y=today.getFullYear();
m = home.correctDigit(m);
s = home.correctDigit(s);
document.getElementById('time').innerHTML = "<br><h1
class='large'>"+h+":"+m+":"+s+"</h1> <span
class='dark'>"+d+",</span class='dark'> <span
class='dark'>"+mo+"</span> <span class='dark'>"+y+"</span>";

var t = setTimeout(function(){home.getTime()},500);
};

home.correctDigit = function(i){
if (i<10)i = "0" + i;  // add zero in front of numbers < 10
return i;
};
```

When you refresh your page, the home clock script should still work.

Creating utility functions

Now that the home content script is still running, move on to some utility functions. We next want to begin creating scripts that provide utility functions.

Creating a services layer for AJAX

These will all be contained in a `services` object, so at the end of the script, create a new object variable called `services`.

```
var services = {};
```

The first thing the services layer will handle will be an AJAX call. We want to be able to use this to get the content asynchronously and placed into a DIV element. So, to demonstrate this, let's break the app into some separate concerns.

Creating and using the file structure

Let's start building out our application structure now, shall we? Inside your app folder is where all the pages for the Single Page Application will live. Each page will live in its own folder with everything it needs.

Working with the home structure

Inside the app directory, add a new directory named `home`. Inside it, create a new HTML page named `home.html`. We will begin putting together the home page section next.

Putting the content in the new file structure for the home

Next, open the `index.html` file and select all of the content within the body tag and cut it out. In the `home.html` file, create a new HTML5 MAIN element and inside it, paste the contents of your clipboard. This is going to create a new layer in your markup, so it will break your CSS. Let's fix that before we move on.

```
<main >
    <section>
        <div class="time color-0" id="time">FOO</div>
        <div>
        <div class="news color-1 scroll">
```

Modifying index.html and CSS

Conversely, modify the body to have the `color-0` class. Add a new child `DIV` element with the ID `content` to it. We use this in the script to insert the AJAX-ified content into the page.

```
<body onload="home.getTime()" class="color-0">
    <div id="content"></div>
</body>
```

Now, if you refresh your page, the application is broken. Well, that's good, as we have something to fix now. This is a good direction to go in. We will fix it using the `services.getPage` function.

Modifying the JavaScript to use the structure

With the `services.getPage` function, we will get the AJAX content. The most important part of a Single Page Application is the asynchronous loading of content into the document object model. So, first things first, let us create a function to load content asynchronously. Create a new function as a method of the services object. The function will be a method in the services object, therefore name it `services.getPage`:

```
services.getPage = function(){
//Do something here
};
```

Inside it, create a new variable called `XHTTP` (Extended Hypertext Transfer Protocol), which will be a placeholder variable for a new `XMLHttpRequest`. An `XMLHttpRequest` is an API that provides the browser with the functionality for transferring data between the client and server:

```
var xhttp;
xhttp = new XMLHttpRequest();
```

Following the `XHTTP` variable, create another variable named `url` to contain the URL we will be getting the content from. In this case, it is `./app/home/home.html`. We should also create another variable to define where we want to load the content into. This variable will be used to select the element `id`:

```
var url = "./app/home/home.html";
var id = "content";
```

XHTTP will have an event method, named `onreadystatechange`, that is performed whenever the `readyState` changes. In our case, it is when the server gives us a response. In the event that the `readyState` is 4, which means that the request is finished and the response is present, and the response status code is 200, meaning 'OK', or that the requested file was found, we want the function to perform another function that will load the content into the page. Leave it commented as pseudo-code for now, but do add a `console.log` of the response so we can take a look at it working:

```
xhttp.onreadystatechange = function () {
if (xhttp.readyState == 4 && xhttp.status == 200) {
// function to load the content
console.log(xhttp)
}
};
```

After the XHTTP `readyState` change and `callback`, XHTTP can retrieve the `url` sent to the function using the GET command inside the `open` method. And then finish it with the `send` method.

```
xhttp.open('GET', url, true);
xhttp.send();
```

Then close the function. The complete function will look like the following example:

```
services.getPage = function(){
var xhttp;
xhttp = new XMLHttpRequest();
var url = "./app/home/home.html";
var id = "content";
xhttp.onreadystatechange = function () {
if (xhttp.readyState == 4 && xhttp.status == 200) {
//function to load the content
console.log(xhttp)
}
};
xhttp.open('GET', url, true);
xhttp.send();
};
```

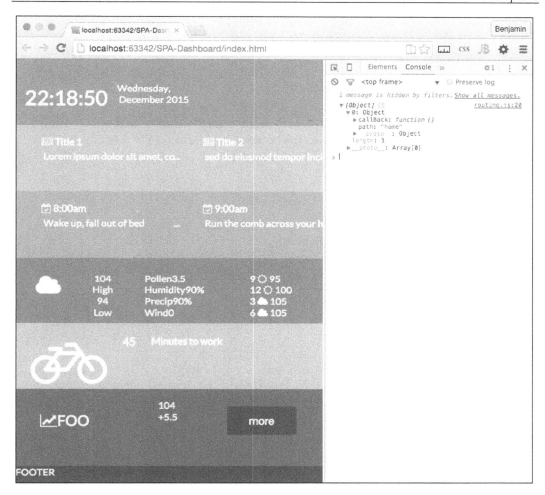

Finish the home to make it work

Good. Now that we see the content loaded, let's create a function to actually load the response text into the HTML. Let's make this a new separate function, as we will want it to be reusable later. Remember that this is a service layer and we eventually want to have a working framework.

Create a new object as a child of the services layer. I want to create a new section for the routing we mentioned earlier. This may be an overcomplication of the namespace, but it keeps the concerns separated at arm's length. It should look like this:

```
services.routing = {};
```

It will have its own methods. The first is to write the HTML into that DIV element. For now, it will write the content into the content DIV element we discussed previously. Create the new method called services.routing.writeHTML like the following example:

```
services.routing.writeHTML = function(){
//Do something
}
We want this function to use the AJAX response we received in the
previous response, and insert it into the DIV element with the id
we just mentioned, the content ID. So feed these parameters to the
function.

services.routing.writeHTML = function(xhttp,id){
//Do something
}
```

Next, go back to the services.getPage and create a function call to this function replacing the commented pseudo-code. It will send the defined variable id and the XHTTP response. You can also remove console.log in that same section:

```
services.routing.writeHTML(xhttp,id);
```

The services.routing.writeHTML function needs something to do. This is pretty simple. First, create a new variable named theHTML equal to the responseText property of the XHTTP that was sent:

```
var theHTML = xhttp.responseText;
```

Now, write a line to get the element by tag name from the document, selecting the id supplied to the function call, and if it is not null, set its innerHtml to equal the XHTTP responseText property:

```
if(document.getElementById(id)!=null)
document.getElementById(id).innerHTML = xhr.responseText;
```

Now, refresh your page again, and you will see this working again; as the content is loaded asynchronously into the content div, this is pretty cool. Before we move forward into breaking the content into more granular pieces, let's do some maintenance. We typically want to break things into smaller tasks as much as possible so they are easier to understand.

Let's first remove some extra lines of code. In the last function we created, `services.routing.writeHTML`, we can condense it further by removing the `theHTML` variable declaration line. In the following line, replace that variable with the value it represented, `xhttp.responseText`. It should look like the following. Now it's a small function, and we can make it more versatile in future:

```
document.getElementById(id).innerHTML = xhttp.responseText;
```

Let's do some more progressive housekeeping. Let's make some of these function calls use `callBack` so we can reuse them later on as a Single Page Application framework. At the bottom of the script, when we call `services.getPage`, we are not sending it anything yet. So let's change that. Let's send it the variables it needs. Let's send it the `url`, the `id`, and the `callBack`. The callback is like sending a function into a function to do some work as a result of something in that function. It's really fun. So right before the function call, set up those variables, except for the function `callBack`, which will go right in the function call parameters. And then add them into the call in that order. Let's precede these lines of code with a reference, TODO, to remove later.

```
//TODO: remove later
var url = './app/home/home.html';
var id = "content";
services.getPage(url, id, services.routing.writeHTML);
```

And don't forget that we need the parameters in the function; `url`, `id`, and `callBack`.

```
services.getPage = function(url,id,callback){
```

And then inside the function, replace the function call:

```
services.routing.writeHTML(xhttp,id)
```

with the following line of code:

```
callback(xhttp,id);
```

This is a good place to show the entire function so you can check yours against mine and correct any problems.

```
services.getPage = function(url,id,callback){
    var xhttp;
    xhttp = new XMLHttpRequest();
    xhttp.onreadystatechange = function () {
        if (xhttp.readyState == 4 && xhttp.status == 200) {
            callback(xhttp,id)
            }
        };
```

```
        xhttp.open('GET', url, true);
        xhttp.send();
};
```

Also, here is the `services.routing` object and its `writeHTML` method:

```
services.routing = {};
services.routing.writeHTML = function(xhttp,id){
    document.getElementById(id).innerHTML = xhttp.responseText;
};
```

So check it again and you can see it working. It should look the same as before, but now it's AJAX.

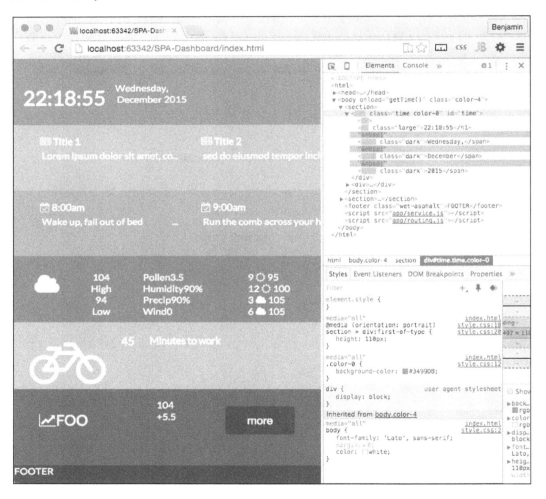

It will get a little more complex from here. But we will use what we have built so far in some new ways. In fact, we have created the base framework for our AJAX loading. Next, we should expand it. To do so, we are going to have to break our working software again. This time, we are going to break out the content into its components. Each section we created will have its own folder, and leave the content framework layout in the home directory.

First, let's start to segment off our services into a separate JavaScript file. In your app directory, create a new JavaScript file named `services.js`. Then cut and paste all of the service object code into it, including the function call at the bottom. Then of course add a link in your HTML file to `service.js` right before the closing `body` tag.

```
<body onload="home.getTime()" class="color-0">
    <div id="content"></div>
    <script src="app/service.js"></script>
</body>
```

Now all the JavaScript we had prepended with the services object is in the services. js file, and all the JavaScript we had prepended with the `home` object will stay in the HEADER SCRIPT for the moment. The `home` object will be moved soon.

Setting up other sections

Next, let's get the content into separate files for the sections. We're going to really break the application now. At least we'll have something to fix again to move forward with our Single Page Application.

Breaking out the content into directories

We already have a `home` directory. Next, add directories for the remaining sections: `news`, `tasks`, `weather`, `travel`, and `stocks`, with the name being the same as the section. Inside each of these directories, add an HTML file named the same as the directory prepended by `home` and a dash, like this: `home-news.html` and `home-stocks.html`. Now, we need to break out the content from the DIV elements and into the directories. First, in `home-home.html` file, only write the text, time, with no markup. As you may recall, the time JavaScript will replace this anyway with the clock. Next, in the `home.html` file, find the DIV element with the class `news`. Add an ID attribute, `news`, to that DIV element.

Then cut its child UL list element from it. Paste it into the home.news.html file inside the /app/news/ directory. The home-news.html file will look like the following:

```
<ul>
<li class="ellipsis">
<h4 class="dark">
<i class="fa fa-newspaper-o"></i>
 Title 1
</h4>
<p>Lorem ipsum dolor sit amet, consectetur adipiscing elit, </p>
</li>
<li class="ellipsis">
<h4 class="dark">
<i class="fa fa-newspaper-o"></i>
 Title 2
</h4>
<p>sed do eiusmod tempor incididunt ut labore et dolore
magna aliqua.
</p>
</li>
<li class="ellipsis">
<h4 class="dark">
<i class="fa fa-newspaper-o"></i>
 Title 3
</h4>
<p>Ut enim ad minim veniam, quis nostrud exercitation
ullamco laboris nisi ut aliquip ex ea commodo consequat.
</p>
</li>
<li class="ellipsis">
<h4 class="dark">
<i class="fa fa-newspaper-o"></i>
 Title 4
</h4>
<p>Ut enim ad minim veniam, quis nostrud exercitation
ullamco laboris nisi ut aliquip ex ea commodo consequat. </p>
</li>
</ul>
```

Follow the same procedure for the tasks starting in the DIV element with the tasks class. Add the ID attribute tasks, and cut out its child content. Paste it into home-tasks.html.

```
<ul>
<li class="ellipsis">
<h4 class="dark">
<i class="fa fa-calendar-check-o"></i>
 8:00am
</h4>
<p>Wake up, fall out of bed</p>
</li>
<li class="ellipsis">
<h4 class="dark">
<i class="fa fa-calendar-check-o"></i>
 9:00am
</h4>
<p>Run the comb across your head</p>
</li>
<li class="ellipsis">
<h4 class="dark">
<i class="fa fa-calendar-check-o"></i>
 10:00am
</h4>
<p>Find your way downstairs and Drink a cup
</p>
</li>
<li class="ellipsis">
<h4>
<i class="fa fa-calendar-check-o"></i>
 11:00am
</h4>
<p>Looking up, notice you are late
</p>
</li>
<li class="ellipsis">
<h4 class="dark">
<i class="fa fa-calendar-check-o"></i>
 12:00am
</h4>
<p>Find your coat and grab your hat
</p>
</li>
</ul>
```

Next, follow the same procedure for the weather section. This is the content that the home-weather.html file will have in it.

```
<ul>
<li>
<ul>
<li>
<h2><i class="fa fa-cloud fa-3x"></i></h2>
</li>
<li>
<ul>
<li class="left">
<span>104</span>
<br>
<span class="dark">High</span>
</li>
<li class="right">
<span>94</span>
<br>
<span class="dark">Low</span>
</li>
</ul>
</li>
</ul>
</li>
<li>
<ul>
<li>
<ul>
<li>
<span class="dark">Pollen</span>
<span>3.5</span>
</li>
<li>
<span class="dark">Humidity</span>
<span>90%</span>
</li>
<li>
<span class="dark">Precip</span>
<span>90%</span>
</li>
<li>
```

```
<span class="dark">Wind</span>
<span>0</span>
</li>
</ul>
</li>
<li>
<ul>
<li>
<span>9</span><i class="fa fa-sun-o"></i> <span>95</span></li>
<li>
<span>12</span><i class="fa fa-sun-o"></i> <span>100</span></li>
<li>
<span>3</span><i class="fa fa-cloud"></i> <span>105</span>
</li>
<li>
<span>6</span><i class="fa fa-cloud"></i> <span>105</span>
</li>
</ul>
</li>
</ul>
</li>
</ul>
```

The travel section:

```
<h2>
<i class="fa fa-bicycle fa-4x"></i>
</h2>
<h3>45</h3>
<h4 class="dark">Minutes to work</h4>
```

And the stocks section:

```
<ul>
<li>
<h2 class="">
<i class="fa fa-line-chart"></i>FOO
</h2>
</li>
<li>
<ul>
<li class="left">
```

```
<span>104</span>
</li>
        <li class="right">
<span>+5.5</span>
</li>
</ul>
</li>
<li>
<button onclick="doSomething()" class="wet-asphalt">more</button>
</li>
</ul>
```

Now, `home.html` will look a bit tidier and easier to manage. Changes to the main template, or the template partials, may be a little easier to work with now. The IDs we added for each content section will be used later to identify which section to load the section templates into. The home template code will look like this:

```
<main class="color-4">
    <section>
        <div class="time color-0" id="time">FOO</div>
        <div>
            <div id="news" class="news color-1 scroll"></div>
            <div id="tasks" class="tasks color-2 scroll"></div>
        </div>
    </section>
    <section>
            <div id="weather" class="weather color-3"></div>
        <div>
            <div id="travel" class="travel color-1 center"></div>
            <div id="stocks" class="stock color-4 center"></div>
        </div>
    </section>
    <footer class="wet-asphalt">FOOTER</footer>
    </main>
```

Refresh your browser and you will see the app is broken. None of the content, except our clock, appears. We can fix this with a few more lines of code.

Separating concerns and making objects

To fix this, we need to make our routing table, which will be a list of our content sections containing information about where to find the various necessary content for it. Create a new JavaScript file in the app directory named `routing.js`.

Include the link to the script in the bottom of the body in the `index.html` file right before the closing BODY tag.

```
<body onload="home.getTime()" class="color-0">
<div id="content"></div>
<script src="app/service.js"></script>
<script src="app/routing.js"></script>
</body>
```

Making the routing registry tables

In `routing.js`, create a new object called `routing`. Inside it a array called `routesArray`. The array is where we will create our routing table.

```
var routing = {};
routing.routesArray = [];
```

The next function will be used to register and store the routes to be used when a link is clicked. Create a new method of the services routing object called `routing.register` as a function. It receives the variables `path` and `callBack`.

```
services.routing.register = function(path, callBack){
//Do Something
}
```

Inside that function, create a new object variable called `routeObject`. It has the properties `path` equaling `path`, and `callBack` equaling `callBack`, both being the variables sent to the function.

```
var routeObject = {};
routeObject.path = path;
routeObject.callBack = callBack;
```

Before closing the function, use the array `push` method to push `routeObject` into the `routing.routesArray` array.

```
routing.routesArray.push(routeObject);
```

Let's quickly move to attempt to see what's going on here, that is, use the functions we are creating. To do so, we want to register our first route. To make it easy, the first route to register in the routing table will be the `home` route. Call the `services.routing.register` function and send the two variable described earlier: the path named `home`, and an anonymous `callBack` function.

```
services.routing.register('home',function(){
//Do something
});
```

Inside the anonymous function, set an undeclared variable, pageRoute, to equal an object with a property: partial. Assign the value to the property: ./app/home/home-home.html. After the object's closing bracket, add console.log to log the string home. This will be helpful later to see when this function is fired.

```
pageRoute = {
partial:"./app/home/home-home.html"
};
console.log('home');
```

Following the services.routing.register call, add console.log to log routing.routesArray and you will see this later:

```
console.log(routing.routesArray)
```

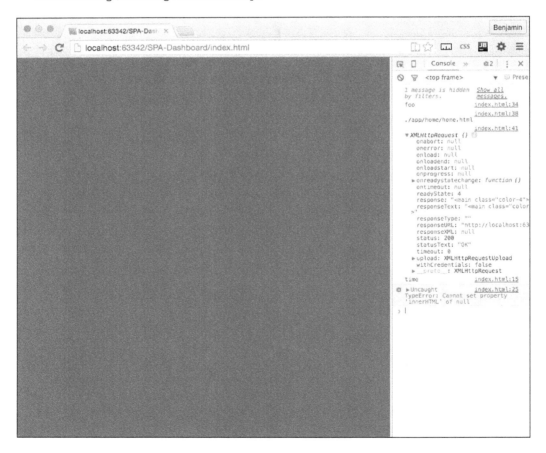

Now you see the routing registration table with the first route. We will of course add more as we move forward, but first, let's make this work. We want to use this to load the home content.

Using routing registry tables to load home content

In the `index.html` file's header, create a new function called `home.loadSections`. This will perform the task of loading the content into the template asynchronously. Inside the function, create a `for` loop that iterates over the `routing.routesArray` array. Add a TODO note to `move this later`.

```
//TODO Move this later
    home.loadSections = function() {
        for (i = 0; i < routing.routesArray.length; i++) {
//Do Something
    }
```

In the loop, call the `routesArray`'s current value's `callBack` using the `call` method. And then call the `services.getPage` function, sending it the values `pageRoute.partial`, which we just initiated in the previous line of code, the `routing.routesArray`'s current values `path` property, which tells the function where to stick it, and then the `callBack` to the function we have already created, `services.routing.writeHTML`, which we know executes the content we called asynchronously in `services.getPage`.

```
routing.routesArray[i].callBack.call();
services.getPage(pageRoute.partial,routing.routesArray[i].path,ser
vices.routing.writeHTML);
```

The function you just created is fully operational and will create the whole page of content asynchronously. All it needs are the values to be sent to it from the routing table. So let's go back and create the routing table for the rest of the home page. You will need to create routing registries for the `weather`, `news`, `tasks`, `travel`, and `stocks`. Then magically they should all load into the home page. Simply follow the model you created for registering the home route.

See the following example:

```
services.routing.register('weather',function(){
    pageRoute = {
        partial:"./app/weather/home-weather.html"
    };
    console.log('weather')
});
services.routing.register('travel',function(){
    pageRoute = {
        partial:"./app/travel/home-travel.html"
    };
    console.log('travel')
});
services.routing.register('news',function(){
    pageRoute = {
        partial:"./app/news/home-news.html"
    };
    console.log('news')
});
services.routing.register('stocks',function(){
    pageRoute = {
        partial:"./app/stocks/home-stocks.html"
    };
    console.log('stocks')
});
services.routing.register('tasks',function(){
    pageRoute = {
        partial:"./app/tasks/home-tasks.html"
    };
    console.log('tasks')
});
```

Now, refresh your screen and you will see how you have fixed the broken page. We have emerged through failure and are again into success! Good work. You will also see that the console log we added earlier is full with an entry for each section.

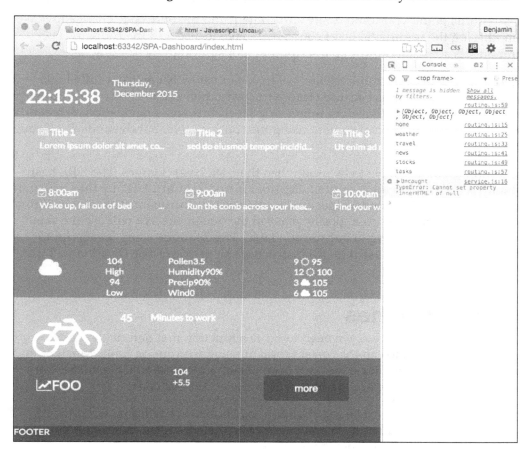

Loading all sections in the structure

That's pretty cool, and a big deal so far. You have created a page that not only loads components asynchronously but also does it through definitions in your routing table. At this point, you could easily add content and the only code change to make is modifying the routing table (of course you have to also add the content). The components are loaded through a script that loops through the routing table.

However, as cool as we think we are, we have not yet truly created a full Single Page Application. This is because there is no navigation yet. It's just a page built up of pieces. So let's make this more interesting by adding some navigation elements. What we want to do is load content using the routing table, but dynamically through navigation and URLs.

We want the routing table to be used when the URL hash changes. The URL hash actually is referring to the fragment identifier introduced in a URL by the (optional) hash mark # in a URL used to specify a portion of the document. That is the original use, to get your browser to a specific place in the document. We will use the same hash to call in our content in our routing table. This requires using JavaScript to 'intercept' the hash and use it to call instructions to perform. The function will use the variable page.

Making #hashes

To use the hash to navigate, we need to write a function that detects the hash fragment and uses it to call the correct content using the routing table. Much of the code is already in place since we have been creating reusable functions. These are mostly ready to use for page loading, with some additional code.

The next code to write will be in your `routing.js` file. We will first write the function to get the location hash and extrapolate the URL from the hash fragment, and then send that URL to another function.

At the end of the `routing.js` file, create a new method of the routing object called `routing.getLocationHash`. The first line of the function is a conditional statement; if the window's location property hash has no value, then change it to equal #home.

```
if (!window.location.hash)
    window.location.hash = '#home';
```

Next, get the hash string and split it at the hash #. From the resulting array values, select the 1 value, and send it to a new function in the services object, called `services.routing`. It can be seen in the next example:

```
var hash = window.location.hash.split('#')[1];
services.routing.useArray(hash);
```

You can also efficiently write this as the following:

```
services.routing.useArray(window.location.hash.split('#')[1]);
```

Then close the function. We next need to call this function in two distinct operations: once when the page initializes, and then any time a new hash, or location, is selected in a link or typed into the URL bar.

 For example, typing in `http://localhost:63342/webtrends-SPA/index.html#tasks` would load the tasks page of the Single Page Application. You should note that this URL and port number are used in my local environment. Yours may be different.

This is an action event, not really reusable services, and because we are trying to keep a separation of concerns, this should be outside of the routing and services JavaScript pages. Therefore, we need to create a whole new JavaScript file, named `app.js`. This is where the actionable things should go. It will only get light use in this framework, but as you build on top of it, more may go here.

First, in the `app.js` file, detect when the window's `onhaschange` method is called and then call the `services.routing.getLocationHash` function. Write another line of code calling the same function for the window's `onload` method. See the following example:

```
window.onhashchange = services.routing.getLocationHash;
window.onload = services.routing.getLocationHash;
```

You have probably realized that I've created a bug, since I have already used the window's `onload` method, and it will not work again. Remember, we used it inline in the `index.html` file's BODY tag to activate the clock. So now we have some more broken application code to fix.

We will have to write some new functions, because we will take advantage of this failure to not only fix but also upgrade the application.

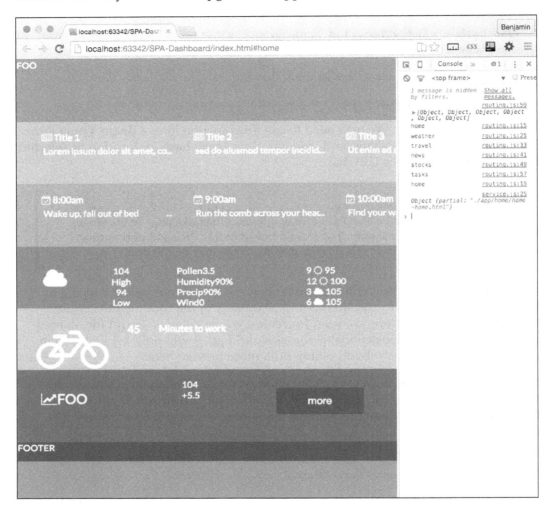

Using #hash for routing

To fix the broken application, let's get this routing table working. It already loads the content in, but we now need it to initialize the application. This will take some mental elbow grease, so let's get moving on it.

In the `services.routing.getLocationHash` function, we called a service method that does not yet exist; we had better fix that problem. So let's create another new services method. You probably can guess what it will be called and what file to write it in; it follows the same conventions.

If you created a `services.routing.useArray` function in the `service.js` file, you are a Jedi Master. If not, just pretend you did and write it quickly while no one is looking. It receives the variable hash. Be sure you are following the definition of the `services.routing` object.

```
services.routing.useArray = function(hash){
//Do Something
};
```

Inside the `services.routing.useArray` function, create a for loop iterating over the `routing.routesArray` array. In each, check that the `routing.routesArray` current value's path property is equal to the hash variable. If it matches, call the `routing.routesArray` current value's `callBack`. This will define, or redefine, to the `pageRoute` value, which is used to load the content into the Single Page Application.

```
for(i=0;i<routing.routesArray.length;i++){
    if(routing.routesArray[i].path===hash)
    routing.routesArray[i].callBack.call();
}
```

Following the `for` loop, we can reconnect full circle to our first service function we created, the `services.getPage` function. The `services.getPage` function will receive four variables, one of which does not exist yet, and we will immediately need to create it to make this work, and it will send more variables than the `services.getPage` function can so far handle, so we now have a new to-do list. This may be a good time to brew some coffee, and then we'll continue.

The `services.getPage` function will receive a new property of `pageRoute` in the routing registration table. The new property is `page`. Inside each registry, you will need to add the new `page` property; each will have the value of the path and page name with the HTML extension. It will essentially give the location of the page to load into the Single Page Application framework when you click the link. So for home, the page property looks like `./app/home/home.html`, and the `weather` page `./app/weather/weather.html`.

The weather `pageRoute` object will look like the following example:

```
pageRoute = {
         page:"./app/weather/weather.html",
         partial:"./app/weather/home-weather.html"
};
```

Pretty slick! Now, add the entry for each router registry. I'll include them all in this example.

```
services.routing.register('home',function(){
    pageRoute = {
        page:"./app/home/home.html",
        partial:"./app/home/home-home.html",
    };
console.log('home')
    });
services.routing.register('weather',function(){
    pageRoute = {
        page:"./app/weather/weather.html",
        partial:"./app/weather/home-weather.html",
    };
console.log('weather')
    });
services.routing.register('travel',function(){
    pageRoute = {
        page:"./app/travel/travel.html",
        partial:"./app/travel/home-travel.html",
    };
console.log('travel')
    });
services.routing.register('news',function(){
    pageRoute = {
        page:"./app/news/news.html",
        partial:"./app/news/home-news.html",
    };
console.log('news')
    });
    services.routing.register('stocks',function(){
    pageRoute = {
        page:"./app/stocks/stocks.html",
        partial:"./app/stocks/home-stocks.html",
    };
```

```
console.log('stocks')
    });
services.routing.register('tasks',function(){
    pageRoute = {
        page:"./app/tasks/tasks.html",
        partial:"./app/tasks/home-tasks.html",
    };
console.log('tasks')
    });
```

You also need to create each of these pages in their proper directory (with the exception of home.html, it should already exist). Let's take a shortcut and simply copy each page partial (excluding home-news.html) into the new page (excluding news.html). This will save a few laborious steps.

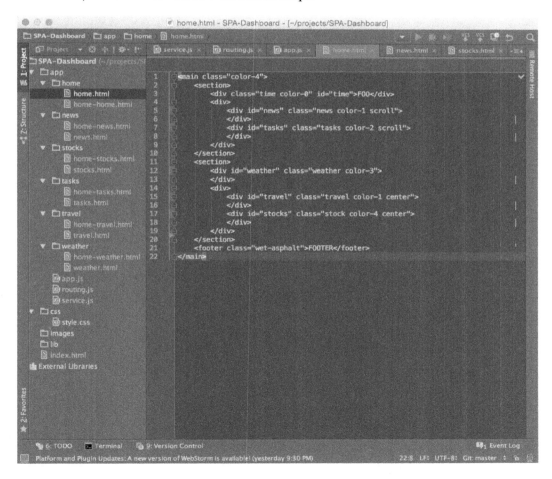

We will not have to further modify our HTML files right now. These are ready to go. It will give us some better testability of our progress. Let's clean up some code that has already been made obsolete by what we just created.

In your `services.js` JavaScript file, look for the `TODO` we created earlier as a reminder to delete some code. It should still be down at the bottom. Find it and remove it.

```
//TODO: remove later
var url = './app/home/home.html';
var id = "content";
services.getPage(url, id, services.routing.writeHTML);
```

Now, it may seem like it's still broken, but in actuality, it's working pretty well. Let's test drive our Single Page Application routing engine we created. Try entering the base URL of the website `http://localhost:63342/SPA-Dashboard/` or `http://localhost:63342/SPA-Dashboard/index.html` (depending on how your server is configured, I am using my IDE as a `localhost`). It will redirect you to the `#home` hash and load the home page like such: `http://localhost:63342/SPA-Dashboard/#home` or `http://localhost:63342/SPA-Dashboard/index.html/#home`.

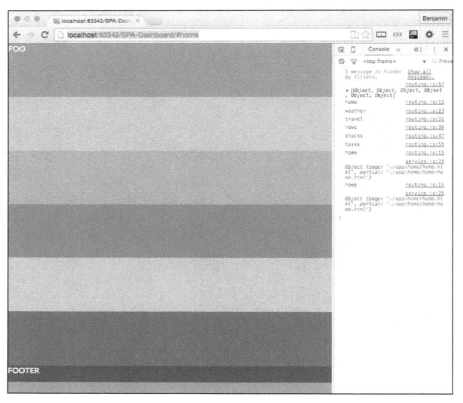

I know you have seen that screen several times already and it's likely irritating you, so let's try a surprise: change the hash from #home to #news. Now you will see the Single Page Application routing table working.

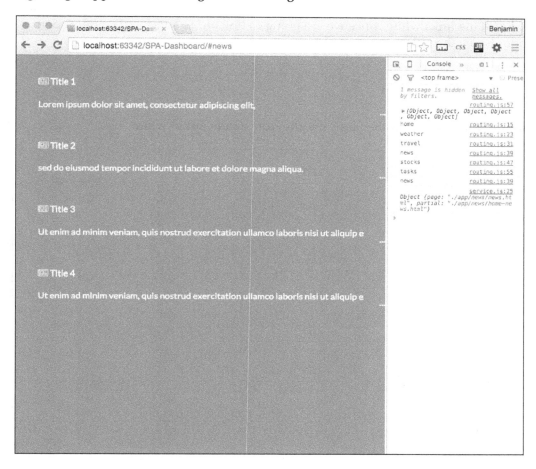

Let's add a bit of navigation to the pages. For now, we will skip creating the navigation on the home page because there is another step we want to perform on that.

In each page HTML (excluding /app/news/news.html) file, add a link that contains a Font Awesome left chevron to the beginning of the page. The link HREF should be pointed to the home page hash. It looks like the following example:

```
<a href="#home"><i class="fa fa-chevron-left fa-3x"></i></a>
```

I do not like the blue arrow; actually, I prefer it to be white. So add a white class to the I Element, and in your CSS add to the color section you created in the *Chapter 2, Flat UI* a white selector (following the wet-asphalt selector), with the attribute color:white. Also, let's do a preemptive strike and a selector for the a to make all the links white, since we are going to link out to some real content soon enough. See the following example:

```
.white, a{
color:white;
}
```

Now when you refresh the page, the chevron stands out in white.

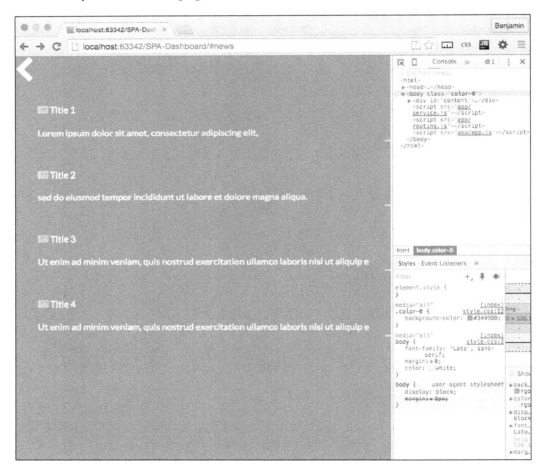

You can now enter any of the paths from the routing table, and they will load up the content into the Single Page Application. Much of the framework is working at this point. It's loading content, but we really also want it to do some things in these new pages. When you load a new page, it's still fairly static. We want more interaction and better active content. One way we could do this is in the routing table; you may recall that there is a `callBack` function that loads in each registry in the routing registration table, and we already employ it to define and refresh the `pageRoute` object, and it gives us a `console.log` to see that it has fired. That is certainly a possibility; however, the main reason I want to not do that is because it will break out of the convention of the separation of concerns that has been working well for us already. If we started loading up the routing registry `callBacks` with functional script, it will become difficult to manage, and difficult to navigate to the code to modify it. The other reason is that we already have an engine that can handle this loading of content from the application directories, so let's use it.

In each section directory, we already have two HTML files that we load up as needed. We can modify the code to load up JavaScript when needed. So, let's add a new JavaScript file in each directory. For example, in the `news` directory, create a new JavaScript file named `news.js`. Do this for every section. In each new JavaScript file, add the code to `console.log` a variable `id` (which we will create soon) so we can confirm it when it works.

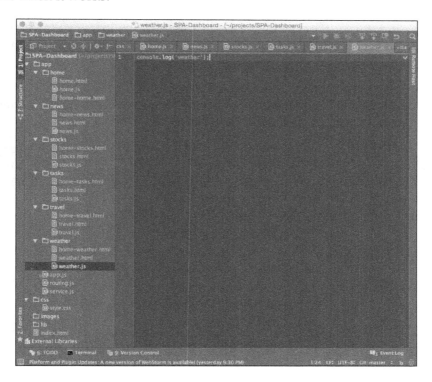

Now you can add these JavaScript files to the routing table. In each routing registry, add a new property to the `pageRoute` object, script. The value for each property id should be the path to the JavaScript you created. For weather's `pageRoute`, the property and value will be script: `./app/weather/weather.js`. See the following example for the full routing registry:

```
services.routing.register('weather',function(){
    pageRoute = {
        page:"./app/weather/weather.html",
        partial:"./app/weather/home-weather.html",
        script:"./app/weather/weather.js"
    };
console.log('weather')
    });
```

Now each routing table registry should have this full set of three paths. Nothing is done with the scripts yet, but we will fix that problem right now.

Performing housekeeping

There are some scripts that are to run on the home page and they are living in the wrong places. The first one is the clock script in the `index.html` HEAD SCRIPT element. We don't want that there. It only runs in the home page, and it isn't in our separation of concerns methodology. So cut the script out of the index script tag and paste it into the `home.js` file.

In the `routing.js` file there is a function called `home.loadSections`. This is also outside of its home. When we created it, we noted it with a TODO to move later. So now cut it out and paste it into the `home.js` file.

Now the `/app/home/home.js` file has the full home object including `home.dayArray`, `home.monthArray`, the `home.getTime` function, the `home.correctDigit` function, and the `home.loadSections` function. It should be followed by calls to the `home.loadSections` and `home.getTime` functions.

The home function should look like the following example without much more modification:

```
console.log(id)
var home = {};
home.dayArray = ["Sunday","Monday","Tuesday","Wednesday",
"Thursday","Friday","Saturday"];
```

```
home.monthArray = ["January","February","March","April",
"May","June","July","August","September","October",
"November","December"];
home.getTime = function(){
var today=new Date();
var h=today.getHours();
var m=today.getMinutes();
var s=today.getSeconds();
var d=home.dayArray[today.getDay()];
var mo=home.monthArray[today.getMonth()];
var y=today.getFullYear();
m = home.correctDigit(m);
s = home.correctDigit(s);
document.getElementById('time').innerHTML = "<br><h1 class='large'>"
+h+":"+m+":"+s+"</h1> <span class='dark'>"+d+",</span class='
dark'> <span class='dark'>"+mo+"</span> <span class='
dark'>"+y+"</span>";
var t = setTimeout(function(){home.getTime()},500);
};
home.correctDigit = function(i){
if (i<10)i = "0" + i;  // add zero in front of numbers < 10
return i;
};

home.loadSections = function() {
for (i = 0; i < routing.routesArray.length; i++) {
routing.routesArray[i].callBack.call();
services.getPage(pageRoute.partial,routing.routesArray[i].
path,services.routing.writeHTML);
}

};

home.getTime();
home.loadSections();
```

Creating a callBack function for the API

The final piece in making this and the other local JavaScript work through the routing table is to wire it into the services.getPage function. This will be easy.

Using the callBack function

Before that, we first need to write a new `callBack` function to do something with the JavaScript that is in the content directories. And when it loads it, it loads into the header's `SCRIPT` element, where it runs. Create a new function as a method of the `services.routing` object called `writeScript`. It will receive the variables `XHTTP`, `id`, and `hash`.

```
services.routing.writeScript = function(xhttp,id,hash){
//Do Something
};
```

Inside it, first create a new variable called `newScript` equal to the document's `createElement` method, creating a `SCRIPT` element.

```
var newScript = document.createElement('script');
```

The `newScript` variable has a `property`, `text`; set it equal to the string `var id="` plus the `hash` variable plus `";`. See the following example:

```
newScript.text = 'var id= "'+hash+'";';
```

Then add to that test property the `XHTTP`'s `responseText`.

```
newScript.text += xhr.responseText;
```

Finally, for this `callBack` function, get from the document the element by tag name (variable) `id`, select its `0`th item, and append to its child your `newScript` variable. This line of code is the magic. It will load the JavaScript into the document's `HEAD` `SCRIPT` element, and that will make it run asynchronously!

```
document.getElementsByTagName(id).item(0).appendChild(newScript);
```

Then, close the `callBack` function.

Using the callBack function

Now that we have written the `callBack` to execute the JavaScript, let's send it as a `callBack` to the `services.getPage` function. At the end of the `services.routing.useArray` function, create a new line of code. Call the `services.getPage` function, sending it the `pageRoute`'s `script` property as the `url` variable, the `head` as the `id` variable, the `services.routing.writeScript` function as the `callBack`, and finally, add a fourth variable, `hash`. The `hash` will be sent to the local JavaScript files to use. In our framework, we are only setting them up to be used to `console.log` the `id` when the page loads.

See the following example to see the function call with the `callBack`.

```
services.getPage(pageRoute.script,'head',services.routing.writeScr
ipt,hash);
```

Almost there! We have to do something with the hash variable: add hash as the fourth variable received by the `services.getPage` function. See the following example:

```
services.getPage = function(url,id,callback,hash){
...
```

Next, in the `services.getPage` function, add `hash` to the `callBack` call as the third variable.

```
xhttp.onreadystatechange = function () {
    if (xhttp.readyState == 4 && xhttp.status == 200) {
        callback(xhttp,id,hash)
    }
};
```

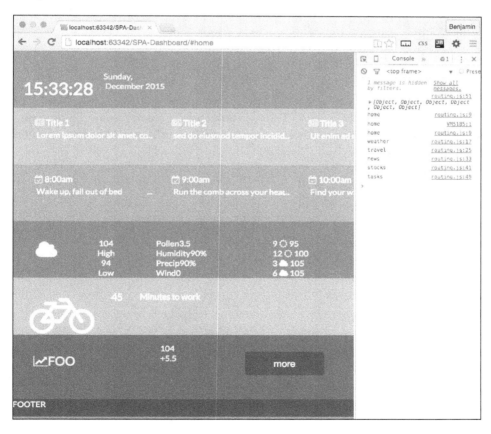

Now, refresh your page, and you can see it is loading all the home page sections. This is happening because you moved all the home page loading script into `home.js`, and the latest fix you crushed loads the local JavaScript files into the head script and runs them.

Adding links that use hashes

Now that the Single Page Application is working, let's add some navigation between the pages of the Single Page Application. You had previously created a link using the font awesome left chevron. Open up one of the local content pages (`news.html`, for example) and copy that link. Then paste it into `home-new.html`. Then, change the HREF attribute to point to `#news` and change the icon class to `fa-chevron-right`.

```
<a href="#news"><i class="fa fa-chevron-right fa-3x
white"></i></a>
```

Do the same for tasks and weather. Refresh your screen, and you will see some broken layout. Here, yet again, is something we need to fix to keep our show on the road. This will be easily fixed with some additional CSS. Add a class to each of these I elements called `right-link` and then open your CSS file style.css. Here's the element with the new class added:

```
<a href="#news"><i class="fa fa-chevron-right fa-3x white right-
link"></i></a>
```

In your `style.css`, add the `right-link` class selector before the media queries. Give it these properties: an absolute position, 0 to the right, a cursor for a pointer, 5% top margin, and 80% opacity. See the following example:

```
.right-link{
position:absolute;
right:0;
cursor:pointer;
margin-top:5%;
opacity:0.8
}
```

Now, refresh your screen and see the links are in a better place. Test them out and you will see the pages are loading up into the Single Page Application!

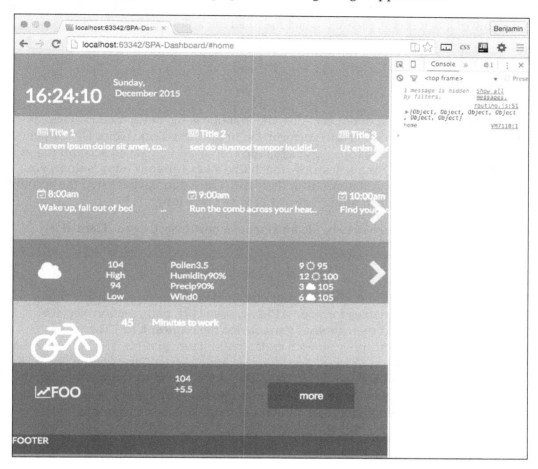

This is really great; it's a working framework. Let's get some real things going here. The remaining problem is that we have not fulfilled our goal, to make a working application; this is all just dummy data. I want you to have a real working Single Page Application. And besides, honestly, you have worked really hard to build a good foundation, and this is the fun part. You've earned some fun, so stick with me.

To get the application working, we need to get real data. There are numerous cool APIs you can play with. I did the homework for you and found ones that are a good fit for the needs of this app. You can replace them with your own if you like, and if you know of a better one, please contact me to let me know.

OK, let's get cracking on the fun stuff.

Using APIs

Let's just go down the list of our sections; the first one is the news section. There is some functional work you need to perform. Go to the New York Times Developer home page at `http://developer.nytimes.com/docs` and create an account to get an API key. The API key is a key string, much like a key for your home's door; you will need to use it to request news from their API. Once you have created the account and received a key, you can move forward. It won't take long.

Open up the `/app/news/news.js` file and create a new object, `news`. There it is, the same pattern again.

```
var news = {};
```

Next, create a new method of the `news` object, called `news.request`. Inside this function, create new variables for your API key, base URL path, section, one for the response format, and then another variable for the request URL. The API documentation should supply you with expanded documentation. The value for the base URL is `http://api.nytimes.com/svc/topstories/v1/`, the section is `world`, and the response format is `json`. The URL variable is equal to the base URL plus the section, plus a period, plus the response format, plus the string `?api-key=`, plus the API key variable. These variables are illustrated in the following example:

```
var apiKey = '1234567890qwerty';
var baseUrl = 'http://api.nytimes.com/svc/topstories/v1/';
var section = 'world';
var responseFormat = 'json';
var url = baseUrl + section + '.' + responseFormat + '?api-key=' +
apiKey;
```

Next, call up the `services.getPage` function and send the variables it wants. It expects the `url` to load the content from, the `id` send to the `callBack`, the `callBack`, and the fourth variable, the `hash`, also to send to the `callBack`, if necessary, but not in this case. It will look like the following example:

```
services.getPage(url,'news-list',news.parseAjax);
```

Then, close the function. It will go through the same functional process as every other asynchronous call we sent through this way before, so I won't need to explain it. What we need to do one last time is write our final function to parse through the AJAX data returned through the function. So in the `news.js` file, create one more function called `news.parseAjax`. It will receive the variables `XHTTP` and the `id`. See the following example:

```
news.parseAjax = function(xhttp,id){
//Do Something
};
```

This function will parse the data and insert it into the list in the news partial template. So first, create a new variable called `data` equal to the result of parsing the JSON object in the response text of the XHTTP response.

```
var data = JSON.parse(xhttp.responseText);
```

Next, create an empty string variable called `newsHTML` as a placeholder. Then, create a `for` loop to go through the first four new stories returned in the JSON object. Each iteration inserts parts of the response object into a list item that we will insert into the template to replace the hardcoded fake news. The API returns a `URL`, a `title`, and a brief `abstract` of the article. Which is everything we need. We just cut the LI list items out of the UL list in the template and replace the content with the data received. See the following example:

```
var newsHtml = '';
for(i=0;i<4;i++){
newsHtml+='<li class="ellipsis"><a href="'+data.results[i].url+'"><h4
class="dark"><i class="fa fa-newspaper-
o"></i> '+data.results[i].title+'</h4>'+'<p>'+data.results[i].
abstract+'</p></a></li>';
}
```

Insert this into the HTML identified by the `id` variable sent and then close the function. See the following example:

```
document.getElementById(id).innerHTML=newsHtml;
```

Finally, call the `news.request` function from the last line of the `news.js` code. This will execute the function when this JavaScript file is loaded asynchronously into the `HEAD SCRIPT` element.

To make this work, we need to add the id to the HTML. So, add the id to the parent UL in the news.html and home-news.html files. You can delete the child list items too. This page now looks like this:

```
<a href="#home"><i class="fa fa-chevron-left fa-3x white left-
link"></i></a>
<ul id="news-list">
</ul>
```

Now you can pull up the URL http://localhost:63342/SPA-Dashboard/#news and see that it has loaded up the content from the API; that's totally awesome. But wait! If you go back home, it does not load! Did I cheat you? Only a little. We still need one tiny piece of code left to finish it and make it load up in the home page.

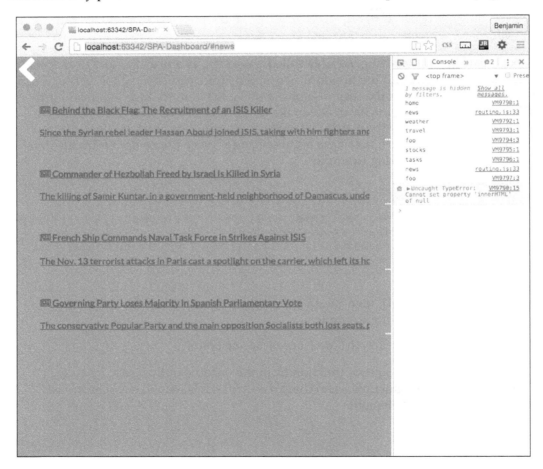

Finally, finally, finally, we need to do one last thing to load up this JavaScript file and the others into the home page header script. So, go back to your `home.js`, and append a conditional `if` statement to the end of the `home.loadsections` function `for` loop. The conditional `if` checks the `routesArray` array's current value, or value in the current `index`, `path` property to not be equal to `home`. If the condition is `true`, or if the current loop in the routing table is not `home`, do something. That something is to call up the `services.getPage` function, sending the `pageRoute`'s `script`, a string `head`, the callBack `services.routing.writeScript`, and finally for the hash value, `routing.routesArray`'s current iteration's `path` value. This will load up each section's JavaScript, so whatever you have written in them will execute here and now. See the following example of the `home.loadSections` function in its entirety:

```
home.loadSections = function() {
for (i = 0; i < routing.routesArray.length; i++) {
routing.routesArray[i].callBack.call();
services.getPage(pageRoute.partial,routing.routesArray[i].
path,services.routing.writeHTML);
if(routing.routesArray[i].path!='home'){
services.getPage(pageRoute.script,'head',services.routing.
writeScript,routing.routesArray[i].path);
}
}
};
```

Now, take a look, and you will see your AJAX news is loading into the page. This works really well.

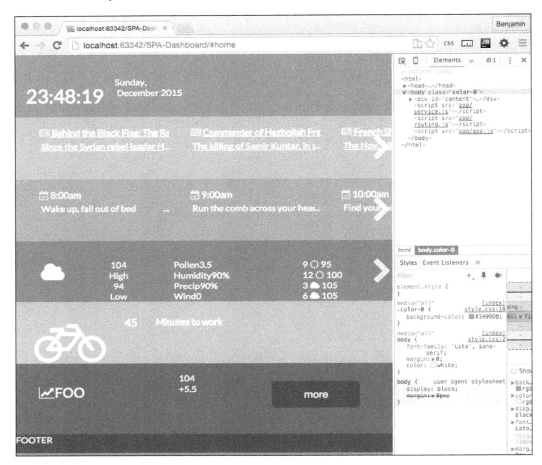

There is still some more coding you can do if you want to finish the page. The rest of the local JavaScript will look very much like news.js. I believe that you are now knowledgeable enough to figure it out, or you can download the rest of the project from GitHub and look.

I will, however, lead you in the right direction to find some more suitable APIs for your data.

For stocks, the most reliable API I found was from Yahoo; here is a sample URL path for returning information on four stocks: `http://query.yahooapis.com/ v1/public/yql?q=select%20*%20from%20yahoo.finance.quotes%20where%20 symbol%20in%20(%22YHOO%22%2C%22AAPL%22%2C%22GOOG%22%2C%22MSFT%22)%0A% 09%09&env=http%3A%2F%2Fdatatables.org%2Falltables.env&format=json`

For tasks, you can access Google Calendar as a JSON object, which will require some familiarity with their authentication model, or you could load it from a JSON file locally, like I have done in the sample project on GitHub.

Travel led me to some interesting places, no pun intended. My first instinct was to look at Google Maps, but the documentation implied that I need to show a map on the screen if I used their API, and then there is their authentication model again. The authentication is not extremely difficult, but it is out of the scope of this book. So I found instead a really cool API at Graphhopper. You need to register to get an API KEY, but it works pretty well, and you can request time to travel for different types of vehicles from two points, or multiple points.

Here is an example key. Try it out!

`https://graphhopper.com/api/1/route?point=49.93 2707,11.588051&point=50.3404,11.64705&vehicle=c ar&debug=true&key=1234567890qwerty&type=json&ca lc_points=false&instructions=false`

Weather was a little more complicated. To get all the information on the screen, I needed to go through three different API services and mix the data. I used Open Weather Map, and two different Wunderground APIs.

Here are the examples I used:

```
http://api.openweathermap.org/data/2.5/weather?q=Houston,tx&APPI
D=1234567890qwerty
http://api.wunderground.com/api/1234567890qwerty
/conditions/q/TX/Houston.json
http://api.wunderground.com/api/1234567890qwerty
/forecast/q/TX/Houston.json
```

Here is a screenshot of what your Single Page Application will look like with all of the pages loading live data from the various APIs.

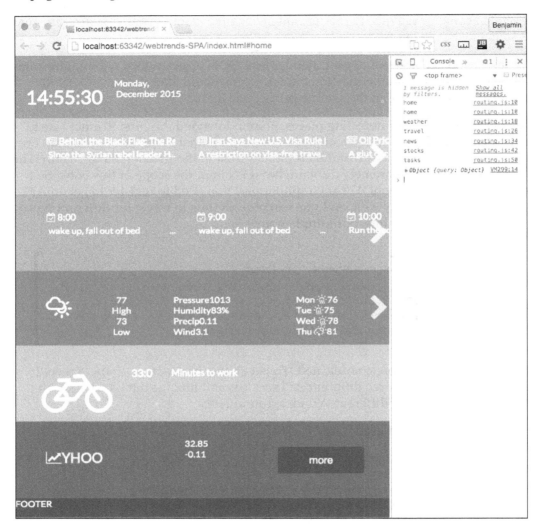

You are on your own from here, and I wish you good luck experimenting with APIs. This chapter has been tremendously fun for me to write, and I hope you have enjoyed it. There are many more cool things you can do with Single Page Applications and the asynchronous web. So live long and prosper!

Summary

Thanks for building this with me. I know it's no small task to build a Single Page Application framework with just vanilla JavaScript. The SPA framework works well with a routing table and utility-loading functions. You can carry this forward and create any sort of application with it. I'll even prove this claim in the last chapter.

5
The Death Star Chapter

Hi, and welcome back. This is the final chapter. This chapter is a special challenge as I was asked to create a project that integrated all of the previous chapters into one final exciting project. I've come up with a project that is a framework for creating a scrolling game with multiple levels that builds on previous code projects from this book. The editorial team liked the concept enough to call this chapter "The Death Star Chapter."

So with that, let's move forward with creating our Death Star Chapter. This chapter will pick up what we built with the Single Page Application and then shove our parallax scroller into it, and make it a responsive, flat UI, multi-level, single page, parallax scrolling game. We are going to modify the structure and add some new stuff to our stack.

Where to begin?

There are so many things to do that you may ask where to even begin. And how can we possibly do it in one chapter? The way to begin a journey is with the first step, so let's get started. The first thing to do will be to get the SPA code open in your IDE. If you don't have it available, and skipped to the last chapter of the book because you just want to do the exciting things, then you could get the code from Packt Publishing, or the GitHib page, `https://github.com/benlagrone`. I'll begin here with checking out my project, webtrends-SPA, and using that as a beginning framework for the chapter. Once you have that project open, you can begin re-crafting it into its new state. The news directory has some repurposable code we will use as a starting point for the application.

Deleting unnecessary features

The first task will be to remove the features from the SPA and leave the framework itself. So first, with the exception of the news directory, delete the `stocks`, `tasks`, `travel`, and `weather` directories. We are left with just this news directory and of course the `home` directory. We will do something with this soon, so leave this aside and open your `routing.js` file in the `app/` directory. Remove all the entries for the directories we removed. You should leave the `home` and `news` registry entries. A registry entry will look like this following code sample:

```
services.routing.register( 'weather', function(){
    pageRoute = {
        page: "./app/weather/weather.html",
        partial: "./app/weather/home-weather.html",
        script: "./app/weather/weather.js"
    };
console.log('weather')
});
```

Your routing table should now only have two entries. Start by renaming the news entry to credits, and refactor it to replace every instance of the text news with `credits`. Including the unchanged home registry; it should look like the following sample:

```
services.routing.register( 'home', function(){
    pageRoute = {
        page: "./app/home/home.html",
        partial: "./app/home/home-home.html",
        script: "./app/home/home.js"
        };
console.log('home')
    });
services.routing.register( 'credits', function(){
    pageRoute = {
        page: "./app/credits/credits.html",
        partial: "./app/credits/home-credits.html",
        script: "./app/credits/credits.js",
        data: "./app/credits/credits.json"
        };
console.log('credits')
    });
```

Adding new routes

Next, add a new registry entry called `leaderboard`. You can copy the credits registry and paste it below. Then, just replace the text `credits` with `leaderboard`. This is fairly simple with the SPA framework we created in the SPA chapter. See the following sample code:

```
services.routing.register( 'leaderboard', function(){
    pageRoute = {
        page: "./app/leaderboard/leaderboard.html",
        partial: "./app/leaderboard/home-leaderboard.html",
        script: "./app/leaderboard/leaderboard.js",
        data: "./app/leaderboard/leaderboard.json"
        };
console.log('leaderboard')
});
```

Adding the directories

As you may recall, to make these work, we need to have the directories and content described inside them. As you recall, we left the `news` directory in place. So, first rename the directory from `news` to `credits`. And then edit the filenames from `news` to `credits`. You should have in the `credits` directory: `credits.html`, `credits.js`, and `home-credits.html`.

We want to be able to use a source of data to retrieve leaderboard and credit information. We won't be adding any new data to our storage, as we are creating a client-side only application, so POSTING and PUTTING are currently outside of our scope. You could instead experiment on your own with putting things in your browser's local storage. That's up to you as it's outside the scope of this book. You will see that we added a new path to the registry, so make sure to add the files `leaderboard.json` and `credits.json`.

My app directory will look like the following image:

Adding levels to JavaScript

I want to continue with our principle of keeping things in JavaScript separate. So, let's create yet another JavaScript file in the `app` directory. Name it `levels.js`. It will be for handling the shared JavaScript specific to the game interaction. We will be creating new code and moving code into this new file. Add a link to the `levels.js` file in your `index.html` at the end of the file.

```
<script src = "app/levels.js"></script>
```

Inside your `levels.js` file, start by defining the `levels` object. We have done this pattern before in the SPA framework, so this should not be a foreign concept. This will use the namespacing conventions to prevent code collisions.

```
Levels = {};
```

Most of the code to be moved will come from the parallax game JavaScript we created in that chapter. But before we move on, let's modify what we have some more. Go to your `home.html` file and open it for editing.

Editing home.html

The `home.html` file is nearly what we want, so this will be easy, but will break some of our CSS.

1. Inside the top section, change the ID and the class of the news DIV element to `level1`.

2. Next, remove the `weather` DIV element, and remove the DIV element that wrapped the `travel` and `stocks` DIV elements.

3. Next, rename the travel DIV element's ID and class from `travel` to `leaderboard`, and do the same for credits.

4. Finally, add the `scroll` class to these. You can take a look at the empty application now.

It should look familiar, as we've seen it in this state before.

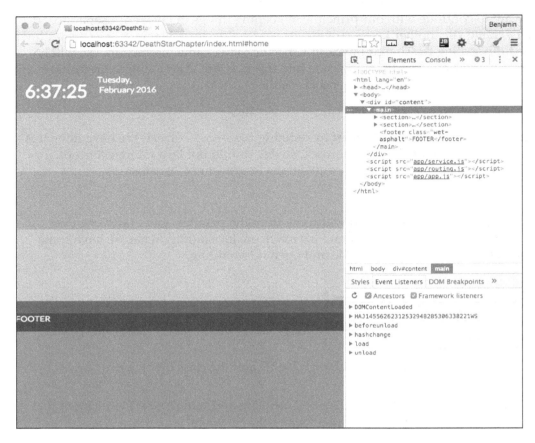

Dropping in the parallax game

Our next step is to jump right into the action and dump your parallax game file into the SPA framework. Since we have a pretty good systematic way to load scripts into the DOM, it should be pretty easy to shim it in and make it work.

We will further be moving the functions around to make them reusable patterns.

1. Create a new directory in your project named `level1`. This is where we will place the work from the parallax project.

2. Copy the `index.html` file into the `level1` directory and then rename it to match the style of the routing registry, `level.html`.

3. Then, create the additional new files `level1.js`, `home-level1.html`, and `level1.json`.

Let's add some CSS files to the directory so we can break it into small pieces. It's not required, but it may help keep things tidy. We will be adding CSS for each partial template. In the `css/` directory, add the CSS files `levels.css` and `level-1.css`.

Since we were last in the `css/` directory, let's work on that. Cut the CSS out of the style tag in your `level1.html` file and paste it into the `level-1.css` file. This will only be used when the `level1.html` file is in the view of the SPA framework. For now, all the CSS goes there. In future, we will find some CSS that needs to be shared with other levels. Then, we can move that code into the shared `levels.css` file.

Next, remove the JavaScript from the `level1.html` file and put it inside the `level-1.js` file. We will do the same later: modify and move functions into a shared state in the `levels.js` file.

We also need to get rid of all the META and BODY tags in the `level1.html` file now that it is shimmed into the framework. So, remove everything that is parent to the MAIN element. Be sure to remove the trailing tags as well. We moved the CSS into a separate directory, and added a new CSS, so let's add links to these so they appear in the HTML of the template partial. Add the link to both new CSS files in the top of the HTML partial template. The links should look like the following sample code:

```
<link type = "text/css" rel = "stylesheet" href = "css/level-
1.css" media = "all">
<link type = "text/css" rel = "stylesheet" href = "css/levels.css"
media = "all">
```

To link this up into our framework, we need to add a routing registration to the routing table. To make it simple, copy the leaderboard registry and replace the leaderboard text with the text `level1`. That's a lot already; we have used our framework to add the first level to our game. It's loading like it should. Let's load it and see what breaks.

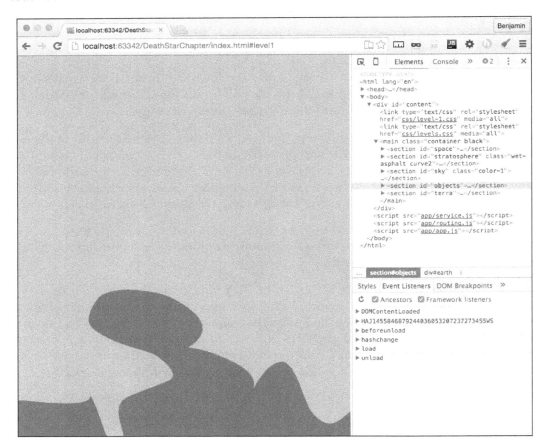

Fixing the broken level

It's a good thing software development is largely based on problem solving, because we have some problems to solve to make this work. You will notice when you load the `level1` partial, the JavaScript for the parallax game is not loading. If you inspect the SPA code in your browser, you will see the JavaScript is loaded into the head, but not firing.

So, let's take a look inside and see what's happening. Most of the JavaScript comprises functions, and we know these won't execute if not called, so we can eliminate them as the original failure point. There is a unique function call at the beginning of our JavaScript, a function that fires when the body loads, which in our previous version fired without a problem. This is your first line of code, and the first executable function, and it's not firing as expected. See the following culprit:

```
document.getElementById("body").onload = function(){...
```

Let's examine the order at which the SPA framework loads this page. First, Index. html loads the HTML BODY into the DOM, Then, the JavaScript fires and then at the end of the chain of functions this loads, so in our normal operations of loading template partials into a view, this would not be expected to work. This is because the body has already loaded at this time, so the JavaScript event listener missed the boat on the body loading.

So, we know this is broken, but don't just go willy-nilly and delete the whole function. It has useful code that you do not want to rewrite later on. For now, just comment out the block of code and save it for later. We will eventually pick this function clean and repurpose its code in other functions.

This is easy to fix. We need something to initialize the first function. Instead of the function executing the loading of the body, let's take a look at the parts involved and see what would be useful to the other levels. We want certain things to happen on each level when it loads. We want to put these things into a function that will call when the template partial loads. So, create a new function, following our SPA framework's namespace method, named level1.load. It should look like the following sample function:

```
level1.load = function(){
//DO SOMETHING
};
```

The first part of the body load, the for loop, gets the row DIV elements and sets each one's height to equal the inner height of the window. This function could reasonably be used to load every game level pages. Move this into the level1.load function.

```
level1.load = function(){
for (i = 0; i < document.getElementsByClassName("row").length;
i++)
{
document.getElementsByClassName("row")[i].style.height =
window.innerHeight + "px";
}
};
```

The next few lines of code send certain objects to the spreadObjects() function, so because these are objects specific to that level, it is not a reusable general function. Therefore, do not move these into the level1.load() function.

After the spreadObject() function calls, the next line of code, calling smoothScrollTo(), scrolls the screen to the bottom. That should be moved into a general pattern since we will want all of the levels to scroll from the bottom to the top this way. The next line of code in the body load function adds an attribute to the BODY element. It adds a function call to the onscroll event to an existing function called updateElement(). And, because it is a reusable pattern, we need to change it so it does not always call the same function, updateElement(), we need this to execute the function we send to it. So, change the value to levelCallBack, because it will function as if we have sent it a proper callBack. This is also a general pattern we will want on every level of the game. Add these lines of code next, and your level1.load function is complete. See the following:

```
level1.load = function(){
for (i = 0; i<document.getElementsByClassName("row").length; i++)
{
document.getElementsByClassName("row")[i].style.height =
window.innerHeight + "px";
}
smoothScrollTo(document.body.scrollHeight);
document.getElementsByTagName("body")[0].setAttribute("onscroll",
levelCallBack)
};
```

We still have not made the change to load the function, as it is only refactored. At the end of level1.js, let's add some code to execute the level1.load function. Let's start it with a conditional statement to check that we are not at the home page. If it's at the home page, we do not want to run this script; if it's not there, then execute the level1.load function. The code should look like this next sample:

```
if(window.location.hash.split('#')[1] === 'home'){
}else{
level1.load('updateElement()');
}
```

Moving the load functions to levels.js

Now, since `level1.load` is a reusable pattern, it has no place in `level1.js`, as that is only loaded on the `#level1` hash. Cut it out of `level.js` and put it into the `app/levels.js` file. Then, rename it `levels.load`.

```
levels.load = function(){
for (i = 0; i<document.getElementsByClassName("row").length; i++)
{
document.getElementsByClassName("row")[i].style.height =
window.innerHeight + "px";
}
smoothScrollTo(document.body.scrollHeight);
document.getElementsByTagName("body")[0].setAttribute("onscroll",
levelCallBack);
};
```

Now, you can launch the URL to the hash `#level1` and see the `level1` parallax scrolling is starting to come back together. There are some things to fix as far as how the objects are rendered, and we will fix that soon. But nevertheless, you can see it's a work in progress in the next screenshot:

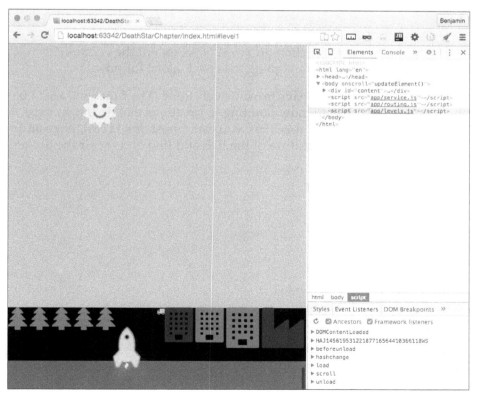

Fixing the namespacing in Level1.js

Before we move further, let's get some maintenance work done. First, in `level.js`, define `level1` as an object. This should be a familiar job as we have done this throughout the SPA framework. Hopefully, I'm not surprising you with this.

```
level1 = {};
```

Most of our functions that we brought over from the parallax site have no object namespacing. They are simply function calls. We want to rewrite them to have the `level1` namespace preceding them. In order to do so, you will need to replace every function call with a namedspace call. See the next example for a proper instruction:

Find this function:

```
function spreadObjects(x, vm, hm, va, ha, p, e){
...
}
```

Change it to this:

```
level1.spreadObjects = function(x, vm, hm, va, ha, p, e){
...
}
```

You should do this to every function on `level1.js`, except the `window.smoothScrollTo` function. We are going to leave it alone for now.

Now, as you would expect, we have broken everything. The functions are to be called by function calls that are now pointing to functions that no longer exist. There are two ways to go about this: first, you can refresh the HTML page and see what breaks, or use the search feature of the IDE and find and repair the broken references in the HTML.

See the following picture with your first error:

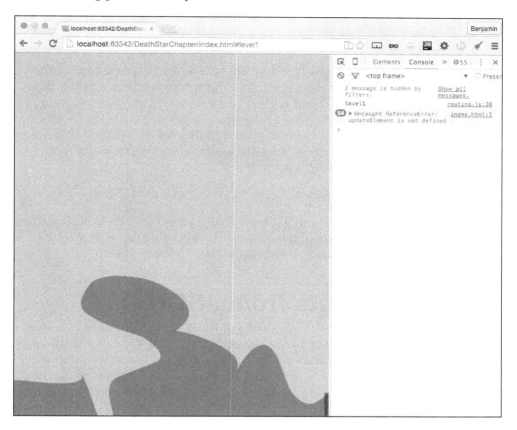

You will see the first error is `updateElement`, which is not defined. We recently broke this, remember? You can fix this at the bottom of the `level1.js` file by prepending the function callback with the text `level1`. See the next example:

```
if(window.location.hash.split('#')[1] === 'home'){
} else {
levels.load('level1.updateElement()');
}
```

This gets us to the next error, `getMovingElements`, which is not defined. You already know what to do. I won't waste your time going through every function. I think you can discover and repair them yourself. But here's a hint: you need to prepend the name with the text `level1`.

This creates another issue to fix early before we see the error; we add an attribute to the body to fire this function on every scroll. But when we are at another page, or level, we don't need this. In fact, it will cause some potential problems later. Let's clean it up by adding a new line of code to `home.js` that will remove the scroll listener from the body. At the end of the JavaScript file, get the element by tag name body, and remove the scroll attribute from it. See the following example for our preemptive strike at fixing broken code:

```
document.getElementsByTagName("body")[0].removeAttribute('onscroll');
```

Take a break, make some coffee, and get busy fixing these function calls. It should only take a few minutes to crush all the little errors and prepend them with the proper namespacing. Once done, you are ready to go to the next step.

Loading elements from JSON

The next big change is to improve the loading of the objects. The old way to load them is to have the HTML already in the template. We want to do it in this improved way that treats the objects like data and loads them as such. We will be removing all the stars, clouds, the rocket, and other objects. These objects will now be stored in the `level1.json` file we created earlier. Let's break the HTML so we have something to fix again. As you can probably tell, I like to break things and then fix them, but I'm not sure which I like more.

In your `level1.html` partial template, start by removing the i element for the moon inside the DIV element with the ID p0.

```
<i class = "fa fa-moon-o fa-5x yellow"></i>
```

In the next DIV element, with the ID p1, remove its child DIV element with the ID stars, and all of the children i elements. Next, there is the `clouds` in the p9, p10, p11, and p12 elements. In addition, remove the plane and Twitter elements. Keep going to remove from inside the objects section the `sun` elements and the `rocket` elements. Finally, do the same for the elements inside the `terra` SECTION. Now the HTML should look pretty sparse in comparison.

See the following example:

```
<section id = "space">
<div id = "p0" class = "row"></div>
<div id = "p1" class = "row"></div>
</section>
<section id = "stratosphere" class = "wet-asphalt curve2">
<div id = "p2" class = "row wet-asphalt curve"></div>
<div id = "p3" class = "row color-4 curve"></div>
<div id = "p4" class = "row color-3"></div>
<div id = "p5" class = "row color-2"></div>
<div id = "p6" class = "row color-1"></div>
</section>
<section id = "sky" class = "color-1">
<div id = "p7" class = "row color-0 curve2"></div>
<div id = "p8" class = "row color-0"></div>
<div id = "p9" class = "row color-0"></div>
<div id = "p10" class = "row color-0"></div>
<div id = "p11" class = "row color-0"></div>
<div id = "p12" class = "row color-0"></div>
<div id = "p13" class = "row color-0"></div>
</section>
<section id = "objects"></section>
<section id = "terra"></section>
```

That felt pretty good, didn't it? I really enjoy deleting code.

Now, we have a blank `level.json` file to fill up with our objects. This file will need to follow the JSON data format. So be careful, it will bomb the JSON parser with will use to insert these objects. First, create an object in the `level1.json` file called `objectgroups`. It will look like this next sample:

```
{
    "objectgroups": {

        }
    }
```

Then, insert the first object, the `stars` object, whose value is an object containing an array.

```
{
    "objectgroups": {
        "stars": {
            "objects": [ ]
            }
        }
}
```

Inside the array, each star must be a separate object, containing all the details the function will need to load it into the DOM. Let's give it a type, an `idclass`, a `sizeclass`, and a `colorclass`. These will be used to build the HTML to call the CSS to place the star in the page. See the following example to fill out the values:

```
{"type": "star", "idclass": "fa fa-star", "sizeclass": "fa-1x",
"colorclass": "yellow"},
{"type": "star", "idclass": "fa fa-star", "sizeclass": "fa-1x",
"colorclass": "yellow"},
```

You can copy and paste the first line into a few hundred lines of `star` objects.

Next, let's add our `moon` object. Even though there's only one `moon` on this level, we will use the same format for the JSON. Follow the stars `objectgroup` with a comma, and then add the `moon` object group.

```
"moon": {
    "objects": [
        {"type": "moon", "idclass":
        "fa fa-moon-o", "sizeclass": "fa-5x",
        "colorclass": "yellow"}
        ]
    },
```

Next, we will add the objects that go into the objects section. Here, we deviate a little by creating a child to the object. There is more depth as we are grouping more different objects together. This `objectgroup` is called `objects`. Its children are the `sun`, the `earth`, and the `rocket`. As you recall, these objects were more complex than the rest as they had richer layers rendered. Each of the child objects has the child objects paired to an array for the value.

The objects in each array follow the same pattern of matching the classes to the `title` as the preceding array objects. See the following sample code for the detail:

```
"objects": {
    "sun": {
        "objects": [
        {"type": "sun", "idclass": "fa fa-smile-o",
        "sizeclass": "fa-1x",
        "colorclass": "green"},
        {"type": "sun", "idclass": "fa fa-circle",
        "sizeclass": "fa-1x",
        "colorclass": "yellow"},
        {"type": "sun", "idclass": "fa fa-sun-o",
        "sizeclass": "fa-1x",
        "colorclass": "yellow"}
        ]
    },
    "earth": {
        "objects": [
        {"type": "earth", "idclass": "fa fa-globe",
        "sizeclass": "", "colorclass": "blue land air"}
        ]
    },
    "rocket": {
        "objects": [
        {"type": "rocket", "idclass": "fa fa-rocket",
        "sizeclass": "fa-5x", "colorclass": "grey-2"},
        {"type": "rocket", "idclass": "fa fa-rocket",
        "sizeclass": "fa-
        5x", "colorclass": "silver"},
        {"type": "rocket", "idclass":
        "fa fa-fire", "sizeclass": "", "colorclass":
        "yellow"},
        {"type": "rocket", "idclass": "fa fa-comment",
        "sizeclass": "fa-5x", "colorclass": "white"}
        ]
    }
},
```

That's it for the objects. Next, it is the objects in the `terra` SECTION. As you recall, the `terra` objects were split to the right and left. The trees were on the left, and the buildings on the right. This follows the same pattern of descendants as the preceding. The objects array are the trees for the left group, and the truck and various buildings on the right.

```
"terra": {
    "left": {
        "objects": [
        {"type": "tree", "idclass": "fa fa-tree", "sizeclass":
        "", "colorclass": "green"},
        {"type": "tree", "idclass": "fa fa-tree", "sizeclass":
        "", "colorclass": "green"},
        {"type": "tree", "idclass": "fa fa-tree", "sizeclass":
        "", "colorclass": "green"},
        {"type": "tree", "idclass": "fa fa-tree", "sizeclass":
        "", "colorclass": "green"},
        {"type": "tree", "idclass": "fa fa-tree", "sizeclass":
        "","colorclass": "green"}
        ]
    },
    "right": {
        "objects": [
        {"type": "tree", "idclass": "fa fa-truck",
        "sizeclass":"", "colorclass": "silver"},
        {"type": "tree", "idclass": "fa fa-building",
        "sizeclass": "small", "colorclass": "grey-1"},
        {"type": "tree", "idclass": "fa fa-building",
        "sizeclass": "small", "colorclass": "grey-2"},
        {"type": "tree", "idclass":
        "fa fa-building", "sizeclass":
        "large", "colorclass": "grey-2"},
        {"type": "tree", "idclass": "fa fa-building",
        "sizeclass":
        "large", "colorclass": "grey-1"},
        {"type": "tree", "idclass":
        "fa fa-industry", "sizeclass":
        "large", "colorclass": "grey-1"}
        ]
    }
},
```

Finally, the `clouds`; this was saved for last, as it's the same object type, split into different groups. Each `cloud` group fits into a different DIV element, therefore the parent grouping is `clouds`, and the child groups, like the left and right `terra` objects, are labeled by the DIV element ID they will be inserted into. The DIV elements we want them to go into are `p9` through `p13`. Then, inside each is the array of the cloud objects to be inserted into the DIV element. See the next example. In the example, there is only one or two `cloud` Objects in each array; you will want about ten in each.

```
"clouds": {
    "p9": {
        "objects": [
        {"type": "cloud", "idclass": "fa fa-cloud",
        "sizeclass":" fa-3x", "colorclass": "white"},
        {"type": "cloud", "idclass": "fa fa-cloud",
        "sizeclass": "fa-5x", "colorclass": "white"}
        ]
    },
    "p10": {
        "objects": [
        {"type": "cloud", "idclass": "fa fa-cloud",
        "sizeclass": "fa-3x", "colorclass": "white"},
        {"type":"cloud", "idclass":"fa fa-cloud", "sizeclass":
        "fa-5x", "colorclass": "white"}
        ]
    },
    "p11": {
        "objects": [
        {"type": "cloud", "idclass": "fa fa-cloud",
        "sizeclass": "fa-3x", "colorclass": "white"},
        {"type": "cloud", "idclass": "fa fa-cloud",
        "sizeclass": "fa-5x", "colorclass": "white"},
        ]
    },
    "p12": {
        "objects": [
        {"type": "cloud", "idclass": "fa fa-cloud",
        "sizeclass": "fa-3x", "colorclass": "white"},
        {"type": "cloud", "idclass": "fa fa-cloud",
        "sizeclass": "fa-5x", "colorclass": "white"},
        ]
    },
    "p13": {
```

```
        "objects": [
            {"type": "cloud", "idclass": "fa fa-cloud",
            "sizeclass": "fa-3x", "colorclass": "white"},
            {"type": "cloud", "idclass": "fa fa-cloud",
            "sizeclass": "fa-5x", "colorclass": "white"}
            {"type": "cloud", "idclass": "fa fa-twitter",
            "sizeclass": "fa-1x", "colorclass": "silver"},
            {"type": "cloud", "idclass": "fa fa-twitter",
            "sizeclass": "fa-1x", "colorclass": "yellow"},
            {"type": "cloud", "idclass": "fa fa-twitter",
            "sizeclass": "fa-1x", "colorclass": "green"},
            {"type": "cloud", "idclass": "fa fa-twitter",
            "sizeclass": "fa-1x", "colorclass": "red"},
            {"type": "cloud", "idclass": "fa fa-plane",
            "sizeclass": "fa-3x", "colorclass": "silver"}
            ]
        }
    } //Remember the closing bracket.
```

You may notice how I slipped in some non-cloud items at the end. These are the plane and birds that flew across the screen. You can place those into any one of the cloud groups.

Using the data requests

We have created the `data` object. Next, we need to load it into the DOM. This will use the `request` function we have already created. The `getPage` function we created previously is well suited for this. We want these objects to be called right after the `levels.load` function. So, add a new line right after `levels.load` calling `services.getPage`. Send it the variables `pageRoute.data`, the path defined in the registry for the JSON, the string `level1`, for the `id`, `level1.parseAjax`, for the callback function (which does not exist yet), and the `id` variable. Now, the end of `level1.js` should look like this next sample code:

```
If (window.location.hash.split('#')[1] === 'home') {

}
else
{
levels.load('level1.updateElement()');
services.getPage(pageRoute.data, 'level1', level1.parseAjax,id);
};
```

As I mentioned before, the `level1.parseAjax` callback does not yet exist, and we have created a new breaking error in our application. You can refresh your browser to see what it's complaining about. It says `callBack is not a function` on `services.js` line 9. See my example picture next:

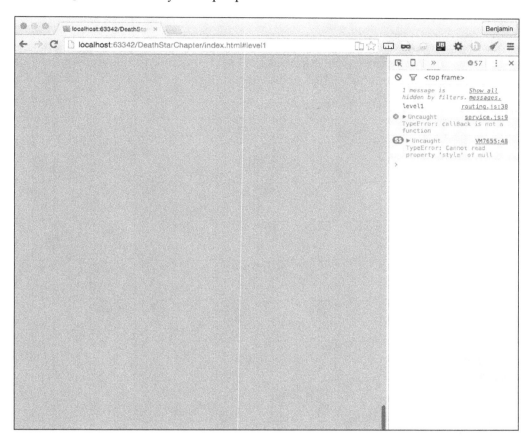

Parsing the AJAX

The `callBack` variable causing the error is referencing the `level1.parseAjax` function we have not yet created. This is easy to fix by creating the function. In your `level1.js` file, create the function `level1.parseAjax` and inside it create a new object, `level1.data`, to hold the response from parsing the AJAX from the `getPage` function. The detail of this were covered in the SPA framework chapter, so I will not go into detail here.

Add a line to `console.log` the response. You can see the following example:

```
level1.parseAjax = function (xhr, id){
    level1.data = JSON.parse(xhr.responseText);
    console.log(level1.data);
};
```

In your browser console, now you will see the data loaded into the DOM as an object. These are ready for you to add to the HTML. This will follow the same pattern as the SPA framework AJAX calls, so again, let's go through it quickly, as there's much more to do.

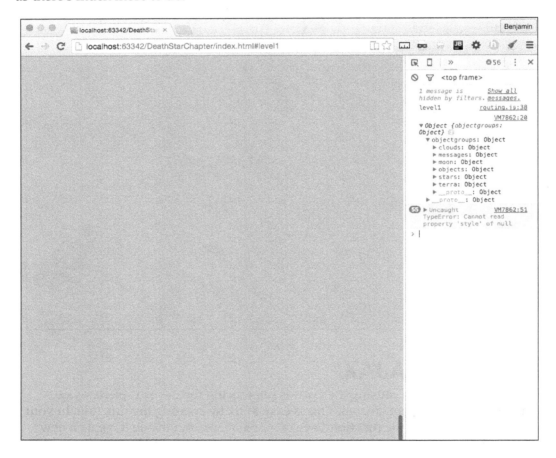

First, let's put the moon and the stars in the sky. The moon object is simple: let's create a new variable, `level1MoonHTML`, equal to a string of the opening `i` element tag and class selector plus the first array item of the `moon` object's `idclass` value plus another string `' '` plus the array item's `sizeclass` plus another string `' '` plus the array item's `color` class, plus the end `>`, and then the closing of the i tag. See the variable next in the example for illustration:

```
var level1MoonHTML = '<i class="' +
level1.data.objectgroups.moon.objects[0].idclass + ' ' +
level1.data.objectgroups.moon.objects[0].sizeclass + ' ' +
level1.data.objectgroups.moon.objects[0].colorclass + '"></i>';
```

Next, get the element selected by the ID `p0` and set its inner HTML to equal `level1MoonHTML`.

```
document.getElementById('p0').innerHTML = level1MoonHTML;
```

You can combine these two lines of code by replacing the variable declaration with the second line of code to have more efficient code. See the following:

```
document.getElementById('p0').innerHTML = '<i class="' +
level1.data.objectgroups.moon.objects[0].idclass + ' ' +
level1.data.objectgroups.moon.objects[0].sizeclass + ' ' +
level1.data.objectgroups.moon.objects[0].colorclass + '"></i>';
```

Adding the stars follows a similar pattern, only a little more complex. Create a new variable, `level1StarsHTML`, equal to a string of an open DIV element with the ID stars. As there are many of the stars in the array, let's create a `for` loop to iterate through the stars array and insert the values into this variable. Inside the loop, add to `level1StarsHTML` the i element created in the same pattern as the moon. Close the loop and follow it by adding to the `level1StarsHTML` variable the closing DIV tag in a string. Finally, insert the `level1StarsHTML` variable into the HTML by getting the p1 element. See the following example for the details:

```
var level1StarsHTML = '<div id="stars">';
for (i = 0; i < level1.data.objectgroups.stars.objects.length;
i++)
{
level1StarsHTML += '<i class="' + level1.data.objectgroups.stars.
objects[i].idclass + ' ' +
level1.data.objectgroups.stars.objects[i].colorclass + '"> </i>';
}
level1StarsHTML += '</div>';
document.getElementById('p1').innerHTML = level1StarsHTML;
```

Refresh your browser again and you will see that the moon and the stars are now in the viewport. See my next screenshot:

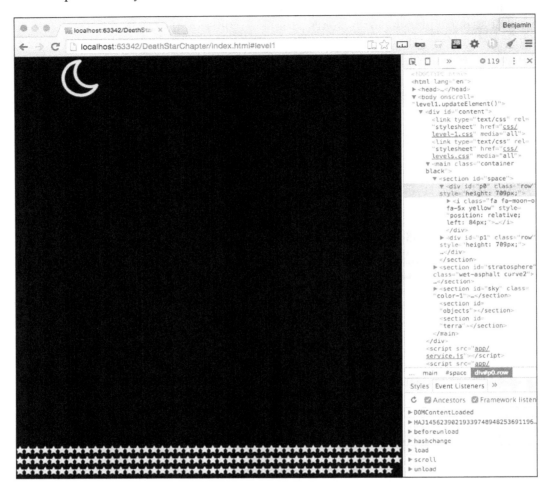

Next, let's go to the next set of objects, the clouds. As this has child objects, we will start with a for in loop going through the clouds object. First, inside the loop, create a new variable for the HTML called cloudHTMLStart equal to an opening DIV element with the class clouds. Next, create a new for in loop with a unique key and iterate through each of the cloud's group children determined by the key of the first loop. Inside the for loop within a loop, add to cloudHTMLStart the i element, much like the moon and stars, only using each of the for in loop keys as an array selector. Outside of the inner loop, add to cloudHTMLStart a string containing the closing DIV element.

Then, get the element selected by the first for loop's key, and set its `innerHTML` to equal `cloudHTMLStart`. These instructions may be difficult to translate into code, so take a look at the following sample code to see how it works exactly:

```
for (var key in level1.data.objectgroups.clouds) {
var cloudHTMLStart = '<div class = "clouds">';
for (var key0 in level1.data.objectgroups.clouds[key].objects) {
cloudHTMLStart += '<i class = "' + level1.data.objectgroups.
clouds[key].objects[key0].idclass + ' ' +
level1.data.objectgroups.clouds[key].objects[key0].sizeclass + ' '
+ level1.data.objectgroups.clouds[key].objects[key0].colorclass +
'"></i>';
}
cloudHTMLStart += '</div>';
document.getElementById(key).innerHTML = cloudHTMLStart;
};
```

The next group of objects, the objects' `objectgroup`, contains the `rocket`, therefore its method of looping will vary further. First, create the variable `objectsHTMLStart` equal to a blank string. Then, initiate the `for in` loop over the objects in `objectgroups`. The next step is to add the opening DIV element as a string to `objectsHTMLStart`, giving it the variable `key` as its ID attribute. Next, add a conditional, `if` the `key` is equal to `rocket`, and add a SPAN element before continuing. We need to iterate through the child objects now, so create another `for in` loop over the objects that are children to the objects and give it a unique `key` variable. Next, add to `objectsHTMLStart` the i element as a string with its attributes supplied by `idclass`, `sizeclass`, and `colorclass`, and close the element. This ends the inner loop. Then, add another conditional `if key` equals `rocket` followed by the closing SPAN tag if `truthy`. Follow this with a closing of the DIV element, and then the closing bracket of the parent for loop. Finally, get the element by the ID attribute objects and set its `innerHTML` to equal `objectsHTMLStart`. See the following sample code:

```
var objectsHTMLStart = '';
for (var key in level1.data.objectgroups.objects) {
objectsHTMLStart += '<div id = "' + key + '">';
if (key === 'rocket')
objectsHTMLStart += '<span>';
for (var key0 in level1.data.objectgroups.objects[key].objects) {
objectsHTMLStart += '<i class="' + level1.data.objectgroups.
objects[key].objects[key0].idclass + ' '
+ level1.data.objectgroups.objects[key].objects[key0].sizeclass +
' ' +
level1.data.objectgroups.objects[key].objects[key0].colorclass +
'"></i>';
```

```
    }
    if (key === 'rocket')
    objectsHTMLStart += '</span>';
    objectsHTMLStart += '</div>';
    }
    document.getElementById('objects').innerHTML = objectsHTMLStart;
```

Only one more layer of objects to load. I'm glad to be nearly done with them. This is the objects in the `terra` SECTION. It is another objects group with children. Start with the new variable `terraHTMLStart` equal to a new DIV element with the ID `ground` as a string. Let's do another `for in` loop for the `terra` objects in the `object` group. The first thing to do in the loop is add a new child DIV element whose class is the `key` variable. Next, add another `for in` loop for the objects in the `terra` arrays. Add to `terraHTMLStart` the i element with the objects `idclass`, `sizeclass`, and `colorclass`, just like the previous examples, and then close the i element. Close the loop. Then close the child DIV element. Then close the outer loop. Close the parent DIV element. Finally, get the element by ID `terra` and set its `innerHTML` to equal `terraHTMLStart`.

Whew! We are done loading objects. I'm glad you stuck with me the whole time. Now, refresh your browser and take a look at the objects loaded into the view. Now it's getting exciting again. By the way, I changed the size of my viewport after I loaded so I could show more objects. Yours may look different.

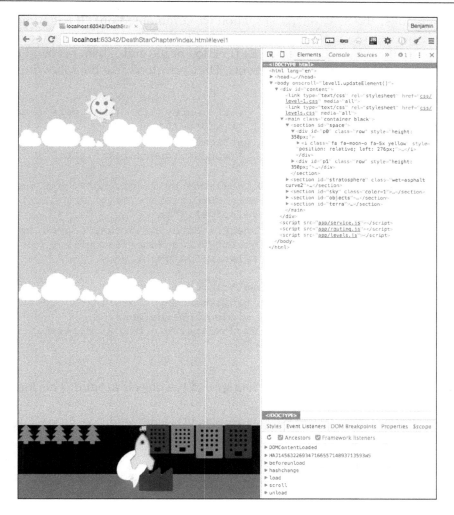

Moving the spreadObjects function to a general pattern

That's awesome so far, but the objects are just lined up, and we want to spread them around the page. So, let's take care of that `spreadObjects` function we already have by moving it into a general pattern. You will want to use this function on every level. Its insides are great as they are, so just cut it out of `level1.js` and put it inside the `levels.js` file. After you move it, you need to rename it from `level1.spreadObjects` to `levels.spreadObjects`.

Do you remember the `body onload` function we commented out? It has some useful code we want to use. I want you to cut out all of the `spreadObjects` function calls and paste them into the `parseAjax` function at the end. Then, prepend the `spreadObjects` function name with levels. They now look like the following sample code:

```
levels.spreadObjects(document.getElementById("stars").getElementsB
yTagName("i"), 150, 100, 1, 1, "fixed", "%");
levels.spreadObjects(document.getElementById("ground").getElements
ByClassName("fa-tree"), 0, 14, -(window.innerHeight / 28), 1,
"relative", "px");
levels.spreadObjects(document.getElementById("ground").getElements
ByClassName("right")[0].getElementsByClassName("small"), 0, 14, -
(window.innerHeight/13), 1, "relative", "px");
levels.spreadObjects(document.getElementById("ground").getElements
ByClassName("right")[0].getElementsByClassName("large"), 0, 14, -
(window.innerHeight/15), 1, "relative", "px");
for (var i = 0; i <
document.getElementsByClassName("clouds").length; i++) {
levels.spreadObjects(document.getElementsByClassName("clouds")
[i].getElementsByTagName("i"),window.innerHeight*.75,
window.innerWidth*.75, 1, 1-(window.innerWidth / 2), "relative",
"px");
}
```

Now, refresh your browser and see it has spread the objects around. This looks much better.

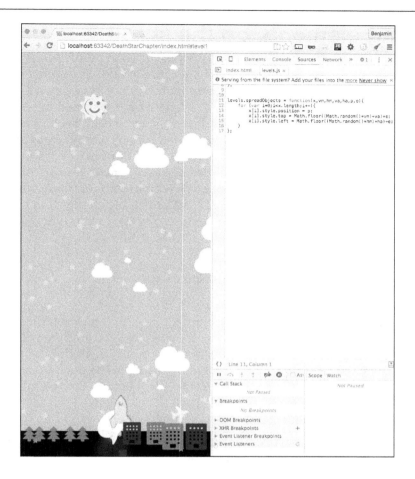

What can be done in the shared levels service

Next, I want to move some more functions from `level1.js` to the general pattern file `levels.js`. We will cut out the `moveRocket` and `moveEarth` functions and paste them into `levels.js`. And of course, rename them to `levels.moveRocket` and `levels.moveEarth`. And be sure to rename the function calls as well. Next, move the `setElementLeftPostion` function to `levels.js`. Rename it `levels.setElementLeftPosition` and the function calls also. This function is called a number of times, so you may want to use a find and replace pattern, or at least find to identify them all. Next, move the `window.smoothScrollTo` function into the `levels.js` file and leave it as is.

Updating elements on the scroll

Let's look at the updateElement function. Most of the code in this needs to stay here; however, I want to add some more functionality that would occur universally on the scroll. So, add a function call to a function that does not yet exist, which we will fix shortly, called levels.updateOnMove(). We will send it something in time, but it does not exist yet, so put a pin in that and we will come back to complete it later. We've created a call for a function that is not there, so we've broken our software and need to fix it. It's an easy fix by adding that function in our levels.js JavaScript file. Once you have added the function, from the level1.updateElement function cut out the function call for levels.moveRocket() with its variable, and paste it into your new function, levels.updateOnMove(). It's not a big change, but it's a change toward more efficient code. Your levels.updateOnMove function now looks like the following sample:

```
levels.updateOnMove = function(){
levels.moveRocket(document.getElementById("rocket"));
};
```

Next, let's get the window's scroll position number and set it into a variable called scrollPosition that we can reuse to activate some new features we will add to improve our gaming experience. Use this formula: round 100 multiplied by the result of the window's page Y offset divided by the difference of the document's scroll height and the document's documentElement's client height. See the following example for clarity:

```
var ScrollPosition = Math.round(100 * window.pageYOffset /
(document.body.scrollHeight-
document.documentElement.clientHeight));
```

I can use this to activate functions based on where the user is, for example the top or bottom. This can be useful if I want to automatically go back home when the user scrolls all the way to the top of the screen. Add a case and switch if the variable ScrollPosition equals 0; call a new function called levels.topOfScroll(), and then if it is 100, call another new function called levels.bottomOfScroll().

```
switch (ScrollPosition){
case 0:
levels.topOfScroll();
break;
case 100:
levels.bottomOfScroll();
break;
default:
}
```

Next, you will need to create these functions in the `levels.js` JavaScript file. They do not need anything just yet. Just make them to look like the following sample:

```
levels.topOfScroll = function(){
};

levels.bottomOfScroll = function(){
};
```

Next, copy these into your `level1.js` file, and replace the `levels` namespace with `level1`. See the following example:

```
level1.topOfScroll = function(){
};

level1.bottomOfScroll = function(){
};
```

Let's actually do something with our `levels.topOfScroll` function. As I mentioned earlier, we need something to happen when the player scrolls to the top of the screen. Let's send the player to the home page after a few seconds, which will give the game some time to execute something significant to show you it's finished. Inside the `levels.topOfScroll` function, add a JavaScript `setTimeout` for 3000 ms and in it set the window's location hash to `#home`, and on the next line `return`. This will send the player back to the home menu.

```
levels.topOfScroll = function(topCallBack){
setTimeout(function(){
window.location.hash = '#home';
return;
}, 3000);
};
```

Great work so far. Since we are in this function, I want to mention something about the app that annoys me. When we load the game, the rocket is at the top, and then scrolls down to the bottom while the player is watching this. It's like arriving at a play and watching them all run around out of costume while the set gets built, and nothing is hidden by a curtain. This is not a great game experience. I want to add a curtain to the transition between screens. This should be a simple class that we can add and take away from a DIV Eeement, which will have the ID `curtain`.

In your `levels.bottomOfScroll` function, add a line to get the DIV element with the `curtain` ID and assign the class name `fade` to it. See the following example:

```
levels.bottomOfScroll = function(bottomCallBack){
document.getElementById('curtain').className = 'fade';
};
```

You will also need to add the code to add the `fade` class to the end of the `home.js` file.

```
document.getElementById('curtain').className = 'fade';
```

You will also need to add this DIV element to `index.html`. Just insert it after the DIV with the ID attribute `content`. See the following example:

```
<body>
<div id = "content"></div>
<div id = "curtain"></div>
<script src = "app/service.js"></script>
<script src = "app/routing.js"></script>
<script src = "app/levels.js"></script>
</body>
```

Let's finish what we started with this transition effect. In the `services.js` JavaScript file, add a new function called `services.routing.transition`. Inside it, get the element by ID `curtain`, and set its class name to be a blank string. This will allow us to add the `curtain` that we will remove when the `fade` class is added. See the next example:

```
services.routing.transition = function(){
document.getElementById('curtain').className = '';
};
```

Modifying the CSS

Before we move on, let's finish this by adding the CSS to make the transition work. Add a selector for the curtain ID and the curtain ID with the fade class. See the following example:

```
#curtain{
}

#curtain.fade {
}
```

When the curtain does not have the `fade` class, it is active and should be blocking everything from view. Give it a fixed position, 0 px from the top and left, make it a dark color like `wet-asphalt`, 100% of the height and width of the viewport, full opacity, a `z-index` of `9999`, and a `0.2` second transition on the opacity. See the following example:

```
#curtain {
position: fixed;
left: 0;
top: 0;
background: #34495e;
width: 100%;
height: 100%;
opacity: 1;
z-index: 9999;
-webkit-transition: opacity 0.2s;
-moz-transition: opacity 0.2s;
transition: opacity 0.2s;
}
```

The `fade` version will change the opacity to 0, and the width to 0, the height to 1%, and the `z-index` to `-1`. See the following example:

```
#curtain.fade {
opacity :0;
width: 0%;
height: 1%;
z-index: -1;
}
```

Now, try it out in your browser and see the `curtain` hiding the transition between screens. It should obscure the loading and downscrolling. You could embellish this any way you want. There are many ways this can improve. You can add a before pseudo selector, and add the text loading as the content of it. Try something like this next example:

```
#curtain:before {
content: "loading...";
position: fixed;
padding: 40%;
top: 0;
left: 0;
font-size: 10vw;
background: #111;
width: 100%;
height: 100%;
}
```

Let's go with it. Before we close the CSS, let's delete all the CSS for these selectors: weather, tasks, news, and stocks. They are no longer used and should be removed.

Adding message objects

Now that we have cleaned up the CSS, let's get back to the scrolling action. I have to admit something I have been hiding from you. I snuck in something and have not mentioned it yet. When we made the JSON file, we added an additional object to the rocket. It was the fa-comment object. That was sneaky of me. Maybe you added it and saw it in your browser. If you thought it was an error and removed it, here's the code in question in this example so you can add it back:

```
"rocket": {
    "objects": [
        {"type": "rocket", "idclass": "fa fa-rocket",
        "sizeclass": "fa-5x", "colorclass": "grey-2"},
        {"type": "rocket", "idclass": "fa fa-rocket",
        "sizeclass": "fa-5x", "colorclass": "silver"},
        {"type": "rocket", "idclass": "fa fa-fire",
        "sizeclass": "", "colorclass": "yellow"},
        {"type": "rocket", "idclass": "fa fa-comment",
        "sizeclass": "fa-5x", "colorclass": "white"}
        ]

    }
```

What is it for? This is for adding messages into the screen in the comment bubble. These will be unique for each level and should be treated like data. You don't want to have to work in the JavaScript business logic to change a message. So, add a new object group to the level1.json objectgroups called messages. Inside its object array, add three objects with the values for text, position, and time. See the following for the details:

```
"messages": {
    "objects": [
        {"text": "3,2,1... SCROLL!", "position": 100,
        "time": 3000},
        {"text": "Keep Scrolling...", "position": 50, "time":
        3000},
        {"text": "finished!! Awesome!", "position": 5, "time":
        6000}
        ]
    },
```

That's awesome! Now they are added into the DOM automatically already. Let's do something with them. We want these to be loaded at certain points in the scrolling action. In the preceding sample code, these will be loaded at the bottom for three seconds, the middle for three seconds, and near the top for six seconds. But how, you ask? In your `level1.updateElement` function call to the `levels.updateOnMove` function, send another variable, the `level1.data.objectgroups.message` object. See the following example code for the new version of the function call:

```
levels.updateOnMove(level1.topOfScroll, level1.bottomOfScroll,
level1.data.objectgroups.messages);
```

Now, in your `levels.updateOnMove` function, add a third variable, `messagesObject`.

```
levels.updateOnMove =
function(topCallBack,bottomCallBack,messagesObject) {
...
```

At the end of this function, add a `for` loop that iterates over the messages in the array of the object. If the current message object's position value equals the `ScrollPosition` we defined earlier, then let's call a new function called `levels.showMessage` and send it the current message object. We will need to create that function next, but first, look at the next example to verify your code for the `for` loop:

```
for(i = 0; i < messagesObject.objects.length; i++) {
if (messagesObject.objects[i].position === ScrollPosition) {
levels.showMessage(messagesObject.objects[i])
}
}
```

K, did you get it? Let's move on to make this new function. Create the new function called `levels.showMessage`, and give it the variable name `messageObject`. We need to modify the comment bubble first. So, select the element by the ID `rocket`, and its first of the child elements by the class name `fa-comment` two times. First, set its style display attribute to `inline`, which implies that elsewhere it is hidden. Second, set its inner HTML to a SPAN containing the `messageObject` text value. See the next example:

```
document.getElementById('rocket').getElementsByClassName('fa-
comment')[0].style.display = "inline";
document.getElementById('rocket').getElementsByClassName('fa-
comment')[0].innerHTML = '<span>'+messageObject.text + '</span>';
```

Next, in this same function, use the JavaScript `setTimeout` to set the `fa-comment` element style's display attribute to none, and the time interval is the `messageObjects time` value. See this in the next example:

```
setTimeout(function() {
document.getElementById('rocket').getElementsByClassName('fa-
comment')[0].style.display = "none";
}, messageObject.time);
```

Now, open your browser and see the messages flashing on the screen. You can tell it needs some CSS work to make this complete.

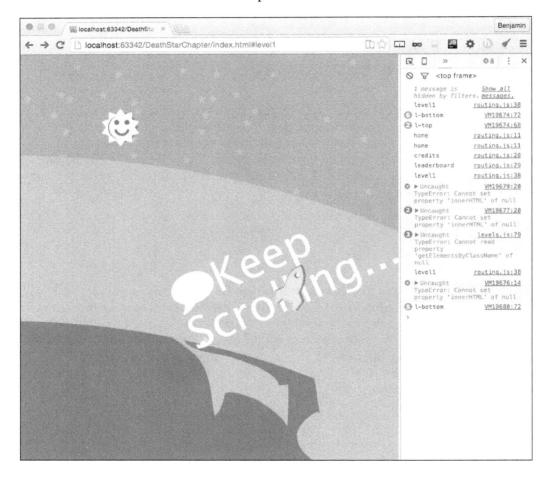

Let's open our `level-1.css` file and get some of the code out of there. Because the `rocket` is going to be used in every level, let's cut that out of the `level-1.css` file and put it into the `levels.css` file so it can be used later by the other levels. So, cut out every CSS for the `rocket` selector and paste it into `levels.css`. Also, make sure you moved the CSS for the `fa-fire` selector.

You will need to add CSS selectors for the `rocket`'s child `fa-comment`, and its child SPAN.

```
#rocket .fa-comment {
}
#rocket .fa-comment > span {
}
```

In the `fa-comment` selector, set the position to `absolute`, 10px from the bottom, and 100px from the left. Rotate it -315 degrees, set the font-size to 100px, and hide it by setting the display to `none`. Here is the example:

```
#rocket .fa-comment {
position: absolute;
bottom: 10px;
left: 100px;
-ms-transform: rotate(-315deg);
-webkit-transform: rotate(-315deg);
transform: rotate(-315deg);
font-size: 100px;
display: none;
}
```

Next, set its child SPAN selector to have a dark gray color, a `font-size` of 1 relative to the root size, a line height of 1.2 relative to the root size, an absolute position of 28px from the top and 18px from the left, with a bold font-weight. See the following example for the detail:

```
#rocket .fa-comment > span{
color: #333;
font-size: 1REM;
line-height: 1.2REM;
    position: absolute;
left: 18px;
top: 28px;
font-weight: bold;
}
```

That covers the messages. Open up the browser again and take a look.

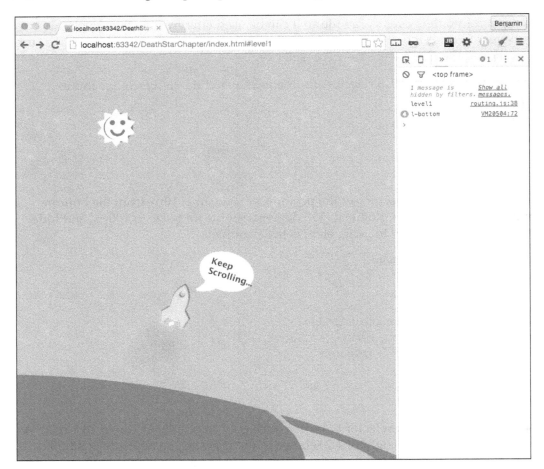

Creating a clickable object

This is great so far. We have the scrolling game into the framework, have it loading data, and there are reusable components. It's missing something still: there's not much fun in only being able to go up or down. I know it's cool to have made this, but it won't be very exciting for a player. It's not *PONG*. So we need to add some left and right controllers.

Let's start by adding some buttons to the screen the player can press to make the rocket go left and right while scrolling up. In your level1.html, add a new SECTION at the end of the MAIN element with the ID attribute controller. Inside the section, add a DIV element with the ID attribute controls. See the following example for the exact code:

```
<section id = "controller">
<div id = "controls">
</div>
</section>
```

Inside the DIV element, add two new I elements. The first is for a font awesome circle arrow to the left, and the second is for a font awesome circle arrow to the right. Give the first the ID attribute leftClick, and the second the ID attribute leftClick. Next, for both, add these three event listeners: onmousedown, onmouseup, and onmouseout; each equaling the function levels.click.internalMove().
See the following example:

```
<div id = "controls">
<i id = "leftClick" class = "fa fa-arrow-circle-o-left"
onmousedown = "levels.click.intervalMove()"
onmouseup = "levels.click.intervalMove()"
onmouseout = "levels.click.intervalMove()"
></i>
<i id = "rightClick" class = "fa fa-arrow-circle-o-right"
onmousedown = "levels.click.intervalMove()"
onmouseup = "levels.click.intervalMove()"
onmouseout = "levels.click.intervalMove()"
></i>
</div>
```

Look on your screen; they are so small and puny. This won't do. Let's add some CSS to make them better. In your levels.css file, add these selectors #controls for the position, #controls i for the actual icons, #controls i:hover to resize when you hover over them, and #controls i.fa.small for JavaScript to add a class for more interaction.

```
#controls {
}
#controls i {
}
#controls i:hover {
}
#controls i.fa.small {
}
```

In the #controls selector, set the position to fixed at 60px from the bottom, and 70% from the left, their width is 30%, and have a z-index of 100. See the following example:

```
#controls {
position: fixed;
bottom: 60px;
left: 70%;
width: 30%;
z-index: 100;
}
```

In the #controls i selector, set the opacity to 75%, the font-size to 15% of the viewport width, an easing transition for all, and a pointer cursor. See the following example:

```
#controls i {
opacity: .75;
font-size: 15vw;
-webkit-transition: all 0.1s ease;
-moz-transition: all 0.1s ease;
-o-transition: all 0.1s ease;
-ms-transition: all 0.1s ease;
cursor: pointer;
}
```

In the hover version, set the opacity to 1, and the font size to 17% of the viewport width. And for the small version, set the opacity to 65%, a 16% font-size, and a silver color. All will have the   override. The example is next:

```
#controls i: hover {
opacity: 1;
font-size: 17vw;
}
#controls i.fa.small {
opacity: .65;
font-size: 16vw;
}
```

Next, we need to wire in the functionality of these buttons. In `levels.js`, add a `levels.click` object to hold the next few functions we will create. The first one being the `intervalMove` function in the onscreen controls.

```
levels.click = {};
levels.click.intervalMove = function() {

}
```

First, inside the function, create a variable, `eventAction`, to hold the click event. Next, start a switch case operation on the event type, as the variable. In the case it's `mousedown`, call a function that will be inside this scope, `controlsAdjustTimer`, which contains an interval operation to call another function. In the case that it is `mouseup` or `mouseout`, call the function `stopAdjustTimer` to clear the interval. See the following example:

```
var eventAction = event;
switch (eventAction.type) {
    case 'mousedown':
    controlsAdjustTimer();
    break;
    case 'mouseup':
    stopAdjustTimer();
    break;
    case 'mouseout':
    stopAdjustTimer();
    break;
    }
```

Let's not forget about touch events. These are a little bit trickier to add. It seems we can't just put them into the HTML like we did; we will need to add them through JavaScript. But first, let's add the event handlers in this `case switch`. The two touch events we will add are `touchstart` and `touchend`. `touchstart` will call the function `controlsAdjustTimer()`, and `touchend` will call the function `stopAdjustTimer()`. See the following example for these additional cases:

```
case 'touchstart':
controlsAdjustTimer();
break;
case 'touchend':
stopAdjustTimer();
break;
```

We will add the listener shortly after we finish the timer functions.

Let's create those two functions just mentioned. These are inside the `levels.click.intervalMove` function following the switch case. First, the `controlsAdjustTimer` function, which contains `theTimer`, equaling a `setInterval` operation with a function call to another function, `levels.click.controlsAdjust`, sending it the event target ID. Set the interval to 50, and return false. Next, `stopAdjustTimer`: inside it, write the `clearInterval` operation in `theTimer`, and `return false`. See the following example:

```
function controlsAdjustTimer() {
theTimer = setInterval(function() {
levels.click.controlsAdjust(eventID.target.id)
}, 50);
return false;
}
function stopAdjustTimer() {
clearInterval(theTimer);
return false;
}
```

You may see that the event listeners are not yet firing for your mobile devices. It may register a `mousedown` if you hold down on the controls, but that's not a great gaming experience. We need to add the listener to the controls. Let's get out of the `levels.click` functions and find a levels function that we can load this event listener after the HTML partial is loaded. The function `levels.load` looks like a favorable place to add this. Append to the `levels.load` function code to get the element by ID controls and set it to equal the variable controller. If it is not null, add the event listeners `touchstart` and `touchend`, both calling the `levels.click.internalMove` function. That's it. See the following example:

```
var controller = document.getElementById("controls");
if (controller) {
controller.addEventListener("touchstart",
levels.click.intervalMove, false);
controller.addEventListener("touchend", levels.click.intervalMove,
false);
}
```

Now, back to the `levels.click` functions.

We've done it again: made some broken software. We are calling a function that does not exist. So, create the function `levels.click.controlsAdjust` and make sure it receives the click target we sent it.

```
levels.click.controlsAdjust = function(clickTarget){
};
```

Creating a moving object

First, let's do some forward movement. We want to scroll up about a quarter of the current screen height; call the `smoothScrollTo` function with a quarter of the window's inner Height subtracted from the window's `pageYOffset`. This will give us a nice velocity forward. Next, let's get the rocket elements first SPAN and set it as a new variable called `sprite`. We are going to turn it into a moveable object, moving left and right as it scrolls up the page. To operate this, we want to have a switch case operation on the variable, `clickTarget`, sent to this function. In the case the `clickTarget` variable is `rightClick`, set the sprite's style left attribute equal to a function call to `levels.setElementLeftPosition`, which you moved over to this file earlier, sending the sprite and the integer 2. In case it is `leftClick`, do the same, except change the variable to a negative two. Finally, let's add some CSS for visual effect. When there is a click, we want to add the class small to `clickTarget`, the icon you clicked, then remove it after a brief time. So, get the element by the ID `clickTarget` variable, and add to the `classList` small, then set a JavaScript Timeout function to remove the small class after 200 ms. Take a look at the following example to see the details of the code:

```
levels.click.controlsAdjust = function(clickTarget) {
    console.log(clickTarget)
    smoothScrollTo(window.pageYOffset - (window.innerHeight /
    4));
    var sprite =
    document.getElementById("rocket").
    getElementsByTagName("span")[0];
    switch (clickTarget){
    case 'rightClick':
    sprite.style.left = levels.setElementLeft
    Position(sprite, 2);
    break;
    case 'leftClick':
    sprite.style.left = levels.setElementLeft
    Position(sprite, -2)
```

```
        break;
        }
document.getElementById(clickTarget).classList.add('small');
setTimeout(function() {
    document.getElementById(clickTarget)
    .classList.remove('small')
    }, 200);
};
```

Now, let's open our browsers and take a look at our controls!

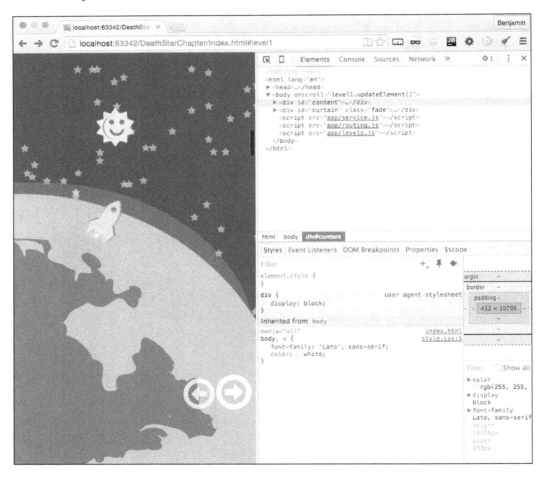

This is pretty cool, but honestly, pressing on the icons is a little sluggish on the desktop. So, let's add the left and right keyboard keys to the controls. Just pretty simple stuff to follow; at the end of the `levels.js` file, add an event listener for the document event on `keydown` that equals a function called `levels.click.checkKey`. See the following example:

```
document.onkeydown = levels.click.checkKey;
```

Broken software again, so let's fix it. Create the function in question in the same file. The function will receive e. In the first line, it will be equal to e, or `window.event`. Let's invoke a switch case operation on the event's `keyCode`. In the case the result is 37, the left arrow key, call the function `levels.click.controlsAdjust` with the string `leftClick`. In the case it's 39, the right arrow key, call the function with the string `rightClick`. See the next example for the code details:

```
levels.click.checkKey = function(e){
e = e || window.event;
switch (e.keyCode) {
case 37:
levels.click.controlsAdjust('leftClick');
break;
case 39:
levels.click.controlsAdjust('rightClick');
break;
}
};
```

Now you can use the keyboard for desktop interaction control. We are done with controls! Actually, we are done with modifying these general patterns for the framework. This is nearly fully operational. Let's move on to some clean-up of the home menu.

Editing the home JavaScript

The home screen is the starting point and where the user will select the levels he wants to go to. Here, he can also see things like the credits and leaderboard. Here is where I lament that there isn't enough time to make a scoring function. Sorry, it's just not in the scope of this book. Maybe we'll make a sequel, or a prequel.

Let's take a look again at our home page. It's empty. Actually, it's not exactly empty: its components are loading, but there's nothing to load. See the following screenshot of our beautiful colors:

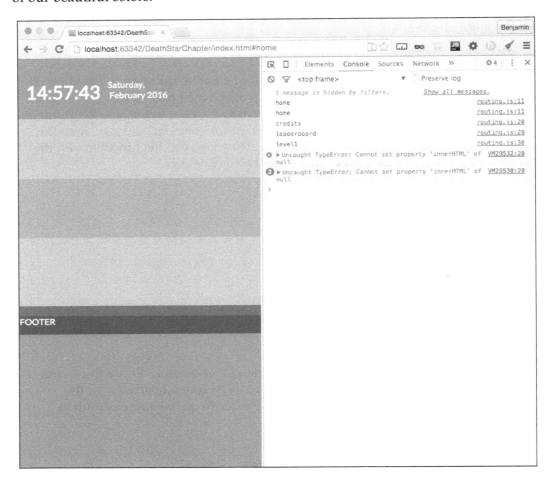

Adding more to make the home interesting

Let's focus on our home page so we can say that the framework is 100 percent operational. Now, the home page is mostly empty, so we want to load up a little bit of content and spread it around in the small section allocated to it. We know that the level1.js file is loaded into the DOM and executed in the header, but that no functions are actually executed.

We want to change that; we want to load a scaled-down version of the objects list into the scaled-down space. So, at the bottom of the page, we have a conditional statement that did nothing if the browser was on the home page, but executed two functions if not at the home page. Let's update it to call a script if the has is at home. Copy the `services.getPage` call in the else condition and paste it into the `home` condition. Change the second variable from `level1` to `home`, and the second variable, the `callBack`, to `level.parseAjaxHome`. See the following sample:

```
if(window.location.hash.split('#')[1] === 'home'){
services.getPage(pageRoute.data, 'home', level1.parseAjaxHome,id);
}else{
levels.load('level1.updateElement()');
services.getPage(pageRoute.data, 'level1', level1.parseAjax,id);
}
```

We need to create this function, `parseAjaxHome`. Simply copy the `parseAjax` function to begin, and scale it down from there. I suggest only loading the `moon` and `stars` to keep it simple, and loading them into the same HTML variable. You can try to add more on your own. You will need to add more CSS to fit it all together. Here's my scaled-down version loading the `moon` and `stars` in the following sample code:

```
level1.parseAjaxHome = function (xhr, id) {
level1.data = JSON.parse(xhr.responseText);
var level1StarsHTML = '<i class="' + level1.data.objectgroups.moon.
objects[0].idclass + ' ' +
level1.data.objectgroups.moon.objects[0].sizeclass + ' ' +
level1.data.objectgroups.moon.objects[0].colorclass + '"></i>';
level1StarsHTML += '<div id="stars">';
for (i = 0; i < level1.data.objectgroups.stars.objects.length / 4;
i++) {
level1StarsHTML += '<i class = "' +
level1.data.objectgroups.stars.objects[i].idclass + ' ' +
level1.data.objectgroups.stars.objects[i].colorclass + '"></i>';
}
level1StarsHTML += '</div>';
document.getElementById('p0').innerHTML = level1StarsHTML;
levels.spreadObjects(document.getElementById("stars").getElementsB
yTagName("i"), 150, 100, 1, 1, "fixed", "%");
};
```

The `spreadObjects` function is a useful function that spreads the objects based on the parameters sent. The parameters sent will spread the stars across the page. That's not really what we are looking for, we just want them spread throughout the small section. And, don't forget our responsive template. The portrait and landscape views are responsive. They need to spread differently to be optimized for both views, as we are using an absolute position to spread them programmatically. Let's replace this function call with a simple if else on whether the window's inner height is larger than its inner width, and if true, send different variables, than if false. The parameters are See my version next and test it out:

```
If (window.innerHeight > window.innerWidth) {
levels.spreadObjects(document.getElementById("stars").getElementsB
yTagName("i"), 100, window.innerWidth, 100,1 ,"absolute" ,"px");
} else {
levels.spreadObjects(document.getElementById("stars").getElementsB
yTagName("i"), 30, 25, 20, 1, "absolute", "%");
}
```

There has to be a template for this to insert into. Remember we created a new HTML partial in the `level-1` folder called `home-level1.html`? This is the partial called when we load the home page. Let's add the link to the `level-1.css` file, then it needs a DIV element to insert the HTML, and it needs the ID attribute p0. Third, it needs a link to the level with a right-link class and inside has a font-awesome right chevron, is 3x the size class and white. See the following sample code:

```
<link type = "text/css" rel = "stylesheet" href = "css/level-
1.css" media = "all">
<div id = "p0" class = "row"></div>
<a href = "#level1" class = "right-link"><i class = "fa fa-
chevron-right fa-3x white">Level 1</i></a>
```

We are getting there. All of these changes are requiring us to do some CSS maintenance. We need to do this as the responsive layout for the SPA framework is breaking apart our game layout in landscape mode. Create a new CSS file called `home.css`. Next, open the `style.css` file. We are going to cut out everything below the color selectors, starting at the first media query, and everything down to right before the curtain selectors, and paste them into the `home.css` file. In addition, in the `style.css` file, change the right-link class selector's style attributes to a relative position, right float, and 9999 z-index. Make a new selector for its child `fa` class with a relative position, 78 pixels from the bottom. See the following example:

```
.right-link {
position: relative;
float: right;
```

```
z-index: 9999;
}
.right-link > .fa {
position: relative;
bottom: 78px;
  }
```

Creating the other pages – credits and leaderboard

Now that we have tamed that, the rest will be easy. Let's move on to the leaderboard and credits. These will be very easy compared to the levels. Most of the hard work is done already. We will work on them simultaneously, as they are so similar. So, let's start with the JSON objects. They copy the same format we used to load the objects in level1.json. Only use one object set, and the data set includes person and credit. I'll use my family, because they deserve the credit for allowing me to write the book. See my following example:

```
{
    "objectgroups": {
        "credits": {
            "objects": [
            {
                "person": "Ben LaGrone",
                "credit": "Author"
            },
            {
                "person": "Anel LaGrone",
                "credit": "Wife"
            },
            {
                "person": "Daphne LaGrone",
                "credit": "Daughter"
            },
            {
                "person": "Darby LaGrone",
                "credit": "Daughter"
            }
            ]
        }
    }
}
```

Next, open your `leaderboard.json` in the `leaderboard` directory, and create something similar, but instead of `credits`, we will have `leaders`, and the values will be `person` and `score`. See the following example:

```json
{
    "objectgroups": {
        leaders": {
            "objects": [
            {
                "person": "BSL",
                "score": 100
            },
            {

                "person": "AK",
                "score": 999
            },
            {

                "person": "SOS",
                "score": 500
            },
            {

                "person": "BSL",
                "score": 100
            },
            {

                "person": "AK",
                "score": 999
            },
            {

                "person": "SOS",
                "score": 500
            }
            ]
        }
    }
}
```

In your `credits` directory, edit the `credits.html` file. It will start with a link back to `home` containing a `fa chevron` to the left with the classes `white`, and `left-link`. Next, we need a title in a Header 3 element, followed by an opening unordered list with the ID `credits-list`, and then close your list. See the simple example next:

```
<a id = "back" href = "#home">
<i class = "fa fa-chevron-left fa-3x white left-link"></i>
</a>
<h3>Credits</h3>
<ul id = "credits-list"></ul>
```

```
In this same directory, the home-credits.html file looks the same,
only instead of the H3 header having the title, we have the text
Credits inside the HREF's child i element, and the i element is a
right chevron, not a left. The HREF follows the UL. See the following
example:
<ul id = "credits-list"></ul>
<a href = "#credits" class = "right-link">
<i class = "fa fa-chevron-right fa-3x white">Credits</i>
</a>
```

To tie it together, we need the `credits.js` JavaScript. In the `credits.js` file, start by making the familiar patterns object, `credits = {};`. Then, create the function to parse the AJAX, `credits.parseAjax`, which gets the variables `xhr` and `id`. This pattern should be so familiar it's boring by now. Inside, create a new variable called `data` equaling the parsed `xhr response text`. Next, create a new variable called `creditsLength`. This function can give us a limited preview of the credits for the home page, then a full credits list for the credits page. The variable is equal to a ternary statement; if the location hash is home, then 4, otherwise, the length of the credits object. Let's take a look at the setup code so far before we start building the HTML. See the following sample code:

```
credits.parseAjax = function (xhr,id) {
var data = JSON.parse(xhr.responseText);
var creditsLength = window.location.hash.split('#')[1] === 'home'? 4 :
data.objectgroups.credits.objects.length;
//TODO write more code
}
```

Next, create a new variable, `creditsHTML`, equaling a blank string. Then, iterate with a `for` loop for the `creditsLength` number, adding to `creditsHTML` for each iteration a LIST ITEM containing a SPAN with a font awesome element for a bullet point and the `person` value, followed by another SPAN with their `credit` value, then close the LIST ITEM, and close the `for` loop. Next, get the element by the ID `credits-list`, and add to its inner HTML `creditsHTML`. Finally, add the `fade` class to the element with the ID `curtain`. See the next example for the remainder of the `credits`. `parseAjax` function:

```
var creditsHTML = '';
for (i = 0; i < creditsLength; i++) {
creditsHTML += '<li><span><i class = "fa fa-fighter-
jet"></i> ' + data.objectgroups.credits.objects[i].person +
'</span>: ' + '<span>' + data.objectgroups.credits.objects[i].
credit + '</span></li>';
}


document.getElementById('credits-list').innerHTML = creditsHTML;
document.getElementById('curtain').className = 'fade';
```

Almost there. The function will not call unless we call it. Create a conditional statement just like `level1.js` if the location hash is `home`, else call the `services.getPage` function with `pageRoute.data`, the string credits, `credits.parseAjax` `callBack`, and the `id` variable. If the first condition is true, it is the home page, call the same function, but supplying the path to the data. See the following example code:

```
if(window.location.hash.split('#')[1] === 'home'){
services.getPage("./app/credits/credits.json",'credits',
credits.parseAjax, id);
} else {
services.getPage(pageRoute.data, 'credits', credits.parseAjax,
id);
}
```

Replicating credits for the leaderboard

Do the exact same for the leaderboard. In `leaderboard.js`, replace everywhere the text credits with leaderboard, and `leaderboardHTML` will have a `score` value instead of the `credit` value.

See the following JavaScript:

```
var leaderboard = {};

leaderboard.parseAjax = function (xhr, id) {
var data = JSON.parse(xhr.responseText);
var leaderboardLength = window.location.hash.split('#')[1] ===
'home'? 4 : data.objectgroups.leaderboard.objects.length;
var leaderboardHTML = '';
for (i = 0; i < leaderboardLength; i++) {
leaderboardHTML += '<li><span><i class = "fa fa-fort-
awesome"></i> ' +
data.objectgroups.leaderboard.objects[i].person + '</span>: '
+ '<span>' + data.objectgroups.leaderboard.objects[i].score +
'</span></li>';
}
document.getElementById('leaderboard-list').innerHTML =
leaderboardHTML;
document.getElementById('curtain').className = 'fade';
};

if (window.location.hash.split('#')[1] === 'home') {
services.getPage("./app/leaderboard/leaderboard.json",
'leaderboard', leaderboard.parseAjax, id);
} else {
services.getPage(pageRoute.data, 'leaderboard',
leaderboard.parseAjax, id);
}
```

Follow the same routing for the `home-leaderboard.html` and `leaderboard.html` files.

Now, let's take a look at the home page! Open up your browser and refresh it:

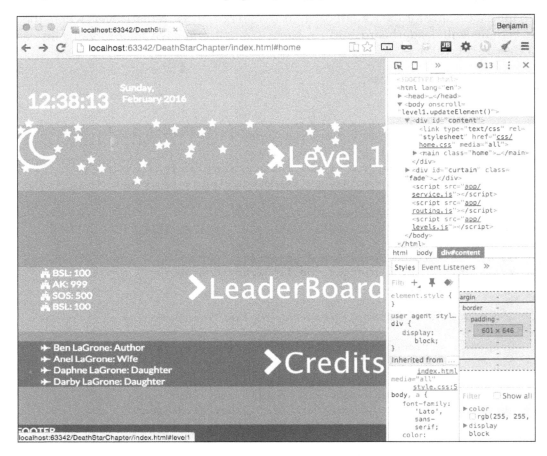

Creating the second level

We've finally arrived at the most exciting part of this chapter. I saved it for last for this reason, because it will be the coolest to see in action. We are going to add a second level to our game that will function much like the first and fit well into the home page format.

The first thing we want to do is discuss what we want this to do and look like. I want to stick with the reusable patterns we've worked so hard to create, such as the scrolling up, the rocket, and the space objects. But we can make some cool changes to it.

In the second level, you are already in space and will scroll up and face the big boss of the level and defeat it with one shot. Since this is the Death Star Level, I want to borrow some objects from Star Wars. We will not be using so many font awesome objects, but instead some SVG icons.

Getting SVG objects

I found a good collection of SVG icons over at `https://www.iconfinder.com` when searching for space icons. It gave me a cool selection of spaceships for the second level. Out of the selection, I found a Death Star, a satellite, a Millennium Falcon, a rocket, Saturn, a Tie-Fighter, and an X-Wing, all in SVG format. So search for and download these. Create a new directory in your `lib` directory called `space-icons`, and move them there.

You will need to edit each of these SVG icons. Inside each SVG file, there is a code for the PATH; inside the opening for the path, add a gray fill attribute. See the following for an example. This is from the `tie-fighter.svg` file:

```
<?xml version = "1.0" ?>
<!DOCTYPE svg  PUBLIC '-//W3C//DTD SVG
1.1//EN'  'http://www.w3.org/Graphics/SVG/1.1/DTD/svg11.dtd'>
<svg enable-background = "new 0 0 28 24" version = "1.1" viewBox =
"0 0 28 24" xml:space = "preserve" xmlns =
"http://www.w3.org/2000/svg" xmlns:xlink =
"http://www.w3.org/1999/xlink"><g id = "Layer_1">
<g>
<path fill = "#ccc" d = "M8,14.5c-0.133,0-0.261-0.019-0.389-
0.039L4.033,24h7.933l-3.577-
9.539C8.261,14.481,8.133,14.5,8,14.5z"/>
<path fill = "#ccc" d = "M5.55,12.5H013.103,11.135l3.571-
9.523C6.106,13.755,5.689,13.18,5.55,12.5z"/>
```

You can see that on each path object in the file, you will need to add the fill attribute.

Creating the directory structure and routes

Follow the familiar pattern we have established time and time again. Create your level2 directory containing your HTML template partials, your JavaScript file, and the JSON file. You will also need to create a level-2-specific CSS file in the `css/` directory. This should be "old hat" by now.

Also, in your routing table in `routing.js`, add the route registry for these files. See my next example:

```
services.routing.register('level2', function() {
    pageRoute = {
        page: "./app/level2/level2.html",
        partial: "./app/level2/home-level2.html",
        script: "./app/level2/level2.js",
        data: "./app/level1/level1.json"
        };
});
```

Creating the new JSON for each level

Excellent! Now that we have the objects, let's build out the JSON object to contain the data for these. Let's start by copying our `level1.json` object into this one, as it's going to run fairly similarly. Once it's pasted in, let's start by removing what we don't want. We do want to keep the messages, the stars, and the objects. The moon and everything after the objects, the terra group and the clouds, can be deleted.

Now, let's start editing out the JSON object, as it's the backbone of what's going into our next level. This time, I want to have seven message objects in the messages. So, create four more messages and give them the positions 100, 75, 30, 25, 20, 10, and 1. See my next example for the text I put in mine:

```
"messages": {
    "objects": [
        {"text": "Many Bothams died to get these plans!",
        "position": 100, "time": 4000},
        {"text": "Be Carefull, there's some fighting ahead!",
        "position": 75, "time": 5000},
        {"text": "That's No Moon!", "position": 30, "time": 6000},
        {"text": "It's a trap!", "position": 25, "time": 6000},
        {"text": "Almost there!", "position": 20, "time": 6000},
        {"text": "Almost there!", "position": 10, "time": 6000},
        {"text": "It's as easy as shooting Womp Rats in Beggars
        canyon", "position": 1, "time": 6000}
        ]
},
```

The next object is the `stars` object. Leave it as it is.

Next up is the objects. These are all the objects that will be on the screen on level two. These are divided into subgroups, similar to the `level1.json` objects. The first group is the `death_star` group. There are four objects in this group: some are font awesome fonts and the `death_star` is an SVG. They all have the same attributes keys, `type`, `idclass`, `sizeclass`, and `colorclass`. See the following details for each object in the example:

```
"death_star": {
    "objects": [
        {"type": "death_star", "idclass": "death_star",
        "sizeclass": "", "colorclass": "silver"},
        {"type": "cloud", "idclass": "fa fa-bullseye",
        "sizeclass":
        "deathStarAdd fa-5x", "colorclass": "red"},
        {"type": "cloud", "idclass": "fa fa-sun-o", "sizeclass":
        "deathStarAdd fa-5x", "colorclass": "yellow"},
        {"type": "cloud", "idclass": "fa fa-crosshairs",
        "sizeclass":
        "deathStarAdd fa-5x", "colorclass": "yellow"}
        ]
}
```

Next, we will have a collection of the starships. The name of the objects is `starships1`. These starships will be encountered by the rocket pilot as you scroll through space. These are the rocket, the falcon, the x-wing, and tie fighter SVG files we downloaded. In my example, I will repeat some of these several times. See the following example:

```
"starships1": {
"objects": [
    {"type": "rocket2", "idclass": "rocket", "sizeclass":
"smallship", "colorclass": "silver"},
    {"type": "falcon", "idclass": "falcon", "sizeclass":
"smallship", "colorclass": "silver"},
    {"type": "x-wing", "idclass": "x-wing", "sizeclass":
"smallship", "colorclass": "silver"},        {"type": "satellite1",
"idclass": "satellite", "sizeclass": "smallship", "colorclass":
"silver"},
{"type": "satellite2", "idclass": "satellite", "sizeclass":
"smallship", "colorclass": "silver"},        {"type": "satellite3",
"idclass": "satellite", "sizeclass": "smallship", "colorclass":
"silver"},
{"type": "tie-fighter", "idclass": "tie-fighter", "sizeclass":
"smallship", "colorclass": "silver"},
```

```
{"type": "tie-fighter", "idclass": "tie-fighter", "sizeclass":
"smallship", "colorclass": "silver"},
{"type": "tie-fighter", "idclass": "tie-fighter", "sizeclass":
"smallship", "colorclass": "silver"},
{"type": "tie-fighter", "idclass": "tie-fighter", "sizeclass":
"smallship", "colorclass": "silver"},
{"type": "tie-fighter", "idclass": "tie-fighter", "sizeclass":
"smallship", "colorclass": "silver"}
]
}
```

As implied by the name of the subgroup, starships1, there will be a starships2 and starships3. Make these a copy of starships1. See the following example:

```
"starships2": {
"objects": [
{"type": "rocket2", "idclass": "rocket", "sizeclass": "smallship",
"colorclass": "silver"},
{"type": "x-wing", "idclass": "x-wing", "sizeclass": "smallship",
"colorclass": "silver"},
{"type": "satellite1", "idclass": "satellite", "sizeclass":
"smallship", "colorclass": "silver"},
{"type": "satellite2", "idclass": "satellite", "sizeclass":
"smallship", "colorclass": "silver"},
{"type": "satellite3", "idclass": "satellite", "sizeclass":
"smallship", "colorclass":" silver"},
{"type": "tie-fighter", "idclass": "tie-fighter", "sizeclass":
"smallship", "colorclass": "silver"},
{"type": "tie-fighter", "idclass": "tie-fighter", "sizeclass":
"smallship", "colorclass": "silver"},
{"type": "tie-fighter", "idclass": "tie-fighter", "sizeclass":
"smallship", "colorclass": "silver"},
{"type": "tie-fighter", "idclass": "tie-fighter", "sizeclass":
"smallship", "colorclass": "silver"},
{"type": "tie-fighter", "idclass": "tie-fighter", "sizeclass":
"smallship", "colorclass": "silver"}
]
},
"starships3": {
"objects": [
{"type": "rocket2", "idclass": "rocket", "sizeclass": "smallship",
"colorclass": "silver"},
{"type": "x-wing", "idclass": "x-wing", "sizeclass": "smallship",
"colorclass": "silver"},
{"type": "satellite1", "idclass": "satellite", "sizeclass":
"smallship", "colorclass": "silver"},
```

```
{"type": "satellite2", "idclass": "satellite", "sizeclass":
"smallship", "colorclass": "silver"},
{"type": "satellite3", "idclass": "satellite", "sizeclass":
"smallship", "colorclass": "silver"},
{"type": "tie-fighter", "idclass": "tie-fighter", "sizeclass":
"smallship", "colorclass": "silver"},
{"type": "tie-fighter", "idclass": "tie-fighter", "sizeclass":
"smallship", "colorclass": "silver"},
{"type": "tie-fighter", "idclass": "tie-fighter", "sizeclass":
"smallship", "colorclass": "silver"},
{"type": "tie-fighter", "idclass": "tie-fighter", "sizeclass":
"smallship", "colorclass": "silver"},
{"type": "tie-fighter", "idclass": "tie-fighter", "sizeclass":
"smallship", "colorclass": "silver"}
]
},
```

The next object group in this list of objects is `saturn`, and it is only one object in the list of objects. Give it a `colorclass` of `purple`, and leave the `sizeclass` blank. See my example:

```
"saturn": {
"objects": [
{"type": "saturn", "idclass": "saturn", "sizeclass": "",
"colorclass": "purple"}
]
}
```

Finally, the `rocket`, which was already defined in `level1`, so just copy it over like my next example:

```
"rocket": {
"objects": [
{"type": "rocket", "idclass": "fa fa-rocket", "sizeclass": "fa-
5x", "colorclass": "grey-2"},
{"type": "rocket", "idclass": "fa fa-rocket", "sizeclass": "fa-
5x", "colorclass": "silver"},
{"type": "rocket", "idclass": "fa fa-fire", "sizeclass": "",
"colorclass": "yellow"},
{"type": "rocket", "idclass": "fa fa-comment", "sizeclass": "fa-
5x", "colorclass": "white"}
]
}
```

Now, make sure the JSON object is well formed and we are done with our objects for level 2.

Creating the level 2 HTML

Excellent work so far. We are so close I can almost taste how awesome this game application will be. We need to create the `level2.html` partial for the game to load into. So, open the file and begin editing it.

Let's start with links to the style sheets it will use. Link to `levels.css` for general CSS style, and link to `level-2.css` that will only be for this level.

```
<link type = "text/css" rel = "stylesheet" href = "css/levels.css"
media = "all">
<link type = "text/css" rel = "stylesheet" href = "css/level-
2.css" media = "all">
```

Next, create a MAIN element with the ID body and classes `container` and `black`. Inside it, add six SECTION elements with the IDs `boss`, `mid`, `first`, `saturnObject`, `rocketObject`, and `controller`. See my next example:

```
<link type = "text/css" rel = "stylesheet" href = "css/levels.css"
media = "all">
<link type = "text/css" rel = "stylesheet" href = "css/level-
2.css" media = "all">
<main id = "body" class = "container black">
<section id = "boss"></section>
<section id = "mid"></section>
<section id = "first"></section>
<section id = "saturnObject"></section>
<section id = "rocketObject"></section>
<section id = "controller"></section>
</main>
```

Inside each of `boss`, `mid`, and `first`, place about eight DIV elements with the class `row`. See the following example:

```
<section id = "boss">
<div class = "row"></div>
<div class = "row"></div>
<div class = "row"></div>
<div class = "row"></div>
<div class = "row"></div>
<div class = "row"></div>
<div class = "row"></div>
<div class = "row"></div>
</section>
```

In the `boss` SECTION element, inside the first `row` DIV element, add a new DIV element with the ID attribute `deathStarObject`. See the following example:

```
<div class = "row">
<div id = "deathstarObject"></div>
</div>
```

In the `boss` SECTION element, again, inside the third `row` DIV element, add a new DIV element with the ID attribute `object3`. See the following example:

```
<div class = "row">
<div id = "objects3"></div>
</div>
```

Next, in the `mid` SECTION element, in the first `row` DIV element, add a new DIV element with the ID attribute `starsObject`. See the following example:

```
<div class = "row">
<div id = "starsObject"></div>
</div>
```

In the fifth `row` element in the `mid` SECTION element, add a new DIV element with the ID attribute `objects2`. See the following example:

```
<div class = "row">
<div id = "objects2"></div>
</div>
```

Looking good so far. Now, in the first SECTION element, in the middle row element, add a new DIV element with the ID attribute `objects1`. See the following example:

```
<div class = "row">
<div id = "objects1"></div>
</div>
```

Do nothing to the SECTION elements with the ID attributes `saturnObject`, or `rocketObject`. Those will be modified by the JavaScript only.

In the SECTION element with the ID attribute `controller`, copy the controls HTML from the `level1.html` template partial. This will look exactly like the `level1.html` controller SECTION.

That went fast. Let's move on to the next, and final, big thing. We will create the JavaScript file, and then fix it up with some CSS wizardry to prettify it.

Creating the level2 JS

This is the home stretch, and I hope you are as thrilled as I am. The `levels.js` file needs to accomplish only three things inside it: get the elements, update on scroll, and move the elements. Everything else is managed by patterns in other files. It's a framework that is ready to load and execute. We are going to go through our similar method of making broken JavaScript and then fixing it. So first, add to the bottom of the JavaScript the familiar executable condition. In fact, it's so familiar, you can just copy it from `level1.js` and modify it. Change the text `level1` to `level2`. See the following example below:

```
If (window.location.hash.split('#')[1] === 'home') {
services.getPage(pageRoute.data, 'home', level2.parseAjaxHome,
id);
} else {
levels.load('level2.updateElement()');
services.getPage(pageRoute.data, 'level2', level2.parseAjax, id);
}
```

Next, let's create the crucial functions that will operate on this page. Start with the `level2` object at the top, and then declare the `level2.data`.

```
var level2 = {};
level2.data;
```

Next, declare the functions `level2.updateElement`, `level2.getMovingElements`, `level2.parseAjax`, and `level2.parseAjaxHome`.

```
level2.updateElement = function() {};
level2.getMovingElements = function(callback) {};
level2.parseAjax = function (xhr,id) {};
level2.parseAjaxHome = function (xhr,id) {};
```

Let's load the objects first with filling in the `level2.parseAjax` function. It receives `xhr` and `id` from `services.getPage`. Inside the function, just like the `level1` version, add the parsed data to the `level2.data` object.

Parsing the AJAX

Placing these objects is much like we did in `level1.parseAjax`, only it's even simpler. First, let's put the `saturn` Object into the HTML. Working with an SVG does not change this very much. Create a new variable, `level2SaturnHTML`, equal to the string opening a `DIV` element with the ID equal to the `level2.data`'s saturn object's `type` plus the string class equal to the object's `idclass`, plus a space, plus the `sizeclass` data, plus a space, plus `colorclass`.

Next, we add to the temporary variable `level2SaturnHTML` this string, opening an object type of `image/svg+xml`, with the data equaling the path to the object's `idclass`, plus the extension `svg`, closing the open tag. Add to this the object's type, and then close the `OBJECT` element, and `DIV` element. See this in the following example:

```
var level2SaturnHTML = '<div id = "' +
level2.data.objectgroups.objects.saturn.objects[0].type + '"
class="' +
level2.data.objectgroups.objects.saturn.objects[0].idclass + ' ' +
level2.data.objectgroups.objects.saturn.objects[0].sizeclass + ' '
+ level2.data.objectgroups.objects.saturn.objects[0].colorclass +
'">';
level2SaturnHTML += '<object type = "image/svg+xml"
data="lib/space-icons/' +
level2.data.objectgroups.objects.saturn.objects[0].idclass +
'.svg" >' +
level2.data.objectgroups.objects.saturn.objects[0].type +
'</object></div>';
```

Next, copy over from `level2.parseAjax` the lines inserting the `stars` object. Replace the `level1` text with `level2`, and replace the text `p1` with `starsObject` to insert it into the `DIV` element with the ID attribute `starsObject`. See the following example:

```
var level2StarsHtml = '<div id = "stars">';
for (i = 0; i < level2.data.objectgroups.stars.objects.length;
i++) {
level2StarsHtml += '<i class = "' +
level2.data.objectgroups.stars.objects[i].idclass + ' ' +
level2.data.objectgroups.stars.objects[i].colorclass + '"></i>';
}
level2StarsHtml += '</div>';
document.getElementById('starsObject').innerHTML =
level2StarsHtml;
```

The next operation will load the `rocket` into the HTML. Create a new variable, `rocketObjectHTML`, equal to the string containing a new `DIV` element with the ID attribute rocket, with a child `SPAN` element. Next, a `for` loop iterates over the `rocket` object `objects`, adding to `rocketObjectHTML` the i element with the data from the JSON object in the same way as `level1.parseAjax`. Close the `for` loop, then add to `rocketObjectHTML` a string closing the `SPAN` element and `DIV` element. Set `rocketObjectHTML` as the inner HTML of the element with the `rocketObject` ID.

See the following example:

```
var rocketObjectHTML = '<div id="rocket"><span>';
for (var key in level2.data.objectgroups.objects.rocket.objects) {
rocketObjectHTML += '<i class = "' +
level2.data.objectgroups.objects.rocket.objects[key].idclass + ' '
+ level2.data.objectgroups.objects.rocket.objects[key].sizeclass +
' ' +
level2.data.objectgroups.objects.rocket.objects[key].colorclass +
'"></i>';
}
rocketObjectHTML += '</span></div>';
document.getElementById('rocketObject').innerHTML =
rocketObjectHTML;
```

Next, let's work on the objects in space. We will create three operations that will be very similar. The first starts with a new variable called `objects1HTMLStart`, equal to an empty string. Then, loop over the `starships1` object in the `levels2.data`. Add to the `objects1HTMLStart` variable, just like you did in the `saturn` example; the first line is the DIV element with its attributes. On the next line, add to `objects1HTMLStart` an object with the attributes similarly built in the `saturn` object. Then, close the OBJECT and DIV elements. Then, after closing the `for` loop, set `objects1HTMLStart` to equal the inner HTML of the element with the ID `objects1`. See the following example to check your own:

```
var objects1HTMLStart = '';
for (var key in
level2.data.objectgroups.objects.starships1.objects) {
objects1HTMLStart += '<div id = "' +
level2.data.objectgroups.objects.starships1.objects[key].type + '"
class="' +
level2.data.objectgroups.objects.starships1.objects[key].idclass+'
' +
level2.data.objectgroups.objects.starships1.objects[key].sizeclass
 + ' ' +
level2.data.objectgroups.objects.starships1.objects[key].colorclas
s + '">';
   objects1HTMLStart += '<object type="image/svg+xml" data =
"lib/space-icons/' +
level2.data.objectgroups.objects.starships1.objects[key].idclass +
'.svg" >' +
level2.data.objectgroups.objects.starships1.objects[key].type +
'</object></div>';
}
document.getElementById('objects1').innerHTML = objects1HTMLStart;
```

Repeat this two times to load the `starships2` objects into the `objects2` element, and the `starships3` objects into the `objects3` element. I'll provide the following example:

```
var objects2HTMLStart = '';
for (var key in
level2.data.objectgroups.objects.starships2.objects){
objects2HTMLStart += '<div id = "' +
level2.data.objectgroups.objects.starships2.objects[key].type + '"
class="' +
level2.data.objectgroups.objects.starships2.objects[key].idclass +
' ' +
level2.data.objectgroups.objects.starships2.objects[key].sizeclass
+ ' ' +
level2.data.objectgroups.objects.starships2.objects[key].colorclas
s + '">';
objects2HTMLStart += '<object type = "image/svg+xml" data =
"lib/space-icons/' +
level2.data.objectgroups.objects.starships2.objects[key].idclass +
'.svg" >' +
level2.data.objectgroups.objects.starships2.objects[key].type +
'</object></div>';
}
document.getElementById('objects2').innerHTML = objects2HTMLStart;
var objects3HTMLStart = '';
for (var key in
level2.data.objectgroups.objects.starships3.objects){
objects3HTMLStart += '<div id = "' +
level2.data.objectgroups.objects.starships3.objects[key].type + '"
class = "' +
level2.data.objectgroups.objects.starships3.objects[key].idclass +
' ' +
level2.data.objectgroups.objects.starships3.objects[key].sizeclass
+ ' ' +
level2.data.objectgroups.objects.starships3.objects[key].colorclas
s + '">';
   objects3HTMLStart += '<object type = "image/svg+xml"
data="lib/space-icons/' +
level2.data.objectgroups.objects.starships3.objects[key].idclass +
'.svg" >' +
level2.data.objectgroups.objects.starships3.objects[key].type +
'</object></div>';
}
document.getElementById('objects3').innerHTML = objects3HTMLStart;
```

The last object to load is the DEATH STAR. This is a little different, but not unfamiliar, as we've done similar operations. The death star object combines SVG elements and font awesome icons, and there will be a condition in the loop to handle it. So, start with a new variable called `deathStarObjectHTML` equal to an empty string. Then, start a `for in` loop with the variable `key` looping over the `death_star` objects. In the first line, add to the `deathStarObjectHTML` variable the DIV element plus the data like the previous example, with one exception: enumerate ids by adding `key` to the data type. In the next line, add a condition: `if` the type is not `cloud`, then add to `deathStarObjectHTML` an OBJECT of type `image/svg+xml` also like previous examples. Then, close the conditional, and close the DIV element, and close the `for in` loop. Finally, get the element by the ID `deathStarObject`, and set its inner HTML equal to `deathStarObjectHTML`. See the following example:

```
var deathStarObjectHTML = '';
for (var key in
level2.data.objectgroups.objects.death_star.objects) {
deathStarObjectHTML += '<div id = "' +
level2.data.objectgroups.objects.death_star.objects[key].type
+  key + '" class = "' +
level2.data.objectgroups.objects.death_star.objects[key].idclass +
' ' +
level2.data.objectgroups.objects.death_star.objects[key].sizeclass
+ ' ' +
level2.data.objectgroups.objects.death_star.objects[key].colorclas
s + '">';
    if (level2.data.objectgroups.objects.death_star.objects[key].type! =
'cloud') {
deathStarObjectHTML += '<object type = "image/svg+xml" data
= "lib/space-icons/' + level2.data.objectgroups.objects.death_star.
objects[key].idclass +
'.svg" >' + level2.data.objectgroups.objects.death_star.objects[key].
type +
'</object>';
}
deathStarObjectHTML += '</div>';
}
document.getElementById('deathstarObject').innerHTML =
deathStarObjectHTML;
```

The final part of the `level2.parseAjax` function is spreading the objects. Send the `stars` object's child i elements to the `spreadObjects` function just like the `level1` version with these numbers: 150,100,1,1,"fixed", "%". Send the `objects1`, `objects2`, and `objects3` child objects gotten by class name `smallship` with the same numbers, but relative instead of fixed.

See the following example:

```
levels.spreadObjects(document.getElementById("stars").getElementsB
yTagName("i"), 150, 100, 1, 1, "fixed", "%");
levels.spreadObjects(document.getElementById("objects1").getElemen
tsByClassName("smallship"), 150, 150, 1, 1, "relative", "%");
levels.spreadObjects(document.getElementById("objects2").getElemen
tsByClassName("smallship"), 150, 150, 1, 1, "relative", "%");
levels.spreadObjects(document.getElementById("objects3").getElemen
tsByClassName("smallship"), 150, 150, 1, 1, "relative", "%");
```

Now, when you reload your browser and see the viewport, you will see that even
though the curtain has yet to be removed, you can look in your HTML code and see
the objects have loaded.

Updating the elements

We can say this is broken again, and we need to fix it. We can move forward with the `level2.updateElement` function. This function executes on every scroll as it is attached as an `onscroll` event listener on the `BODY`. First, call a new nonexisting function, `levels.updateOnMove`, a callback, `level2.topOfScroll`, another callback, `level2.bottomOfScroll`, and the `level2` data messages object. This calls the generalize movement patterns for all levels. These callBacks will be added shortly as well as the function they are sent to. Next, get the element by ID `saturn` and the first of its child objects, and send it to a function called `levels.moveSaturn`. This function does not yet exist, but it gives us something to do next. Get the elements by ID `objects1` and `objects2` and send them to another nonexistent function, `levels.setElementBottomPosition`. Now we have a growing TODO list. Next, call `level2.getMovingElements` with a callback function calling `theObject`, and increment. In the callback, `theObject` style's position attribute is equal to relative, and its left style is equal to a call to the function `levels.setElementLeftPosition` sending `theObject`, and increment (wait for the example). See the following example:

```
level2.updateElement = function(){
levels.updateOnMove(level2.topOfScroll, level2.bottomOfScroll,
level2.data.objectgroups.messages);
levels.moveSaturn(document.getElementById("saturn").getElementsByT
agName('object')[0]);
document.getElementById('objects1').style.bottom =
levels.click.setElementBottomPosition(document.getElementById('obj
ects1'), 1);
document.getElementById('objects2').style.bottom =
levels.click.setElementBottomPosition(document.getElementById('obj
ects2'), 1)
level2.getMovingElements(function (theObject, increment){
theObject.style.position = "relative";
theObject.style.left =
levels.click.setElementLeftPosition(theObject, increment);
});
};
```

As I mentioned, we have a growing TODO list, so let's mitigate that problem before we move on. We need to create a function called `levels.moveSaturn` and `levels.setElementBottomPosition`.

So, over in `levels.js`, create these new functions. First, `levels.moveSaturn`; it receives a variable that we will just call `orb`. Inside the function, set the `orb`'s style left attribute equal to the `rocket` element's bounding client rectangle's bottom attribute divided by the window's inner height, subtracted from the number of rows, then multiplied by the window's inner height, then add to that the number of rows multiplied by negative six, and add the string px. I'll show you the example for that because it's convoluted.

```
orb.style.left =
(((window.innerHeight*(document.getElementsByClassName("row").leng
th) -
document.getElementById("rocket").getBoundingClientRect().bottom)
/ window.innerHeight) +
document.getElementsByClassName("row").length * -6) + "px";
```

The next operation on the orb is to set its style height attribute. First, get the number of rows, multiplied by the window's inner height attribute, then subtract the window's page Y offset, and divide by the window's inner height, plus 0.5, and then add the % sign as a string. Here is the sample code:

```
orb.style.height = (window.innerHeight *
(document.getElementsByClassName("row").length) -
window.pageYOffset) / window.innerHeight + .5 + '%';
```

The last operation on the `orb` element is to set its style bottom position. Start again with the number of rows, multiplied by the window's inner height attribute, subtracted from 100, and subtract from that the window's page Y offset, and divide by the window's inner height, and subtract 15 from it, then add the % sign as a string. See the following example:

```
orb.style.bottom = (100 - (window.innerHeight *
(document.getElementsByClassName("row").length) -
window.pageYOffset) / window.innerHeight - 15) + '%';
```

You might think I'm writing new common core math skill to make kids hate math, but these, as obtuse as they are, will give the `saturn` element a smooth scrolling presence on the viewport; just wait and see.

Next, we need to create the other function on our TODO list, the `setElementBottomPosition` function. This one is simpler than the previous one, so don't lose heart. First, copy the function `setElementLeftPosition`, and paste it and rename it.

Then, rename the left text to bottom. See the following example:

```
levels.setElementBottomPosition = function(element,increment){
if (isNaN(parseInt(element.style.bottom.split("p")[0]))) {
return ((element.getBoundingClientRect().bottom) + increment) +
"px"
} else {
return ((Math.abs(parseInt(element.style.bottom.split("p")[0]))) +
increment) + "px";
}
};
```

In `levels.js`, we also need to create the function `levels.updateOnMove`
that receives the two `callBacks` and the `messages` object. As I mentioned before,
this is the generalized pattern for moving things on the scroll for every level. In the
first line of code, send the `rocket` element to the `levels.moveRocket` function.
Next, set a new variable, `scrollPosition`, equal to 100*the window's page Y offset
divided by the document's body scroll height minus the document's document
element client height, rounded. Finally, copy the message operation from `level1.
updateElement` and paste it in here, changing the text `level1` to levels. See the
entire function in this sample:

```
levels.updateOnMove = function(topCallBack,bottomCallBack,messagesObj
ect) {
levels.moveRocket(document.getElementById("rocket"));
var ScrollPosition = Math.round(100 * window.pageYOffset /
(document.body.scrollHeight -document.documentElement.clientHeight));
switch (ScrollPosition){
case 0:
levels.topOfScroll(topCallBack);
break;
case 100:
levels.bottomOfScroll(bottomCallBack);
break;
default:
}
var scrollPosition = Math.round(100 * window.pageYOffset /
(document.body.scrollHeight -
document.documentElement.clientHeight));
for ( i = 0; i < messagesObject.objects.length; i++) {
if (messagesObject.objects[i].position === scrollPosition) {
levels.showMessage(messagesObject.objects[i])
}
}
};
```

We created two calls to callbacks back in the `level2.js` file. They do not perform any function, but I want to save this for future development. Back in `level2.js`, create the empty functions `level2.topOfScroll` and `level2.bottomOfScroll`. See the following example:

```
level2.topOfScroll = function() {
};
level2.bottomOfScroll = function() {
};
```

Moving the elements

Let's move on to the final big piece of interaction, the moving element. This is much like `level1.getMovingElements`. So, let's blaze through since you are a pro already! First, create a `for` loop over the rows. Then, if the window's page Y offset plus the window's inner height is greater than the current row in the viewport's top offset, and the page Y offset is less than the current row's top offset plus two-thirds of the window's inner height, then perform the next check. If the current row has any elements with the class `smallship`, then perform an operation. But first, let's handle an `else` operation. If there are no `smallship` elements, then add an else it to check if there is an element in the viewport with the class `deathStarAdd`, and if the `rocket`'s bounding client bottom divided by the product of the window's inner height and the number of rows equals or is greater than .999. If these conditions are true, `console.log` the text explode, and we will come back to this later. Let's take a look at this deep operation before moving forward with the other condition. See the following example:

```
level2.getMovingElements = function(callback) {
for (var h = 0; h < document.getElementsByClassName("row").length;
h++) {
if ((window.pageYOffset + (window.innerHeight)) >
document.getElementsByClassName("row")[h].offsetTop &&
(window.pageYOffset) < (document.getElementsByClassName("row")[h].
offsetTop +
(window.innerHeight / 2 * 3))){
if (document.getElementsByClassName("row")[h].getElementsByClassName(
"smallship").length > 0) {

} else if
(document.getElementsByClassName("row")[h].getElementsByClassName(
"deathStarAdd").length > 0 && (document.getElementById("rocket").
getBoundingClientRect().bottom)
/ (window.innerHeight*(document.getElementsByClassName("row").length
)) >= .995) {
```

```
console.log('explode')
    }
  }
}
};
```

Next, inside the first `truthy` condition, start a `for` loop over the current `row`'s `starship` elements list. In each, add a `switch` `case` operation getting the current `row`'s current `smallship` element's ID attribute. The cases are `rocket2`, `falcon`, `x-wing`, `tie-fighter`, `satellite1`, `satellite2`, and `satellite3`. In each case, call the callback, sending it the current `row`'s current `smallship`, and a number. I assigned a positive number to the rebel fleet, and a negative number to the Empire. I'll show you the entire version of the function in the following sample:

```
level2.getMovingElements = function(callback) {
for (var h = 0; h < document.getElementsByClassName("row").length;
h++) {
if ((window.pageYOffset + (window.innerHeight)) >
document.getElementsByClassName("row")[h].offsetTop &&
(window.pageYOffset) < (document.getElementsByClassName("row")[h].
offsetTop +
(window.innerHeight / 2 * 3))) {
if (document.getElementsByClassName("row")[h].getElementsByClassName(
"smallship").length > 0) {
for (j = 0; j < document.getElementsByClassName("row")[h].
getElementsByClassName("
smallship").length; j++) {
switch(document.getElementsByClassName("row")[h].getElementsByClas
sName("smallship")[j].getAttribute('id')) {
case 'rocket2':
callback(document.getElementsByClassName("row")[h].getElementsByCl
assName("smallship")[j], -4);
break;
case 'falcon':
callback(document.getElementsByClassName("row")[h].getElementsByCl
assName("smallship")[j], -3);
break;
case 'x-wing':
callback(document.getElementsByClassName("row")[h].getElementsByCl
assName("smallship")[j], -2);
break;
case 'tie-fighter':
callback(document.getElementsByClassName("row")[h].getElementsByCl
assName("smallship")[j], 2);
break;
```

```
case 'satellite1':
callback(document.getElementsByClassName("row")[h].getElemen
tsByClassName("smallship")[j], 7);
break;
case 'satellite2':
callback(document.getElementsByClassName("row")[h].getElementsByCl
assName("smallship")[j], 3);
break;
case 'satellite3':
callback(document.getElementsByClassName("row")[h].getElementsByCl
assName("smallship")[j], 2);
break;
default:
;
}
}


} else if
(document.getElementsByClassName("row")[h].getElementsByClassName(
"deathStarAdd").length > 0 &&
(document.getElementById("rocket").getBoundingClientRect().bottom)
/
(window.innerHeight*(document.getElementsByClassName("row").length
)) >= .999) {
console.log('explode')
}
}
}
};
```

Wow, that was some heavy lifting. I'm glad we are done. It's all downhill from here. Let's add some style to make it flow a little better.

Adding some CSS

A while ago, we created the `level2.css` file and then left it blank. Now, let's get to work on it. First, style the mid SECTION's stars DIV child i elements with a 5 z-index. Next, the `saturn` element object will have a 10 z-index, a width of 120%, a fixed position, to the left negative 76%, 40% from the bottom, and rotate it 319 degrees. Next, give the boss, mid, first SECTION's rows' child DIV elements a 100% height. Rotate the `falcon` class selector 50 degrees. For the elements with the class `smallship`, assign a width of 20 vw, a z-index of 99, and float them to the left. Assign to the `death_star` selector a z-index of 30. Give the elements with class `death_star` and `saturn` an absolute position 0% to the right. Finally, make the `rocketObject`'s rocket's child span a z-index of 999.

See all this in the following example:

```css
#mid #stars > i {
z-index:5;
}
#saturn object{
z-index: 10;
width: 120%;
position: fixed;
left: -76%;
bottom: 40%;
transform: rotate(319deg);
}
#boss .row > div,
#mid .row > div,
#first .row > div{
height: 100%;
}

.falcon {
-ms-transform: rotate(50deg);
-webkit-transform: rotate(50deg);
    transform: rotate(50deg);
}
.smallship {
width: 20vw;
z-index: 99;
float: left;
}
.death_star {
z-index: 20;
}
.death_star, .saturn{
position: absolute;
right: 0%;
}
.fa-crosshairs {
position: absolute;
right: 324px;
top: 212px;
z-index: 99;
}
#rocketObject #rocket span{
z-index: 999;
}
```

There, that's just a little bit of CSS to pull it all together. Now, take a look in your browser and see it in action.

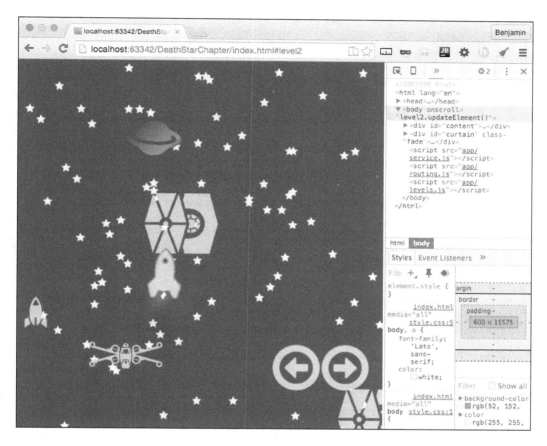

Creating the home page version

Now, let's wrap this up by putting together the home page partial. Copy from the `level2.parseAjax` function the `level2.data` definition, and then the `starships3` for in loop, and the `death_star` loop. Have them all build into a new variable, `homeObjectsHTMLStart`. Get the element by ID `homeObjects`, and set its inner HTML to equal `homeObjectsHTMLStart`. Next, copy from `level1.parseAjaxHome`'s `spreadObjects` calls for the responsive spread into here.

Replace the element by ID call with `homeObjects`, and the children with get elements by class name `smallship`. See the entire function in the following example:

```
level2.parseAjaxHome = function (xhr, id) {
level2.data = JSON.parse(xhr.responseText);
var homeObjectsHTMLStart = '';
for (var key in level2.data.objectgroups.objects.starships3.objects) {
homeObjectsHTMLStart += '<div id = "' + level2.data.objectgroups.
objects.starships3.objects[key].type + '"
class = "' +
level2.data.objectgroups.objects.starships3.objects[key].idclass +
' ' +
level2.data.objectgroups.objects.starships3.objects[key].sizeclass
+ ' ' +
level2.data.objectgroups.objects.starships3.objects[key].colorclas
s + '">';
homeObjectsHTMLStart += '<object type = "image/svg+xml" data =
"lib/space-icons/' +
level2.data.objectgroups.objects.starships3.objects[key].idclass +
'.svg" >' +
level2.data.objectgroups.objects.starships3.objects[key].type +
'</object></div>';
    }
for (var key in level2.data.objectgroups.objects.death_star.objects) {
homeObjectsHTMLStart += '<div id="' +
level2.data.objectgroups.objects.death_star.objects[key].type + '"
class="' +
level2.data.objectgroups.objects.death_star.objects[key].idclass + ' '
+
level2.data.objectgroups.objects.death_star.objects[key].sizeclass
+ ' ' +
level2.data.objectgroups.objects.death_star.objects[key].colorclas
s + '">';
if (level2.data.objectgroups.objects.death_star.objects[key].type!='c
loud') {
homeObjectsHTMLStart += '<object type = "image/svg+xml" data =
"lib/space-icons/' +
level2.data.objectgroups.objects.death_star.objects[key].idclass +
'.svg" >' +
level2.data.objectgroups.objects.death_star.objects[key].type +
'</object>';
        }
homeObjectsHTMLStart += '</div>';
}
document.getElementById('homeObjects').innerHTML =
homeObjectsHTMLStart;
if (window.innerHeight > window.innerWidth) {
levels.spreadObjects(document.getElementById("homeObjects").getEle
mentsByClassName("smallship"), 120, window.innerWidth, 210, 1,
"absolute", "px");
```

```
} else {
levels.spreadObjects(document.getElementById("homeObjects").getEle
mentsByClassName("smallship"), 30, 25, 20, 1, "absolute", "%");
}
};
```

There, it's coming together even more. Let's put some final touches on the CSS so it looks stitched together.

Adding final touches

Here, we are going to put together the final touches of CSS. First, in your `style.css`, cut out the footer selector and paste it into `home.css` in the `portrait` and `orientation` media queries. In the `portrait` media query footer selector, remove the clear both attribute. In the same file, remove the media query for the min-width 838px. In the `portrait` orientation, add selectors for `leaderboard-list` and `credits-list`, giving them the styles 0 padding and 0 margins except for left, which will have a 15% margin. See the following sample for this CSS:

```
footer{
height: 34px;
}
#leaderboard-list,#credits-list{
margin: 0 0 0 15%;
padding: 0;
}
```

Copy the `leaderboard-list` and `credits` list style and paste it into the `orientation` landscape media query, adding a left-float to it. Then, add a selector for the `leaderboard` and `credits` IDs, giving them a height of 144px. Also, add selectors for the `homeObjects` child `death_star` 20% to the right. See the following sample for these changes:

```
#leaderboard-list,#credits-list{
margin: 0 0 0 15%;
padding: 0;
float: left;
}
#leaderboard,#credits{
height: 144px;
}
#homeObjects .death_star {
right: 20%!important;
}
footer{
```

```
height: 34px;
clear: both;
}
```

Finally, outside the media query, add these selectors. For the `homeObjects` child `death_star` class object, a width of 100px and 50% to the right. For the child clouds of `homeObject`, display `none`, and for the `smallship` child of `homeObjects`, add a width of 5 vw. See the following example:

```
#homeObjects .death_star object{
width: 100px;
right: 50%;
}
#homeObjects #cloud{
display: none;
}
#homeObjects .smallship{
width: 5vw;
}
```

See the screenshot of the responsive home page:

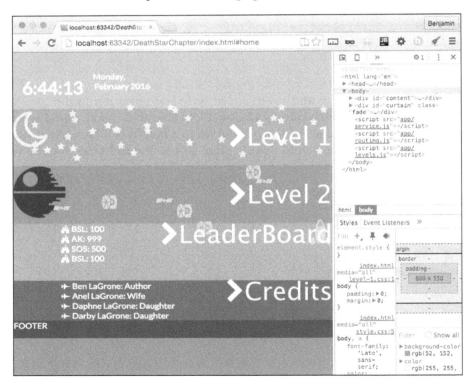

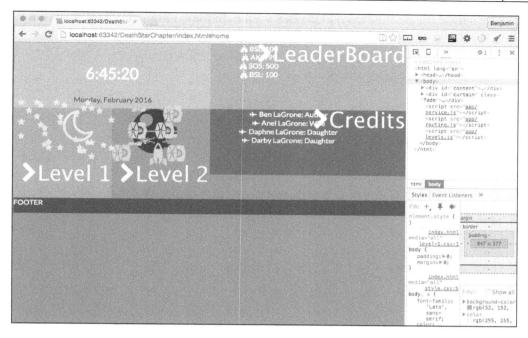

Creating explosive final touches

Remember way back when we made `level2.getMovingElements` and we left the `if else` condition empty except for `console log explosion`? Let's do something quick and effective about it. Let's add a new variable called `deathStarExplodes` equal to the current `row`'s elements by class name `deathStarAdd`, and do a `for` loop over their length, and for each, add the class `show`. See the following example:

```
var deathStarExplodes =
document.getElementsByClassName("row")[h].getElementsByClassName("
deathStarAdd");
for (var i = 0; i < deathStarExplodes.length; i++) {
deathStarExplodes[i].classList.add('show')
}
```

Great! That is the last of the last of the last of JavaScript. Let's just add a few little pieces of CSS. In `level-2.css`, add a selector for `fa-sun-o` giving it an absolute position 55% to the right, 15% from the top, a z-index of 999, a font-size of 4vw, and the color orange. And one more selector for `fa-bullseye`, with an absolute position, 47% to the right, 7% from the top, a z-index of 999, a font-size of 65vw, and a red color.

Also, let's hide the `deathStarAdd` classes with a display: none, and then display: inline when the show class is added. See the following example:

```css
.fa-sun-o {
position: absolute;
right: 55%;
top: 15%;
z-index: 999;
font-size: 40vw;
color: orange;
}
.fa-bullseye {
position: absolute;
right: 47%;
top: 7%;
z-index: 999;
font-size: 65vw;
color: red;
}

.deathStarAdd{
display: none;
}
.deathStarAdd.show{
display: inline;
}
```

Now you have a pretty cool little explosion when the rocket gets close to the Death Star and shoots a little missile into the exhaust vent. See the following screenshots:

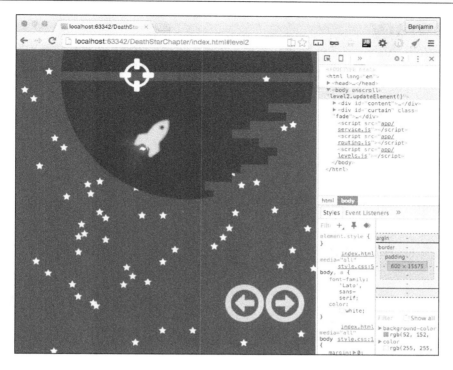

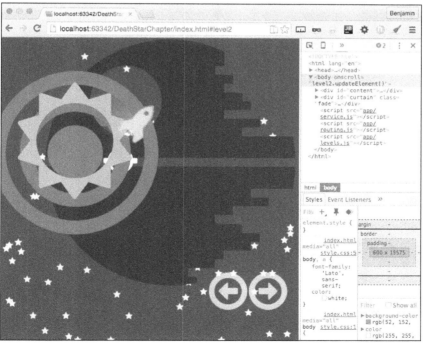

Summary

If you made it this far, then you have done great work. Thanks for reading this book. Please feel free to contact me if you have any ideas about, or corrections for the project. I look forward to hearing from you.

Index

Symbols

B

C

D

E

F